Cambridge Oriental Series No. 4

THE BATTLES OF COXINGA

Published on behalf of the Faculty of Oriental Studies
in the University of Cambridge

PLATE I. THE YOUTHFUL COXINGA BATTLES THREE UNRULY DUTCHMEN

THE BATTLES OF COXINGA

Chikamatsu's Puppet Play, Its Background and Importance

BY DONALD KEENE

WITH A PREFACE BY MARK VAN DOREN

CAMBRIDGE
AT THE UNIVERSITY PRESS
1971

ISBN: 0 521 05469 9

FIRST PUBLISHED IN 1951 BY TAYLOR'S FOREIGN PRESS
REPRINTED 1971 FOR THE FACULTY OF ORIENTAL STUDIES, CAMBRIDGE

First printed by Lund Humphries & Co. Ltd., London and Bradford
Reprinted in Great Britain by Lewis Reprints Limited, London and Tonbridge

To

KIM GWAN LIE

RYUSAKU TSUNODA

MASAKATSU YOKOYAMA

PREFACE

The Battles of Coxinga *is a play in which a Chinese general at the Emperor's court suddenly drives a knife into his left eye, turns it round along the lids, draws out the crimson ball, and ceremonially offers it to the Great King of Tartary's envoy, who accepts it reverently. In the same play a Chinese princess drifts in a small boat to the shores of Japan, where she is found by the hero and his wife in lamentable condition: her sleeves are wet with the sea-winds and the rouge and powder have been washed from her face, which nevertheless still looks like an hibiscus flower. Later on, back in China, the hero's sister needs to send a message to him from the interior of a castle which she cannot leave and he cannot enter. He is expecting either a red signal or a white one. Circumstances are such that Kinshōjo, the sister, can send only her own blood. She does so, through a conduit, and determines the destiny of an empire. This destiny has previously been served in an even more astonishing fashion: the Empress of China having been murdered while pregnant, a statesman of the court kills his own child and substitutes it for the royal child whom a Cæsarean operation has left living; for it must appear to the Tartars that the Empress has died without issue.*

The justification of these horrors, even for a Western reader who knows Œdipus Rex *and* King Lear, *is that* The Battles of Coxinga *is a puppet play, performed to the continuous accompaniment of instrumental music and the trained voice of a narrator who does all the speaking. Which calls for a great deal of exegesis, both critical and historical; and Mr. Keene, along with his admirable translation of Chikamatsu's masterpiece, has amply responded to the call. His accounts of Chikamatsu, of the narrator who chanted the text, of the theatre at Osaka where the play was given with such success in 1715, of the Jōruri dramas which it exemplified, of the patriotic and other sentiments which it satisfied in the audience, of the puppet tradition in general, and of Coxinga's career in history—he died in 1662, but it is not known whether from wounds, fatigue, a bad cold, disappointment in his son, excitement over the approach of the Dutch Navy to the Philippines, or madness promoted by over-indulgence in wine and women—all of these accounts add up to much indeed, further fortified as they are by Mr. Keene's excellent understanding of English literature in which he discovers so many parallels and contrasts. As for the translation itself, Mr. Keene admits how much is lost when the music, the spectacle, and the chanter's voice are missing; but what remains is fascinating in its own right, and the best equivalent we are likely ever to have in the West of this remarkable Japanese classic.*

MARK VAN DOREN

PREFATORY NOTE

THIS BOOK was begun no more ambitiously than as a translation of Chikamatsu's celebrated puppet play *The Battles of Coxinga*, but it soon became apparent that unless the general reader were supplied with some account of the Japanese puppet theatre and of the historical background of the play, a good part of its interest would be lost. I endeavoured, then, to give a Westerner such information as a Japanese reader would need to know of corresponding English institutions and people in order to appreciate fully an historical play by Shakespeare. But I found I could not easily stop at this point, for I discovered that Coxinga was treated as a dramatic hero even in professedly historical works, and *The Battles of Coxinga* was thus the culmination of many imperfect attempts, both of fictional history and historical fiction, to give a dramatic coherence to the life of the famous warrior.

As I have intimated, the book is designed for the general reader, the person interested in literature but not necessarily familiar with the languages or history of Japan and China. The book may thus be read without previous knowledge of the subject and without recourse to the notes, which are often technical and apt to be dull. The notes are for the benefit of specialists in Japanese who may wish to learn the sources of some of my statements or who seek further elucidation of some particular point. The Chinese characters have also been relegated to the notes, for it was my experience before being initiated into their mysteries that their appearances in a text were like the family jokes of other people's families, bewildering and rather irritating. A glossary of technical terms of the Japanese theatre is appended, as is a bibliography in which the Chinese characters for the authors and titles of works consulted are given.

Before proceeding to the pleasant task of expressing my thanks to various scholars and friends who have helped me, I should like to utter one fiercely operatic *maledizione* on the head of the thief who stole a large part of the only copy of my manuscript from a railway carriage in Milan. I trust that his disappointment in finding typed sheets of paper instead of cigarettes and wrist-watches upset him at least a fraction as much as the loss did me at the time.

My thanks must go first to the trustees of the Sino-American Cultural Fellowship and of the Henry Fellowship for having provided me with the financial support necessary to complete my work on the various aspects of the subject. Among my friends, thanks are due especially to Mr. E. B. Ceadel for having read with great care a large part of the manuscript, and for having offered innumerable useful suggestions. It would be ungracious to acknowledge the help of others except alphabetically, as follows: Professor Hugh Borton, Professor C. R. Boxer, Mr. C. J. Dunn, Professor Serge Elisséeff, Professor L. C. Goodrich, Mr. Hugh Hanmer, Professor H. G. Henderson, Dr. William Hung, Mr. Piet van der Loon, Professor C. C. Wang, Mr. Gurdon Wattles and Professor C. M. Wilbur. To innumerable others who have helped me at one stage or another, I express my thanks and the regret that considerations of space forbid my naming them all.

To three friends in whose particular debt I stand, I offer this book. Their names will be found on the dedicatory page.

TABLE OF CONTENTS

ILLUSTRATIONS

PLATE I. THE YOUTHFUL COXINGA BATTLES THREE UNRULY DUTCHMEN

(frontispiece)

From *The Life of Coxinga* by Kanagaki Robun (see page 84). The hero is depicted in the act of disposing with his bare hands of three armed Dutchmen who have insulted his aged father.

PLATE II. BEHIND THE SCENES AT AN EDO PUPPET THEATRE OF 1690

(pages 18 and 19)

From *Seikyoku Ruisan* by Saitō Gesshin. The illustration shows a puppet theatre of 1690, that of Yamamoto Tosa-no-jō (see page 27). To the right are the puppets not in use. The chanter and the samisen player sit on a low dais. To the left are two puppet operators holding the puppets over their heads, while they themselves remain out of sight. The inscription above the picture notes that at the time the chanter did not appear before the public, and that the puppets, which did not have any feet, were operated by one man each.

PLATE III. THE BATTLES OF COXINGA SUMMARISED IN A 1715 ILLUSTRATION

(facing page 100)

From *Seikyoku Ruisan*. A contemporary (1715) illustration for the play-book of *The Battles of Coxinga*. The action of the play may be followed from right to left in the two registers: Watōnai's mother riding the subdued tiger, accompanied by the hero and his newly won followers; the scene on the wall of Kanki's castle, with Kinshōjo holding her father's portrait to the right; the suicides of Kinshōjo and Watōnai's mother, with the hero receiving homage; Go Sankei watching the battles of the four seasons while the old men play at chess; and, finally, the victory of Coxinga and the punishment of his enemies.

(Illustrations reproduced by courtesy of Cambridge University Library.)

I

INTRODUCTION

ON THE first day of the eleventh moon of 1715 a new play was performed by the puppets at the Takemoto Theatre in Osaka. The manager of the theatre might well have been anxious about the reception which was to be accorded the piece, for the company, faced by severe competition from its rival, the Toyotake Theatre, and crippled by the death of its chief chanter, Gidayū, was threatened with collapse if the new work proved a failure. Already the members of the company had shown signs of dissatisfaction with the young and inexperienced successor of the great Gidayū and some had deserted to the flourishing rival troupe. For the staff playwright, Chikamatsu Monzaemon, the new work was also to be his greatest test. His last productions had been failures, and he laboured long over the latest one, in a resolute attempt to save both the theatre and its young director, Masatayū, for whom he had much personal affection.

The new work, *Kokusenya Kassen*, or *The Battles of Coxinga*[1], scored a success of a magnitude difficult for us to realise to-day when plays of slight merit sometimes run for years. It was performed every night for seventeen months at the Takemoto Theatre, a record for the puppet theatre in Japan.[2] It was adapted for performance by actors, and was kept playing simultaneously at several theatres in each of the chief cities of Japan by the insatiable demands of a Coxinga-mad public. Nothing was deemed too great or too small to be honoured with the magic name: plays, novels, poems, children's toys, sweets, textile patterns, dolls, and numerous other objects found a wider public when called "Coxinga".[3]

It goes without saying that after such a success the prestige and finances of the Takemoto Theatre were restored. The usually harried playwright, who had been known to turn out a completed work in a week, had a holiday of a year and a half. Although no one ever said that Masatayū's rather thin voice had the quality of the old master, Gidayū, his recitation of the touching scenes of the third act left nothing to be desired, and those critics who found interpretation as important a factor in singing as the natural beauty of a voice declared that Masatayū was in no way inferior to his predecessor.[4] So vigorously were the puppets put through their parts that three sets of costumes were worn out during the course of the run. And it was a matter of only a few years before the puppet play was revived, either for the sake of those who had not already seen it, or for others who longed to share again in the excitement of a perform-ance of *The Battles of Coxinga*.[5] The proud Toyotake Theatre, like the Great King of Tartary in the play, was thoroughly humbled, and it had its own staff playwright turn out a demi-monde version of *The Battles of Coxinga* to catch the trade of those turned away at the Takemoto Theatre.[6]

The reasons for the success of *The Battles of Coxinga* are usually given as its patriotic appeal, its exoticism, and the quality of the writing. Each of these factors and its contribution to the success of the play will be discussed below.

1. Patriotism

The subject of *The Battles of Coxinga*, the blending of Japanese and Chinese civilisation, is the central theme of Japanese history, if such a theme can be said to exist. From earliest times the Japanese have expressed a boundless admiration for China, the source of their civilisation, to which is added a seem-ingly contradictory pride in that which is non-Chinese, the pure Yamato elements of Japanese culture. Again and again in Japanese history, literature and art arises this curious and unresolved struggle between the worship of the philos-ophy, literature, arts and sciences of China and the " Japanese spirit", the mysterious power that emanates from the mountains and waters of the Land of the Rising Sun. It is not unusual to find in the same man an orthodox Con-fucian and a believer in the peculiar claims to blessedness of the Japanese. Indeed, it is rare to find a Japanese thinker who does not embody the two dis-parate conceptions. One man like Ogyū Sorai, might call himself an "Eastern barbarian" and adopt a Chinese name. Another of an opposite sort, like Hirata Atsutane, might make light of Chinese learning and even seek to produce Japanese writing antedating the ideographs imported from China. But there were many hundreds who repeated variants on the formula "Chinese tech-niques and Japanese spirit".

In *The Battles of Coxinga* there is more of the Japanese spirit than of the Chinese techniques, but a balance is maintained in other ways. A quality in which the Japanese have always taken much pride is their bravery. The philos-opher Yamazaki Ansai had declared that the Japanese were superior to the Chinese because they excelled in bravery and were also more benevolent than the Chinese, bravery and benevolence and wisdom having been considered the three great virtues. In the play, the Japanese carry off the chief honours in bravery, the Chinese are much more wise, while benevolence or love is evenly divided.

Japan is exalted in *The Battles of Coxinga* as the land of great bravery,

bravery of the kind associated with the samurai code now commonly known as *bushidō*. Chikamatsu tells us in the play, "Weakness is the way of the women of China. Neither Watōnai nor Ikkan wept; that is the way of a Japanese warrior."[7] Chinese courage, as shown in the persons of Coxinga's two lieutenants, Go Sankei and Kanki, is not so spontaneous as Japanese bravery, but is tempered with wisdom. Go Sankei and Kanki counsel Coxinga with their clever plans, but Coxinga, Japanese hero that he is, has no use for elaborate stratagems, and prefers to dash in against the enemy with no other weapons than his bare hands. The distinction here made is fundamentally the same as the one between spirit and technique. The Japanese are willing to admit that the Chinese are learned and clever, but they claim for themselves the virtues of the spirit—sincerity and directness. This Japanese view of themselves accords very poorly with their reputation for slyness, or, at best, inscrutability, but it is exactly their opinion. The audience must have been moved by Go Sankei's loyalty and steadfast devotion and by the high nobility of the gallant Kanki, but it was with the impetuous Coxinga that every Japanese, however little inclined to martial pursuits, must certainly have identified himself. The spectator was impressed when told that the castles in China are much more formidable than those in Japan, and he knew that China was a country filled with marvellous things, but he was confident that the spontaneous bravery and directness of Coxinga would find no barrier too great to overcome. In the final analysis, Japanese spirit must prevail over Chinese techniques.

The appeal to patriotism is thus a complex one, and not the sort that would have been popular in an English theatre, for example. John Dryden's play *Amboyna: Or, the Cruelties of the Dutch to the English Merchants*, staged some forty years before *The Battles of Coxinga*, was a typical English approach. Some of the sentiments might have been found in Chikamatsu's play: "Would you have English wives show less of bravery than their children do? To lie by an Englishman's side, is enough to give a woman resolution."[8] Or, in response to the Dutch villain's threat of torturing an English boy with fire after torture by water has failed, the boy declares, "You think my father got me of some Dutchwoman, and that I am but of a half-strain courage; but you shall find that I am all over English, as well in fire as water".[9] The audience would have revolted, however, at the scene that "discovers the English tortured, and the Dutch tormenting them" in which an English captain is ordered to be burnt from the wrists up to the elbows. The Dutchman cries, in limping iambic pentameters:

> Boy, take that candle thence, and bring it hither;
> I am exalted, and would light my pipe
> Just where the wick is fed with English fat.[10]

3

This matter has been discussed at some length, in order to show the particular kind of patriotism that appealed to the Japanese audience. It was not so much a question in the play of Japan versus China, with a triumph for the men of Yamato, as would have been the theme of a Western patriotic play. Although Coxinga makes much more of his Japanese ancestry than of his Chinese lineage, even to the point of flying the banners of the shrine of Ise over a city that he has captured, it is essential to the play that he be half-Chinese, and that his Chinese half be by no means contemptible. Chikamatsu seems to have tried to make it a good contest between the two nations, rather than to present the black-and-white view of a Dryden. Coxinga's female counterpart is not Komutsu, his countrified Japanese wife, for all her bravery and sincerity, but rather his Chinese half-sister, Kinshōjo. Chikamatsu makes the weakness of Kinshōjo most appealing, for "weakness is the way of the women of China", but she later demonstrates that she has great courage, when by her suicide she serves as an inspiration to her husband. Chikamatsu had insight enough to realise that it was only by making China and the Chinese worthy of admiration that dimension could be given to the feats of his Japanese hero.

The ceaseless Japanese insistence on their spiritual supremacy resulted from a deeply felt awareness of Japan's position of continued inferiority to China. The Chinese attitude toward Japan was invariably that of the unique power of the world looking at one of many tributary barbarian nations. The Japanese were powerless to retaliate, or even soften the insult, although sometimes the Chinese chose to "soothe" instead of to "subjugate" the barbarians. With what desperate eagerness the Japanese relate the cases of a few men who were accepted on a footing of equality among Chinese scholars or artists! Seldom was there a suggestion that China was not the centre of the world; the Japanese sought instead to prove that however small and insignificant their country might appear, it was really just as good as China.[11] It would obviously have been impossible to maintain such a thesis in face of Chinese material superiority if the Japanese had chosen to defend themselves on any grounds less shadowy than those of the "spirit", the so-called *Yamato-damashii*.

In Chikamatsu's play the spiritual supremacy is made concrete. Although Coxinga is equipped with one "secret Japanese weapon" of a purely military nature, at the key points in the play it is the spiritual help of the Japanese gods which is responsible for success. In the Bamboo Forest of Senri a sacred charm from the Great Shrine at Ise suffices to subdue a tiger. The gods then so strengthen the tiger that it fights for Coxinga with fabulous strength. The most spectacular demonstration of the power of the gods is saved for the fourth act. The imperial party, in dire straits, seeks divine assistance. Go Sankei and the boy prince pray to the spirit of the first Ming emperor without

4

apparent effect. Komutsu and the Princess Sendan, who had already been helped by the god Sumiyoshi to cross from Japan to China, pray to him for assistance. At once a miraculous cloud bridge spans the abyss, permitting the loyal supporters of the emperor to cross safely. When the villainous Tartars attempt to follow them over the bridge, it disintegrates, plunging them to their deaths below. The Japanese gods were evidently behind the restoration of the Ming!

The patriotism which helped make *The Battles of Coxinga* popular was a patriotism designed to show the possibilities of the union of the great central country of the world with the land of the gods. The play is a celebration of the marriage of the two countries, and not a shout of triumph.[12] The Japanese spectator might have felt a surge of national pride when he heard Coxinga exclaim, "You low creatures who despise the Japanese because we come from a small country! Have you seen how even tigers are struck with awe by Japanese prowess?", but he would not have felt the anti-foreign sentiment associated with patriotism in the West.

2. Exoticism

During the third decade of the seventeenth century a number of shogunate edicts had been promulgated which effectively reduced Japan's once flourishing commerce with the rest of the world to a thin stream, and brought back to Japan the merchants who had lived in lands of great opulence. Most of these merchants settled in the port cities, like Hakata in Kyūshū, or Sakai near Osaka. They returned with many treasures from China, Siam, and the Indies, and with a taste for a life infinitely more luxurious than anything that Japan had to offer. Economic prosperity brought about by the establishment of peace made it possible for such merchants to gratify their desires, and it is to the spread of this influence in later years that must be credited a good part of the brilliant flowering of high life in Japan which culminated in the Genroku era (1688-1703).

Because Japan had never seriously considered herself the centre of the universe and the fountainhead of all civilisation, she was readier to take up foreign ways and wares than was China. During the sixteenth century, when the Portuguese were at the height of their power and influence in the East, Japanese dandies affected the balloon breeches and melon hats of the Lusitanians. The Japanese were also quick to approve of Portuguese cooking, and *tempura*, a standard Japanese dish of to-day, dates from the same time. Dutch wares enjoyed great popularity; there are eighteenth-century prints which show fashionable demi-mondaines wearing sashes of Dutch calico over their splendid silken robes. The wealthy merchants of Osaka were willing to pay tremendous sums for anything sufficiently unusual, whether it was a strange animal or a European scientific instrument.

China was even more interesting. It was almost as exotic as a European country and had the advantage of being more readily intelligible to the Japanese because of their familiarity with Chinese legends and literature. Japanese artists of the eighteenth century were eager to learn of new trends in Chinese painting.[13] It may seem curious that China was not made the scene of many plays, but playwrights seldom ventured beyond Japanese themes. About 1700 a minor dramatist named Nishiki Bunryū wrote a play entitled *Kokusenya Tegara Nikki*, or *A Diary of Coxinga's Achievements*.[14] The work is of little intrinsic importance, but it may have had enough success in its time to attract Chikamatsu's attention to the story of Coxinga. He must have sensed the dramatic possibilities of a play with a Chinese background. It was probably after looking into histories of the real Coxinga that he discovered new material which appealed to him more than what he had found in Bunryū's play.

Chikamatsu spares no efforts in exploiting the exotic possibilities of the story of Coxinga. To throw into highest relief the strange qualities of China, he cleverly alternates Chinese scenes with familiar Japanese ones. The first act depicts the Chinese court at the height of its brilliance. The audience must have been dazzled by the costumes of the members of the court, costumes as bizarre as the actions of the characters. Then, lest the audience grow accustomed to the unfamiliar, Chikamatsu opens the second act with a scene which affords the greatest possible contrast. Coxinga and Komutsu are walking on the beach of Matsura in their fisherfolk clothes. Komutsu is a simple girl whose ready laugh is likely to give way to the sharp barbs of her tongue when her jealousy is aroused. On the heels of one of her earthy jokes, she and her husband spy the strange, brightly-painted Chinese boat that bears within it the beauteous Princess Sendan. The audience is startled when the princess, her pale and drawn face contrasting with her splendid Chinese robes, sets foot on the humble beach of Matsura. The princess then addresses Coxinga and Komutsu in a bizarre Chinese-sounding language. The first reaction is the natural one: Komutsu shrieks with laughter at the curious noises she hears. For a moment at least the exotic becomes humorous.

In the third act Chikamatsu reverses the situation. Coxinga's mother is the only character in Japanese clothes, and the strangeness of their cut is the subject of gossip of the Chinese maid-servants. The *michiyuki* of the fourth act has another interesting example of costuming—Komutsu dressed as a young Japanese warrior. Later in the act we see the two old men who play chess on the mountain. They are presumably attired in strange and ghostly raiment, one last variety of dress that Chikamatsu presented to capture the interest of his audience.

6

The costuming of the characters was only one of the ways in which Chikamatsu utilised the unfamiliarity of China (and the familiarity of Japan) for his dramatic ends. In the language, the sentiments and the actions a similar pattern could be traced. This one example should suffice, however, to indicate the appeal that the exoticism exerted.

3. Quality of the Writing

Although patriotism and exoticism undoubtedly enhanced the attractions of *The Battles of Coxinga*, its success rested finally with the quality of the writing. Even the cleverest use of patriotism and exoticism would not have sufficed to ensure the reception that the play was accorded. As proof of this, it is necessary only to cite the two sequels written by Chikamatsu on Chinese themes, *The Later Battles of Coxinga* and *The Chinese Boat: A Modern Coxinga*.[15] The first of these was modelled on *The Battles of Coxinga* in the attempt to repeat its success, but though patriotism and exoticism were both present in abundance, the play was an utter failure. Some critics have ascribed this failure to the saturation of the public's craving for the exotic,[16] but the repeated revivals of *The Battles of Coxinga* prove that the public was not necessarily averse to a Chinese theme. The failure of both sequels can be attributed mainly to the inferior quality of the inspiration and writing.

The success of *The Battles of Coxinga* lay in Chikamatsu's text, both in the beauty of individual passages and in the effect of the whole. It was said that there was no one, educated or ignorant, who could not recite the *michiyuki* in the fourth act.[17] This passage begins, "For the Chinese style of hairdress they use Satsuma combs; for the Shimada style of hairdress they use Chinese combs. Thus are Yamato and Cathay united." To appreciate the qualities of these words, they must be read in the original. In Japanese the sentence runs, "Kara-ko-wage ni wa Satsuma-gushi, Shimada-wage ni wa Tō-gushi to, Yamato Morokoshi uchimazete". Literally, this is, "In the Chinese hairdressing Satsuma combs, in the Shimada hairdressing, Chinese combs, thus mix Japan, China". In the Japanese the phrases have a pleasant cadence which is much lighter than the antithesis of the English translation. There is another charm to the original that is hard to recapture in translation. The name "China" is rendered by three different Japanese words, *Kara*, *Tō* and *Morokoshi*. Each of these words has a slightly different flavour, *Kara* usually being used for China, the land of fashionable things, *Tō* as a general name for the country, and *Morokoshi* for the faraway and strange land over the seas.[18]

These lines became so popular that Chikamatsu felt entitled to refer to them in a later play.[19] The learned Hozumi Ikan (1692-1769), Chikamatsu's friend and commentator, attempted to trace a profound meaning for them in

7

the writings of the Chinese philosophers,[20] but the lines would seem to be no more than a particularly graceful rendering of the theme of the play, the union of Japan and China.

Chikamatsu was extraordinarily skilled in the use of allusion, both in small details and in the incorporation of whole passages from other plays in his own works. There is nothing quite like this latter use of allusion in European literature. If, for example, part of the balcony scene from *Romeo and Juliet* were to be used almost word for word in a modern play, with only a substitution of names and a few new twists, we should have a rough parallel of a common practice in Chikamatsu's plays. The intent is not parody, nor may this practice be termed plagiarism; it is, rather, a literary equivalent of the virtuosity of a coloratura soprano or a violinist. An opera goer who attends a performance of *Rigoletto* expects that the soprano delivering the *Caro Nome* will stay fairly close to the version with which he is familiar, but he will be delighted if the singer is talented enough to add dazzling leaps and trills of her own. When Chikamatsu used a dozen lines from an earlier play, it was with the expectation that the audience would be familiar with the original work and would applaud him for his skill in fitting the old lines into the new context of his play. There are some passages of this description in *The Battles of Coxinga*, particularly the scene in which Coxinga plays the part of the hero Benkei at the barrier.

Another feature of Chikamatsu's style which it is difficult to communicate in translation is his use of puns and plays on words. Here again usage in Japan and the West differs markedly. In recent years certain English poets have made serious use of word-plays to expand the meaning of lines,[21] but in general the pun is considered a kind of joke, and a bad one at that. In Japan plays on words are used for comic purposes, but they are also found in highly tragic contexts where they serve to lend complexity to the expression. Perhaps the most effective word-play to be found in Japanese drama is *senkata namida*. The pun involves the words *senkata nami*, meaning "hopeless" or "impossible to help", and the word *namida*, meaning "tears". Thus, in one word-play we have a situation and its reaction: faced with a helpless predicament one is moved to tears.

In *The Battles of Coxinga* Chikamatsu shows his great ingenuity in the use of puns. The description of the sea shells which occurs at the beginning of the second act is a virtuoso exhibition which must have delighted his audiences. It is ostensibly little more than a list of fairly common sea shells, tied together with a number of short phrases. If the meaning of the names of the shells is taken into account, the passage is turned into a love scene of considerable charm. The *michiyuki* in the fourth act also abounds in verbal dexterity, as was the convention in the travel description. The nature of the word-plays in the *michiyuki* was determined by usage; they were almost invariably on the names of places passed on the journey.

Above any individual excellences of Chikamatsu's style, there is the effect of the whole. Solemn spectacle, low comedy, pathos, wild combat, terrible suspense and final exultation are all treated in one play. It is fortunate that the Japanese of 1715 were of no more sensitive natures than, say, the Elizabethan audiences. Modern Japanese spectators are more inclined to be squeamish. One critic, able to watch with equanimity the spectacle of Ri Tōten gouging out his left eye, declared that the scene in which Go Sankei performs a Cæsarean operation on the dead Empress would be intolerable to-day.[22] The same critic, however, did not consider worthy of mention certain other blood-lettings, notably the scene in which one unfortunate Tartar is crushed "like a ripe persimmon against a rock".

As far as the presentation of *The Battles of Coxinga* was concerned, the chanting of Masatayū and his five associates was judged excellent, the puppets were operated by Tatsumatsu Hachirobei, the master of his art, and his capable assistants, and the scenic effects were supervised by Takeda Izumo, who was always anxious to achieve spectacular results. It is small wonder that the play scored so great a triumph.

It would be wise at this point to give a summary of the plot of *The Battles of Coxinga* so that discussions of the play's particular scenes in the following chapters may more easily be followed.

The Battles of Coxinga opens at the court of the Ming sovereign, Shisōretsu. An envoy has come from the Tartars (Manchus) to ask that the Lady Kasei, one of the emperor's consorts, be turned over to the Great King of Tartary. The court is astounded at the request, but the General of the Right, Ri Tōten, comes forward to second it, revealing that Tartary had helped China in the time of famine, and should now be recompensed. The President of the Council of War, Go Sankei, angrily denounces Ri Tōten and defies the Tartars. When the envoy is on the point of leaving in a rage, Ri Tōten gouges out his left eye and presents it to the Tartar as a peace offering. The envoy, appeased, returns to Tartary.

Later, Go Sankei attempts to reveal to the emperor the treachery planned by Ri Tōten, but his advice is spurned. Just at this moment cries outside the palace reveal the arrival of the Tartar armies. In the fighting that ensues Go Sankei acquits himself nobly, but he is unable to prevent the killing of the emperor by Ri Tōten and the subsequent death of the empress. The empress was in the last stages of pregnancy, and Go Sankei manages to deliver her child. He kills his own baby and substitutes it in the womb of the dead empress so that the Tartars will think the imperial heir is dead. The Princess Sendan, younger sister of the emperor, is aided by Go Sankei's wife, and manages to escape to the coast, where she boards a little boat that is blown out to sea.

At the beginning of the second act the scene shifts to the beach at Hirado in Japan, where we find Watōnai (Coxinga's early name), a youth of twenty years or so, and his wife Komutsu. Watōnai is a fisherman by trade, but has learned about military strategy from his father Rōikkan (or simply Ikkan), who had served as a minister at the court of Shisōretsu. After a humorous scene between husband and wife, the boat bearing Princess Sendan arrives, and Watōnai, who understands Chinese, learns from her of the disasters that have overtaken the Ming supporters. Rōikkan and his Japanese wife enter, and it is then decided that Watōnai and his parents will journey to China to help restore the dynasty. The Princess remains behind with Komutsu in Japan. After various adventures Watōnai, with the aid of a divinely guided tiger, subdues a group of Chinese soldiers, and they become his military strength.

The third act opens with the meeting of Watōnai and Rōikkan in China at the castle of Kanki, who is the husband of the daughter Rōikkan left behind when he departed China for Japan years before. A tender recognition scene ensues between Rōikkan and the daughter, Kinshōjo. She cannot admit her father to the castle because of the strict prohibition on the admission of strangers. It is agreed finally to allow the old mother to be brought in, bound like a prisoner. Kinshōjo promises to send a signal to Rōikkan and Watōnai to let them know if they can come into the castle. A white signal will be used to denote success, and a red one for failure. Kanki returns and, after some discussion with the mother, decides that honour will not permit him to go over to Watōnai, especially since it might be thought that he was influenced by his wife's blood relationship to him. Kinshōjo gives the arranged signal by stabbing herself and sending her blood flowing through a conduit to the river where Watōnai is waiting. Watōnai, infuriated at the thought of failure, bursts into the castle. Kinshōjo pleads that Kanki now become an ally of Watōnai, which he does. He then gives Watōnai a new name, Coxinga, with the title of Prince of Yen-p'ing. The mother then commits suicide because she is afraid that people will think that she has been a wicked step-mother who has driven her step-daughter to death. Resolute in their grief, Coxinga and Kanki set out together against the Manchus.

In the fourth act, we return to Japan. Komutsu has been drilling herself in the military arts in preparation for a voyage to China. She and Princess Sendan set out and are helped on their journey by the god Sumiyoshi.

The scene then shifts to the Mountain of the Nine Immortals, where Go Sankei is wandering with the infant prince in his arms. There he observes two old men playing a game of *go*.[23] They tell him of the mystic significance of the game and the powers one gains through playing it. Go Sankei is then enabled to see the campaigns waged by Coxinga over a period of five years. He is startled to find that while he has been watching time has been passing very quickly, so much so that the prince is now a boy of seven. Go Sankei later meets Rōikkan, by this time joined by Komutsu and the Princess Sendan. The Tartars discover them, and it is only by the intercession of Sumiyoshi that they are saved and the Tartars destroyed.

The last act takes place outside the walls of Nanking. Coxinga listens to the plans of Go Sankei and Kanki for capturing the city. Rōikkan is taken prisoner by the Tartars when he goes off by himself to challenge them. When Coxinga and his forces storm up to the gates of the city, Ri Tōten and the Great King of Tartary use Rōikkan as a shield, and Coxinga is unable to bring himself to attack. By a trick Go Sankei and Kanki overcome the Tartars, and the day goes to Coxinga. Ri Tōten is executed, the Great King beaten and driven back to Tartary, and the little prince acclaimed as the Emperor Eiryaku.[24]

II

(a) A SHORT HISTORY OF THE JŌRURI

A RECENT Japanese critic declared that *The Battles of Coxinga* was one of two Chikamatsu masterpieces which represent the climax of a hundred years of the *jōruri* theatre.[1] An adequate comprehension of this statement requires, of course, some knowledge of the history of the *jōruri*,[2] and I shall attempt to present in concise form the significant features of its development.

Very little is known about what theatricals existed in Japan in the Heian Period (794-1185) or before. We may find it surprising that a civilisation as refined as that portrayed in the *Tale of Genji*[3] (*c.*1000 A.D.) had no theatre worthy of the name, or, indeed, anything more than the caperings of acrobats and the broad humour of the simple farce. Such were the forms of entertainment available at the court. There are records, however, even in this early period, of performers called *kugutsu-mawashi*, or "puppet-turners", who wandered about the countryside. The name *kugutsu* is apparently of Central Asiatic origin, and may originally have been derived from a Greek word for "puppet".[4] An account of the "puppet-turners" written in the Heian Period by Ōe Tadafusa (1040-1111) has been preserved. It is entitled *Kairaishi-ki* or *Chronicles of the Puppeteers*.

> The *kugutsu-mawashi* have no fixed place of residence nor permanent homes. They live in tents out in the fields. They move from place to place wherever there is water and grass. Their customs very much resemble those of the northern barbarians. The men all make use of the bow and of horses, and hunt for their subsistence. Sometimes they engage in sword-play with blunt-edged swords, or they make wooden men dance and peach-wood men fight. They are able to reproduce the attitudes of real men. They are just like the famous conjurers of old, and can turn sand and pebbles into gold coins, or grasses and wood into birds and animals.
>
> As for their womenfolk, they have mournful brows and put white powder under their eyes. They sway their hips as they walk, and smile seductively. They use rouge and face powder. They sing lascivious songs to captivate men. Even if their fathers, mothers or husbands know of this,

they do not reprimand them. They are not disinclined to spend a night with even a chance passer-by or traveller.[5]

There were groups of these foreigners, who paid none of the usual allegiances to the various feudal lords, scattered about Japan. The most skilful of them at puppetry were those in the eastern provinces of Mino, Mikawa and Tōtōmi, while the poorest were to be found in Kyūshū.[6] During the Kamakura Period the *kugutsu* came to be attached permanently to shrines and temples, where they performed various services. Puppet plays of a crude sort on the history of the shrine or of a particular festival were staged by the men on feast days, while the women of the tribe continued their old ways, giving the word *kugutsu* its added meaning of "prostitute". Some puppets, ranging in size from seven or eight inches to three or four feet in height and believed to date from this period, have been preserved in a Shintō shrine.[7] There is no record telling how much the art may have improved with time, but puppet performances under the name of *ebisu-kaki* ("barbarian lifting") or *ebisu-mai* ("barbarian dancing") gradually found favour in high places. In the sixteenth century, for example, there are numerous mentions of *ebisu-kaki* in the Imperial presence. It is not clear whether the performers were descendants of the original *kugutsu-mawashi*.

New forms of theatrical entertainment gradually evolved in Japan during the twelfth, thirteenth and fourteenth centuries. The *sekkyō*, or "explanation of sermons", began as simple elucidations of doctrine, gradually grew more dramatic in character, and with the addition of music became a kind of ballad drama. The development of the *sekkyō* after its ballad drama stage closely paralleled that of the *jōruri*.

The Nō drama, after several centuries of development, reached its period of greatest brilliance during the career of Zeami Motokiyo (1363-1443). (A Nō play is a short work chiefly in poetry and usually on a religious or historical theme. There are two leading characters in a Nō play, the *shite*, or principal actor, and the *waki*, or supporting actor. Either the *shite* or the *waki* may have a companion. The only other persons in the drama are the members of the chorus, who may recite for the *shite*.) The Nō was meant for the refined tastes of the court aristocrats. Its poetry is often extremely beautiful, but so complex as to be virtually unintelligible to the uninitiated.[8]

The *kōwaka-mai*, a kind of dance performed while a prose text (*bukyoku*) was chanted, also dates from the same period. *The Tale of Jōruri*,[9] which may be considered the first parent of the art of the *jōruri*, is not mentioned until about 1485. We do not know the name of the author of the original *Tale of Jōruri*; we do not even know what it was like in its original form. Wakatsuki

Yasuji, author of the monumental *Study of the Puppet Jōruri*, was of the opinion that the story was at first concerned entirely with the Princess Jōruri and a love affair she may have had with some man. Later, to gain wider popularity, the man was identified as the celebrated Minamoto no Yoshitsune, and the story of their love gradually evolved.[10]

The Tale of Jōruri, stated in barest form, is the account of the love that grew up between Yoshitsune and the Princess Jōruri while he was recuperating from illness which seized him on his journey from the capital to the remote province of Michinoku. The story was elaborated in various ways, and, in the version which became most famous, was cast in twelve episodes. The form of the work was responsible for an alternative title *The Story in Twelve Episodes*, by which it was frequently known even when a particular version happened to be in five, six, or fifteen episodes, as the case might be. *The Tale of Jōruri* came to be chanted by blind musicians to the accompaniment of the biwa, a four-stringed instrument rather resembling the mandoline. The music at first used was that employed in recitation of *The Tale of the Heike*, but gradually other tunes found acceptance, tunes derived from the Nō, the *bukyoku* or the popular songs of the period. The *jōruri* chanting because or in spite of its rather elementary nature, seems to have gained wide popularity among the common people. This was probably because they could not easily understand the Nō dramas and because they found the *sekkyō* too gloomy and didactic.

The first important development in the *jōruri* came with the introduction to Japan of a musical instrument called the samisen or shamisen.[11] Japanese historians like to trace the path of this three-stringed guitar from ancient Egypt to Arabia, to Central Asia, to Tibet, to South China, to the Ryūkyū Islands, and at last to Japan. The instrument did apparently enjoy considerable popularity in parts of China, especially Fukien, during the Yüan Dynasty (1280-1368) and later times. It was in 1390 that King Satto of the Ryūkyūs had thirty-six musicians from Fukien visit his court. The three-stringed guitar they brought with them was called by the islanders the *jabisen* or "snake-skin strings". When, in the middle of the sixteenth century the instrument reached Japan, the name was corrupted to *shamisen*, and characters used to express these sounds which meant "three flavour strings".[12]

Soon after its arrival in Japan the samisen was taken up by the blind musicians to accompany their recitations, replacing the biwa. It also found favour with the courtesans, and was made familiar by them to the samurai and the nobility. With the adoption of the samisen by the *jōruri* reciters two of the chief elements of the later *jōruri* were joined, the story of the fair princess and its musical accompaniment. The third element, the puppets, were added quite soon afterwards, in the last decade of the sixteenth century.

For our information on the earliest period of the puppet *jōruri* we must depend on the often unreliable accounts of the seventeenth century, which were usually written by dilettantes with no particular interest in accuracy. Contradiction and confusion would seem to be the rule in their writings, but the modern historian has no choice but to attempt to piece together his history from such accounts as the following one in the book *Heaven, Earth and Man in Japan and China, Illustrated.*

There were in the capital two blind musicians named Takino and Sawazumi, who were good both in playing stringed instruments and in singing. Previously, there had been someone who had written about the love of Yoshitsune and Jōruri in twelve episodes, and they used to recite it, beating time with a fan . . . There was later a certain man, a metalsmith by trade, who lived at Higashi-no-Tōin in Shijo, and who was an excellent musician. He persuaded a puppeteer from Awaji to operate wooden puppets while he played a three-stringed instrument to accompany them. The Emperor Go-Yōzei summoned them to the court, and he was thereupon appointed Awaji-no-jō. This art has flourished in recent times, and stories both ancient and modern of various kinds from China and Japan have been sung under the name of *jōruri*.[13]

The metalsmith mentioned in the above passage was a man named Chōzaburō, who ran a *menukiya*, a shop where sword-hilt ornaments were made, whence originated his name, Menukiya Chōzaburō. He was a pupil of the blind musician Sawazumi, and was the first of the puppet *jōruri* chanters of the "stiff" style, a term used to distinguish the recitations of the followers of Sawazumi from the "flexible" school of Takino.[14] About the latter's school we have various accounts, of which the following is quoted from the *Chronicle of Famous Places in the Eastern Circuit Provinces.* The quotation is for the Keichō era (1596-1611).

As for the *jōruri*, it was at this time that a man from the capital named Jirōbei, or some such, persuaded a puppeteer from Nishinomiya to join him. This puppeteer was later granted the title of Awaji-no-jō. In Shijō-gawara he recited the story of Kamato no Masakiyo while the puppets acted it out. Later they performed *The Princess Go-ō, Amida's Sacrifice,* and other stories.[15]

Another version, in the *History of Yōshū Prefecture*,[16] tells us that two pupils of Takino, the above-mentioned Jirōbei and one named Kambutsu, together planned the new *jōruri* with the puppeteer from Nishinomiya. It is curious that the rival schools are both recorded as having made use of the services of a puppeteer later given the title of Awaji-no-jō, and it is possible, as Wakatsuki suggests, that there has been some confusion in the matter of the title, and that it most properly belonged to Menukiya Chōzaburō.[17]

The matter of the title is worthy of note for, as we shall discover, all the celebrated *jōruri* chanters were known as the *jō* or *shōjō* of one or another province, *jō* being a secondary and *shōjō* a third rank position. These titles were purely honorary, of course, and do not mean that the chanters ever performed any governmental service, but in order for them to appear at court it was necessary that they have some court title and rank. It was generally the case that when a chanter achieved some eminence he would be granted a title as a mark of recognition.

The two original schools, the "stiff" founded by the pupils of Sawazumi and the "flexible" founded by those of Takino, continued to find admirers for many years. At first the two styles vied for popularity in the same cities, but gradually the "stiff" style achieved unquestioned supremacy in Edo, (modern Tokyo) while the "flexible" style was characteristic of Kyoto. This difference in styles corresponds to an observable difference in taste and temperament between the inhabitants of the two cities. Edo was the capital of the Shōgun and the stronghold of the samurai, while Kyoto retained its gentler aristocratic tone set by the weak but still prestige-laden court of the Emperor. Osaka, the third of the great cities of Japan, was chiefly a commercial centre, and its real contribution to the *jōruri* did not come until the advent of the domestic tragedies written by Chikamatsu. At various times chanters attempted to combine qualities of both "stiff" and "flexible" styles, and it was the great achievement of Gidayū, the most celebrated of the chanters, to have succeeded in doing so. As his art was closely connected with Osaka, we may consider the typical Osaka style to have been the combination "stiff-flexible" style: however, Japanese critics claim to be able to divide the acts, characters, and sentiments of any Osaka *jōruri* into their component Edo and Kyoto parts.

As the history of the *jōruri* between the time of its early beginnings and the time of its "climax" in 1715 with Chikamatsu's play *The Battles of Coxinga* is a long and complicated one, it has been found convenient to divide it into three periods: 1596-1664, 1664-1686 and 1686-1715. These dates correspond roughly to the periods when Edo, Kyoto and Osaka respectively were the centres of the *jōruri* art.

1596 - 1664

Our earliest recorded performances of puppet *jōruri* date back to about 1610, but it is generally believed that there were *jōruri* plays by about the first year of the Keichō era (1596). A 1614 account records the performance of *The Tale of Jōruri, Amida's Sacrifice* and *The Princess Go-ō*.[18] These were virtually the only plays presented during the first years of the puppet *jōruri*. There are illustrations of the Keichō era which show us what a typical *jōruri* theatre looked like.[19] The theatre was apparently no more than a temporary shack of extreme crudity, at one end of which was an undecorated stage. A big box hid the body of the puppet operator from the view of the audience and his head was concealed by some sort of curtain. The puppets themselves were usually of wood, although we do find occasional mention of clay ones. A screen from the period shows that there were women chanters and women samisen players at the time.[20]

Of the three plays that were most commonly offered, *The Tale of Jōruri* was easily the best in its language, construction and musical qualities.[21] *Amida's Sacrifice* (literally, "The Chest-Splitting of Amida") was more of the *sekkyō* style of morality play. It tells of a rich man who needs a human liver to save his son. It is arranged that the liver of a certain girl will be taken, but Amida[22] gives his own in her stead. *The Princess Go-ō* rather resembled *The Tale of Jōruri* in plot, but had a much more tragic tone.

When *The Tale of Jōruri* was written it was not with any intention of performance. This want of dramatic quality was not felt when the tale was recited, but the original text had to be revised when it was staged as a puppet play. The *jōruri* play, however, was never entirely divorced from the narration, and thus did not become real drama in the Western sense. The narrator (later, narrators) chanted not only the lines for the various puppets, but also bits of descriptive commentary. This feature inevitably detracted from the dramatic quality of the plays, but the alternation of the lyric lines of the descriptions with the *sprach-stimme* of the dialogues helped to prevent monotony in the recitation. Chikamatsu devoted an increasing proportion of his plays to dialogue, but never saw fit to abandon entirely the traditional descriptions.[23]

The *jōruri* apparently originated in Kyoto,[24] but the centre of *jōruri* activity soon shifted to Edo. A pupil of the original Takino, one Sugiyama Shichirozaemon, went to Edo in 1616 and founded the *jōruri* theatre there.[25] Sugiyama, later known as Tango-no-jō, was a partisan of the "flexible" style of singing, and enjoyed considerable success before the taste in Edo had crystallised in favour of the "stiff" style. He performed a number of times before various Shōguns, but little has been recorded of the nature of his performances.

About his more famous rival, Satsuma Jōun, we know a good deal more.[26] Jōun, though a pupil of Takino like Sugiyama, became the leading exponent of the "stiff" style of chanting in Edo. A description of one of Jōun's puppet performances has survived in the writings of the Confucian philosopher Hayashi

人形巻きまわくの人形
ありろびとをゑなりえて
きゅう
うらうにいうえぬ足内
のりもて海るさらやな
ち
さよま
り藤女ぐさからもや
ちらゑ
をゆけろにとよりをせ
世国へ元孫三子七月家坂の人形
初業図喜七の生兵持車り
一て山を糸根らせ右の尽く
せくはき生くらろく人形も
弱はろいくくきめけなきき
人形ず

さかり社

人形巻

PLATE II. BEHIND THE SCENES

18

EDO PUPPET THEATRE OF 1690

Razan (1583-1657). On the twenty-eighth day of the fifth moon of 1647 the old philosopher visited a *jōruri* theatre where he saw wooden puppets dressed as "men, women, monks or laity, immortals, soldiers, horsemen and porters. There were dancers and those who raised fans and beat drums. Some leapt about and some rowed boats and sang. Some had been killed in battle, and their heads and bodies were separated. Some were dressed in the clothes of the gentry. Some shot arrows, some waved sticks, and some raised flags and bore aloft parasols. Some were dragons and snakes, and some were birds. Some were foxes and carried fire in their tails, at which all the spectators marvelled. The performance began at eleven in the morning and lasted until three that afternoon. As far as the voices of those who sang hidden in the bottom of the puppet booth were concerned, there were some good and some poor, some delicate and some powerful. There were drums and flutes and foreign guitars to accompany the movements of the puppets and there were songs...The puppets were just as if they were alive. The man who was in charge of things to-day is the best puppeteer in Edo. His name is Koheita, and he is the most skilled of the puppet operators of recent times."[27]

We may gather what sort of play Razan saw from the list he made of the kinds of puppets and also from the plot of *Hanaya*, a *jōruri* produced by Satsuma Jōun in 1634 which has been preserved. The story tells of a villainous provincial lord who, on being refused the daughter of a certain rich man, determines to win control of her by denouncing her father as a traitor. The rich man flees, sending a message to his family telling of his misfortune. They attempt to go to the capital to plead for him. His son and daughter are deceived by a henchman of the villain and are brought into the villain's house. He tries to detain them there, but that night the girl is stricken with a disease which renders her most ugly, and the villain, no longer interested in the girl, chases out the brother and sister. They reach a river on their journey, where an old man emerges from the water to help them, and where a serpent later appears to prevent pursuing assassins from doing their evil work. It was the deity Kannon who saved them, and when the brother dies of fatigue a while later, the same goddess answers the sister's prayers and restores the boy to life. When the two reach the capital they are told that the Empress is ill and that no one has been able to cure her. The boy goes to the palace, recites the Kannon Sutra, and the Empress is immediately restored to perfect health. She wishes to bestow on him a province as a reward, but he asks instead that his father be brought back to his former honours. He discovers, however, that the father was sentenced to death four or five days before. He rushes with the letter of pardon to his father, arrives just in time, and proves himself a filial son. The rich man goes to the capital where he is granted two provinces. The father and his

children thank Kannon for all her blessings. Then the rich man crushes his
enemy, returns home, and lives there happily ever after.[28]

However the plot of *Hanaya* may strike modern readers, it was easily the
most important play of its time, and may be said to represent the first major
dramatic contribution to the *jōruri*, the earlier works such as *The Tale of Jōruri*
having been, as has been mentioned, originally meant for recitation and not
for stage performance. Several features of *Hanaya* might be especially noted.
The work is in six acts, which remained the custom in Edo until the Gidayū
style of *jōruri* became popular there some seventy-five years later. The second
act is devoted almost entirely to a *michiyuki* or "road-travel", a lyrical descriptive scene telling of the journey of the rich man to refuge in the provinces.
The *michiyuki* of this play or of any subsequent *jōruri* is not intended primarily
to advance the action, much less to afford us any dramatic insights on the characters of the piece. It is intended to intoxicate by its lyrical beauty, and to delight by its clever references to famous places in Japan. No people is more
fascinated by the names of places and their associations than is the Japanese,
and though it may have little dramatic interest, no part of a *jōruri* affords
greater pleasure than the *michiyuki* which caters to this fascination. The
michiyuki is a prominent part of Nō plays as well as of the *jōruri*, but the brevity
of the Nō forbids the great indulgence in the often meaningless beauty of names
that one finds in *jōruri* from Jōun's time on.

Another interesting feature of *Hanaya* is the element of the miraculous.
If the restoration to life of the boy and the cure of the Empress may be interpreted as products of the influence of the proselytising *sekkyō*, the appearance
from the water of the old man and the serpent can only be ascribed to a desire
to delight the public with the tricks of the puppeteer's trade. With the increase
in skill of the puppet operators we find *jōruri* texts which call for more and more
extraordinary miracles.

Satsuma Jōun was a pioneer in the improvement of the techniques of puppetry. We do not know much about the kind of puppets operated by Hikita
from Nishinomiya, the man credited with having been the first to stage a puppet
jōruri. It is doubtful whether he and his puppets had any connection with the
wandering *kugutsu-mawashi* of earlier times. It has been suggested that Hikita's
puppets were of a much more advanced type, and had come from China during
the Muromachi Period.[29] An account of 1617 tells us that already at that date
string-operated marionettes were common, but hand-operated puppets are
also believed to have existed about the same time.[30] Jōun seems to have preferred
the hand-operated puppets. From the account of Hayashi Razan quoted above
it would appear that Jōun (the Koheita of Razan) operated the puppets. It is
possible that he combined the functions of chanter and puppeteer, such a dual

role having been facilitated by the fact that a curtain concealed the operators and musicians from the public. The combination of the two arts was not usual, however, and it is only further testimonial to Jōun's importance in the history of the *jōruri* if he actually succeeded in doing both.

We may notice in *Hanaya* another typically Buddhist feature, the application of the doctrine of "encourage virtue and punish vice". This doctrine was probably in large part responsible for the usual happy endings of the plays, with the villain discomfited and the hero triumphant and joyous. There is a difference, however, in the way the same sort of "encourage virtue and punish vice" or miracle theme would be treated in the *jōruri* and the *sekkyō*. The latter, it will be remembered, began as simple explanations of Buddhist doctrines, but later developed into a form of dramatic recitation. About the same time that puppets were added to the *jōruri* they were also adopted by the *sekkyō* reciters, but we know little of the details since even less attention was devoted by the scholars to the *sekkyō* than to the *jōruri*.[31] The difference in the treatment of a subject by *sekkyō* and *jōruri* writers may be typified in the following example.

In the *jōruri* vice is punished and virtue rewarded when the long-suffering hero slays the villain and crushes his enemies. In the *sekkyō* the hero will forgive the villain his sins and save his enemies, thus winning them over to the side of the angels. If the hero is caught up in a battle he does not massacre the enemy, as his *jōruri* counterpart would do, but instead relies on his virtuous non-resistance to save the day.[32] It is not difficult to see why the lively *jōruri* should have captured the fancy of the seventeenth century Japanese public; it is puzzling if somewhat pleasing that the same pleasure-mad public should have supported for so long a time the pious palaver of the *sekkyō*.

Hanaya and the other surviving *jōruri* of the early period show little trace of the influence of the Nō drama, probably because the *jōruri* was still in too elementary a state to admit either the wraith-like plots or the extremely complex poetry of the Nō. The *bukyoku*, or dance dramas, and the fairy tale were the chief sources of the material of the writers of *jōruri*. A majority of the surviving plays are on religious themes, and the rest are chiefly loyalty and vengeance works.[33] In spite of the fact that the original *Tale of Jōruri* might be regarded primarily as a love story, none of the early *jōruri* plays have love as a central theme, at least of those that have survived.[34] The themes are those of medieval Japanese literature; not until the following period did the effect of the move of the cultural centre of Japan from Kyoto and Osaka to Edo show in the subject matter of the *jōruri*.

The climax of the "stiff" style of Jōun may be found in the Kimpira plays performed by Jōun's pupil, Izumi-dayū.[35] The precise date of the first of the Kimpira plays is not known, but it is believed to have been sometime shortly before the great fire of 1657 which devastated Edo. The disaster created a need for entertainment to distract the minds of the inhabitants from the painful scenes they had witnessed. It is not obvious why the entertainment desired should have taken the form of the Kimpira *jōruri*. One Japanese critic has offered an ingenious if not entirely convincing explanation, as follows.

By the middle of the seventeenth century Japan had experienced for the first time in many hundreds of years a long period of virtually uninterrupted peace. The Tokugawa family, victorious at the Battle of Sekigahara in 1600 and at Osaka in 1615, had ruled Japan with firmness and in peace. With no military pursuits to occupy them, a number of the samurai turned to rowdyism and terrorised the townsmen, who were beginning to prosper as never before. Among the most powerful of these samurai was one Mizuno Jūrozaemon of Edo. Jūrozaemon named his five chief henchmen after those of the leading characters in the Nō play *Ōeyama*, which relates how five heroes set out to subjugate devils. The devils that Jūrozaemon chose to quell were the upstart townsmen. The samurai at first met with little opposition on the part of the devils, for a long tradition of obedience to the military class was still very strong. Gradually some townsmen began to resist the outlawry of the samurai. Two of them, Chōbei and Machiyakko, showed especial courage towards Jūrozaemon. It appears that Jūrozaemon considered himself to have been humiliated by Chōbei one day in a theatre, and he asked Chōbei to come to see him at his home. Chōbei's friends urged him not to accept, and Chōbei himself knew that Jūrozaemon could only be seeking vengeance, but he thought that it would be ignoble to refuse, and went to dinner at Jūrozaemon's house. There he was trapped and slain. This event took place in the fourth moon of 1650.

Chōbei's friends were unable to avenge his death. One night Machiyakko and the others caught Jūrozaemon as he was returning from the pleasure quarter, but Jūrozaemon took to his heels and made his escape. Not until 1664 did the Shogunate government act on the matter, when it ordered the death of the villainous Jūrozaemon.[36]

While Jūrozaemon was still unpunished the townsmen of Edo felt burning within themselves an inchoate rage against the samurai. They were at once too timid and too traditional in their ways of thought to attempt any direct action against the samurai. Only vicariously could they hope to enjoy the vengeance they desired. When they went to the *jōruri* theatre to see the Kimpira plays they could associate themselves with the dashing hero Kimpira, who feared no man, or with his gallant friend Taketsuna, who combined wisdom and bravery. In that way alone (until 1664 at least) were they able to feel themselves victors over Jūrozaemon and the other lawless samurai.[37]

C

The Kimpira plays have their origin in the same Nō play *Ōeyama* that provided Jūrozaemon with such inspiration, but the plot has been vastly expanded, and the heroes are no longer the original five men but Kimpira and Taketsuna, the sons of two of them. Kimpira is the typical Japanese military hero, fearless, quick-tempered, imprudent, simple and rough, a type which was to find its ultimate expression in the person of Chikamatsu's Coxinga. To set off his particular qualities we have the highly admirable but not so Japanese Taketsuna, who was to serve as model for Kanki in *The Battles of Coxinga*. The two of them went through a series of adventures, always triumphant, and always demonstrating their complete loyalty to the Emperor and the Shōgun.

Many of the Kimpira pieces were written by one Oka Seibei, about whom little is known.[38] The quality of the writing was inferior, for it was designed to be immediately intelligible even to the least educated woman or child, and good Japanese writing is usually full of allusions, and difficult. The "stiff" style favoured by the chanter Izumi-dayū and the general roughneck quality of the action were especially congenial to the people of Edo. Another factor which helped to promote the success of the Kimpira plays was the action taken by the government against the *kabuki*. In 1642 women were prohibited from appearing on the stage, and in 1652 this prohibition was extended to female impersonators.[39] Public favour thus was caused to centre on the puppet theatre.

The Kimpira plays continued to be extremely popular in Edo until about 1664 when, possibly because of a natural surfeit with the wild adventures of Kimpira, or possibly because the sentence passed by the government on Jūrozaemon removed the necessity of finding vicarious vengeance or for reasons unknown, they quickly began to lose favour, and the Edo puppet theatre went into a decline from which it never emerged.

1664 - 1686

During the many years that the Edo *jōruri* was supreme there was very little important activity in Kyoto, and virtually none at all in Osaka. For a long time the chief chanter in Kyoto was one Wakasa-no-kami, an exponent of the characteristic "flexible" style.[40] In 1657 Toraya Kidayū arrived in Kyoto from Edo and founded a puppet theatre in Shijōgawara,[41] where he put on *jōruri* combining Kimpira with the prevailing "flexible" flavour. Shortly afterwards another refugee from Edo, Toraya Gendayū, and his more famous pupil, Inoue Harima-no-jō, founded the puppet theatre in Osaka.[42]

The Kimpira plays, however modified, still remained alien to the taste of Western Japan, and when in this period the puppet theatre began to flourish

24

there a new subject found increasing importance in the *jōruri* plays: love. During the period 1664-1686 the theme of love, which had been missing in the Kimpira *jōruri* and other military plays, was treated in a number of romantic pieces. One that may interest Westerners particularly is that called *Aigonowaka*.[43] This is the story of a young stepmother who falls in love with the man who is her son in name only. She is unable to restrain her passion, criminal though it is, and tells her stepson of it. The young man, Aigonowaka, refuses her advances. The stepmother, in anger, joins with her lady-in-waiting to plot against him. They steal a precious sword and scabbard belonging to her husband (Aigonowaka's father) and accuse the youth of the theft. The boy's father has him tied up, but his dead mother's spirit releases Aigonowaka that night. He escapes, but can find no place to take refuge and finally drowns himself, leaving behind a letter to his father. When the father reads it and learns of the guilt of his wife and her servant, he causes them to be killed. The story was often reworked, but the supernatural elements, which interfere with a Westerner's enjoyment of this new approach to the Hippolytus theme, continued to multiply with each recension. There was also a moralising quality in the text which probably resulted from the fact that it had originally (about 1661) been produced as a *sekkyō* puppet play.[44]

Another theme associated with love that we find for the first time in this period is that of jealousy. *The Quarrel of the Consorts of Kazan-in* (1673) is the pioneer work in this field. The play tells of the rivalry of the Ladies Kōkiden and Fujitsubo. Fujitsubo dies an unnatural death, and her revengeful ghost appears to torment Kōkiden, finally driving her to death. Kōkiden is restored to life by prayers, but the vengeful Fujitsubo, unsatisfied, turns herself into a weasel and steals into the palace. When discovered she transforms herself into the shape of a wicked demon and summons a host of other demons to her aid. They are finally quelled by five martial heroes.[45]

The Quarrel of the Consorts of Kazan-in does not strike the modern reader as being essentially a romantic play, but the theme of jealousy and that of the vengeful spirit are both derived from love and are commonly connected in Japanese novels. But it was not long after the play just described that the classic theme of the Japanese theatre of later days made its appearance: the love suicide. Already in 1676 in *Yuya Monogatari*, a *jōruri* performed by Tosa-no-shōjō, the hero and heroine decide on a love suicide, but are unsuccessful in their attempt. In the fourth moon of 1683 there occurred in Osaka a love suicide of two unhappy lovers, and the event furnished the material for a number of dramatic works. This love suicide gained notoriety as the first of many celebrated ones. It was from about this time that the word *shinjū* or "love suicide" gained currency.[46] With the development of the *shinjūmono*, as plays about love suicide were called, the love element came to assume a dominant role in many of the works of the Japanese theatre.

Other important themes of plays of this period included loyalty and filial piety, vengeance, and the miracles of the gods and of Buddha. One feature of the loyalty plays is the self-sacrificing substitutions, designed to save one's lord by taking punishment on oneself. A variant of this appears in *The Tale of Iroha*. The girl Iroha, believing her lover to have been guilty of the murder of his mother, attempts to take the punishment herself, though it was actually the crime of her lover's brother. Just when she is about to be punished, the lady in whose care Iroha had been left, seeking to save her, in turn attempts to substitute herself for Iroha before the real villain is discovered.[47] In *The Battles of Coxinga* we find a different type of substitution, when Go Sankei substitutes his infant son for the imperial child in the womb of the dead Empress.

Very few plays were without a supernatural element.[48] Miracles were wrought by Buddha in his various aspects, by old men, gods, demons, spirits of the dead, and by little children. Such miracles, like those in *The Battles of Coxinga*, were designed to show to the best advantage the art of the puppet operator, and thereby to impress the audience. In this period there was also a marked increase in the proficiency of the stage property handlers. Birds, animals, snakes and even insects populated the scenes, and the sun, the moon, and clouds would pass at appropriate times in natural fashion over the stage, with no direct resort to human hands.[49]

One element of spectacle conspicuous by its absence was scenery. Backgrounds suitable for the action of the play were not employed. None of the accounts of the period indicate that any effort was made to suggest the locale of any scene. This was probably in keeping with the traditions of the Nō drama, in which there is virtually no use of scenery.[50]

As far as puppets were concerned, it is not clear from contemporary accounts whether string- or hand-operated puppets were more widely used. The operators, in any case, remained invisible to the public in Kyoto and Osaka, but were at least partially visible in Edo. The puppets were still primitive, having neither hands nor feet, but already they were being dressed in splendid costumes.[51]

As far as the chanters of the period are concerned, there are several noted ones, including Inoue Harima-no-jō, Uji Kaga-no-jō, and Yamamoto Tosa-no-jō (or Tosa-no-shōjō), who were most popular respectively in Osaka, Kyoto and Edo.

Inoue Harima-no-jō is interesting chiefly because his style influenced Gidayū, but Uji Kaga-no-jō (1635-1711) was a much more considerable figure, and, indeed, one of the leading men in *jōruri* history.[52] It was Kaga-no-jō (also known as Kadayū) who first succeeded in making the tone of the *jōruri* artistic. In the prefaces he wrote to various collections of *jōruri* plays, he showed how deeply he was influenced by Nō drama, and in particular by the aesthetic principles of Zeami, the greatest Nō master. He tried to lay down rules for the performance of *jōruri* which would lift the medium to the level of the Nō. The five-act *jōruri*, which had been traditional in Kyoto and Osaka, as the six-act had been in Edo, was now likened to the five Nō plays customarily performed in one programme. As another parallel to the Nō, short comic plays called *kyōgen* were put on in between the acts of the *jōruri* as they had been staged between Nō plays. Sometimes these *kyōgen* took the form of dances, as a contemporary diary informs us.[53]

Although the plays chanted by Kaga-no-jō incorporated large sections of Nō dramas in their five acts, and although he made extensive use of Nō melodies, these puppet plays were clearly in the *jōruri* tradition, and not mere amplifications of the Nō. He borrowed also from the *kabuki*, adding the flavour of the prostitute quarter to his plays. He is thus credited with having been responsible for the beginning of the so-called *sewa-jidaimono*, or combination mundane and historical play. Chikamatsu wrote some of his early *jōruri* for Kaga-no-jō, including *Yotsugi Soga*, which is considered by some critics to be his earliest surviving play.[54]

The result of the borrowing from the Nō was to lend a literary value to the *jōruri* it had not had before, while the *kabuki* influence led to much greater realism. It is important to remember that Kaga-no-jō achieved his successes in Kyoto, the city where tradition was most highly regarded in Japan. The Edo audiences would probably not have taken kindly to Kaga-no-jō's literary improvements, as we can gather from the quality of the productions of Yamamoto Tosa-no-jō, their long-time favourite.

Tosa-no-jō (*c.* 1647-1712) tried to combine the "stiff" style of the Kimpira with the somewhat more refined tone of Kyoto plays.[55] This he achieved by adding a strongly sentimental tone to all the works he presented. His frequent introduction of brothel scenes would seem to be in step in the direction of realism, but the only changes were on the surface, not in the plots. The woman carried off is no longer a princess but a courtesan, and the abductor a townsman and not a samurai or a feudal baron. Tosa-no-jō was apparently untouched by the influence of the Nō. The works he chanted had no unity of plot, but were mere disconnected incidents. The language of these plays has been termed "a model of the worst possible composition".[56] Yet his school reigned in Edo for many years, and the last echoes of it were heard into the nineteenth century. The art of Kaga-no-jō would have been wasted in a city where so inferior a kind of *jōruri* long held sway.

1686 - 1715

No name in the history of the *jōruri* is more celebrated than that of Takemoto Gidayū (1651-1714).[57] *Gidayū-bushi*, or "Gidayū-music", is a common way of denoting the art of the puppet theatre, so famous did his name become. It may seem unusual that it should be with a chanter rather than with an author or even a celebrated puppet operator that the art was always most closely identified, but the role of the chanter is the one of the greatest importance in the *jōruri*. It is significant that while we know the names of many of the chanters of the early period, the authors of the plays are unknown. Often Japanese books would lead us to believe that the chanter was entirely responsible for the quality of the works he performed, as if the contribution of the author were of negligible value. In a sense this was true. Until the time of Chikamatsu the *jōruri* plays served only as "vehicles" for the chanters to demonstrate their particular talents, as sometimes in the West plays or operas are composed for celebrated artists. The author was in an entirely dependent position on the chanter. If, for example, Oka Seibei, the author of many Kimpira plays, had grown tired of writing the childish adventures usually found in such works he would not have been at liberty to propose a change of subject. The author was expected to produce a variant on some well-known story which would meet the chanter's special requirements. The chanter, who usually also acted as producer, had absolute control over the texts he used. In this sense we may with propriety speak of innovations in *jōruri* texts effected by Kaga-no-jō, or any other chanter, even though he did not actually write the words himself. In this sense also we may speak of Gidayū as the greatest figure in the history of the *jōruri*, though Chikamatsu's masterpieces would make us question such a designation.

Gidayū, the son of a humble peasant family from the area around Osaka, became interested in the style of chanting of Harima-no-jō when he was a young man, and though he never actually studied under him became so proficient that he was known as a "second Harima".[58] About 1675 Gidayū's teacher, Shimizu Ribei,[59] opened a theatre in the Dōtombori in Osaka, and Gidayū was employed as his assistant. It had previously been the custom for one man to chant an entire *jōruri* play, but about this time it became usual for two or three chanters to take turns, the best parts being reserved for the chief chanter.[60] After Gidayū had served as assistant to Shimizu for a few years, he went to Kyoto, where in 1677 he became Uji Kaga-no-jō's assistant. He won a good reputation for his work there, and felt confident enough to open a theatre of his own in Shijōgawara, where he appeared late in the same year under the name of Shimizu Ridayū. He scored a fair sucess with the *jōruri* he chanted there, as may be inferred from the fact that they were printed with his name on them, but his style did not entirely satisfy the Kyoto audiences, who were used to the mellifluous Kaga-no-jō. Gidayū's theatre failed soon afterwards, and we lose track of him for five or six years.

Early in 1684 the manager of Kaga-no-jō's company, a man named Takeya Shōbei, quarrelled with Kaga-no-jō and organised a new company to perform in Osaka. He took with him from Kaga-no-jō's staff the samisen player Takezawa Gonemon, and the puppet operator Yoshida Saburōbei, skilled men in their professions. He chose for his chanter the then Shimizu Ridayū, who thereupon changed his name to Takemoto Gidayū. The Takemoto Theatre was opened on the first day of the second moon of 1684 in the Dōtombori.[61] The *jōruri* presented during the first year were three works by Chikamatsu that had originally been written for Kaga-no-jō, *The Soga Successors*, *Aisome River*, and *The Tale of Iroha*.[62]

Gidayū's company was so successful that it roused the jealousy of Kaga-no-jō, who was already stung by the desertion of three of his company. He accordingly moved from Kyoto to Osaka with his whole company in the first moon of 1685 to demonstrate his superiority to the Osaka public. There he presented Saikaku's *jōruri*, *The Almanac*,[63] to which Gidayū responded with a work by Chikamatsu, *The Wise Ladies' Writing Practice and the New Almanac*.[64] Gidayū triumphed unqualifiedly over his rival. Kaga-no-jō was forced to withdraw *The Almanac*. He managed to regain some of his lost prestige when he presented another play by Chikamatsu, but his theatre was destroyed by fire during the run of the play, and Kaga-no-jō returned to Kyoto, leaving Gidayū with undisputed supremacy in Osaka.[65]

In the following year Gidayū asked Chikamatsu to write a new play for him. The result, *Kagekiyo Victorious*,[66] was a triumph for both men. The collaboration of Gidayū and Chikamatsu ushered in the great period of the *jōruri*. Although Chikamatsu continued to write *jōruri* occasionally for Kaga-no-jō until 1692 or 1693, he seems to have found working with Gidayū more satisfactory, and he wrote three to five plays for him every year thereafter. The outstanding product of their collaboration was *Love Suicides at Sonezaki*,[67] which was written in 1703. The work was so successful that the company recouped all its previous losses. Gidayū found this a good time for withdrawing as manager of the company. He surrendered the position to Takeda Izumo, but continued as a chanter in the theatre until shortly before his death in the ninth moon of 1714.[68]

Certain changes in the techniques of puppet operation had contributed to the success of Gidayū's performances. By about 1690 the puppets had acquired hands and feet, and they had come to be operated most commonly by hand and not by strings. In a picture of that year we see a puppeteer operating a puppet from underneath, with his hands inside the figure.[69] This was the technique used by Tatsumatsu Hachirobei, who was much praised for his manipulation of the puppet of the heroine in *Love Suicides at Sonezaki*. In the Hōei era (1704-1710) the puppeteers began to perform in the open instead of behind curtains, as had been the custom in Kyōto and Osaka. The Japanese audiences, far from finding the presence of the operators on the stage distracting, appreciated the more personal quality one gains when the puppeteers can be seen.[70]

Gidayū had not cared for the spectacular effects possible in the puppet theatre. The miracle element, still so conspicuous in the contemporary *jōruri* performed in Edo, is seldom encountered in the works Gidayū chanted. The new manager of the company, Takeda Izumo, was more interested in spectacle, and it was under his supervision that beautiful decor became a part of the *jōruri* for the first time.[71] After the death of Gidayū, and especially in *The Battles of Coxinga*, Izumo was to have the opportunity of satisfying his fondness for the colourful. The tendency of the *jōruri* theatre under the influence of Izumo was to develop in the direction of greater spectacle but not of greater realism. The audience was always conscious of the unreality of the puppets, especially when they could see the operators manipulating them, but their pleasure in the spectacle was thereby made only the greater. Any attempt to achieve realism would only have exposed the fantastic nature of most *jōruri* plots.

At the end of Gidayū's career the Takemoto Theatre began to suffer competition from the Toyotake Theatre on the same street. The latter's guiding spirit was Toyotake Wakatayū (1681-1764).[72] Wakatayū had at one time been a pupil of Gidayū, but he had taken advantage of the absence of Gidayū's company on a road tour to open a theatre of his own in 1702. This attempt ended in failure, as did another early in the following year. In the seventh moon of 1703 he founded the Toyotake Theatre. This time he had more success because he had the services of a good playwright, Ki no Kaion (1663-1742).[73] He also managed to induce the puppeteer Tatsumatsu Hachirōbei to join his company (but Hachirōbei returned to the Takemoto Theatre in time for the first performance of *The Battles of Coxinga*). Although Ki no Kaion was a very accomplished writer, his plays were not the equal of those of Chikamatsu. It was for this reason that the Toyotake Theatre was never able to offer a serious threat to the Takemoto Theatre except in the critical period immediately following Gidayū's death.[74] This was the first time in the history of the *jōruri* that the author occupied so important a place in the prosperity of a theatre.

Gidayū's successor, as named in his will, was the youthful Masatayū, only twenty-three years old at the time. Masatayū (1691-1744) had made his debut as a chanter at the Toyotake Theatre in 1710. Two years later he was engaged by the Takemoto Theatre. Gidayū was very fond of him and coached him. Masatayū was still by no means a finished artist when he inherited the position of chief chanter of the company, and there was both surprise and dissatisfaction on the part of the other artists. Masatayū was saved by Chikamatsu, who wrote for him *The Battles of Coxinga*. After this triumph Masatayū went on to gain new laurels as chief chanter in the other important works Chikamatsu wrote until his death in 1725.

(b) CHIKAMATSU'S CAREER AND THE PLACE IN IT OF "THE BATTLES OF COXINGA"

A good deal more is known about Chikamatsu's life than of Shakespeare's, for example, but such facts as we have are colourless for the most part, and afford us little clue to the nature of his personality. It is for this reason undoubtedly that there has grown up about the facts a small body of apocrypha, the attempts of later admirers to create an image of this man who once had lived and written over a hundred plays. No less than ten localities have been identified as Chikamatsu's birthplace, with numerous proofs for each in the form of anecdotes and legends; less interest is shown in his final resting place, with only half a dozen claimants for the honour. The few scraps of writing in Chikamatsu's hand have been examined with desperate care by scholars for some fresh insights into his life, but they generally can find no more to say of the holographic material than that a particular piece shows Chikamatsu's "honesty" or his "reverence" or any one of the other virtues.

The early accounts of Chikamatsu's life, unsatisfactory as they are, are sometimes more reliable than later ones, for the elaborate legends had not yet been conceived. This notice appeared in the *Chikuhō Koji*, written in 1765:

> In olden times there was no such thing as a person devoting himself to being a writer of *jōruri*. *Jōruri* were composed by *haikai* masters (or by persons who had nothing better to do) for their own distraction ... Chikamatsu Monzaemon was the first man to make *jōruri* writing his profession. He was a person of wide learning and great literary ability. Moreover, he had an insight into the spirit of his times, and understood everyday life. He wrote over one hundred *jōruri*. His style is one of extraordinary quality.
>
> He was by birth a native of Kyoto, and served the family of a certain court noble. His real family name was Sugimori. He was of good lineage. For certain reasons he became a *rōnin*. Early in the Genroku era he became a

playwright at the Miyako Mandayū *kabuki* theatre and also wrote *jōruri* for Uji Kaga-no-jō. He was the patron saint of playwrights in this country. Later he went to Osaka and served as dramatist to Takemoto Gidayū. He died on the twenty-second day of the eleventh moon of 1724.[75]

So short an account failed to satisfy anyone. Later scholars, by virtue of diligent research and the play of vigorous imaginations, were able to expand the biography considerably. A critic of the Meiji (1868-1912) era wrote:

Chikamatsu Monzaemon was a member of the Sugimori family and was given the name of Nobumori. His name as a boy was Tōshirō. His literary names were Sōrinshi, Heiandō and Fuisannin.[76] He was a native of Hagi in Nagato. His father was named Muramatsu Hachibei (or else one Sugimori). Tōshirō was the third son. When he was young he entered the Chikamatsu Temple in Karatsu, in the province of Hizen. He shaved his head and took the name of Koken. He was gifted with extraordinary talents and was fond of study. After a time he became familiar with all the classics, the Buddhist scriptures, and the writings of the sages ... He was eventually promoted and made the chief priest of a certain temple. He changed his name to Gimon. After a time, however, he realised that the priesthood was not his calling. He left the temple and went to Kyoto, where he stayed at the house of his younger brother, Okamoto Ippō. He later let his hair grow, returned to the laity, and served the Ichijō family.

After he left this position he changed his name to Chikamatsu Monzaemon. He then became the author of romances. He wrote for the *kabuki* theatre of Miyako Mandayū, and *jōruri* libretti for Uji Kaga-no-jō, Inoue Harima-no-jō and others. The puppet theatre was very popular at this time. The music was of the *jōruri* type, but the words and the plots were not distinguished. The *jōruri* plays were limited in variety and none of them was worth seeing. It was inevitable that when Monzaemon, with his genius, appeared in this milieu his talent won him fame. Thus it was that in 1685 he wrote a *jōruri* play called *Kagekiyo Victorious* on order from Takemoto Gidayū. Monzaemon indeed transformed the old theatre and created the new kind of *jōruri* with this first work.

Monzaemon went to Osaka from Kyoto in the first moon of 1688. He wrote a large number of *jōruri* libretti there. It was his work *Love Suicides at Sonezaki*, written in 1703, which was the first example of the domestic tragedy in Japan. It was of divine beauty in its writing. Ogyū Sorai, a Confucian scholar of the time, read the *michiyuki* of this play and praised it, saying that Chikamatsu's most wonderful qualities were to be found in it, and that one could divine all his excellences by reading just this passage and nothing else. This opinion of Sorai, a great Confucian of uncommon talent, shows how much Chikamatsu was admired at that time . . .

He died on the twenty-first day of the eleventh moon of 1724. He is buried at the Hōmyō Temple in Tera-machi, 8 chōme, Osaka. Other accounts have it that he is buried in the Myōsen Temple in Yamaguchi.[77]

It has only been in the last twenty years or so that it has been possible to evaluate these and many other disparate biographies of Chikamatsu. We know now, thanks to recent Japanese discoveries, that Chikamatsu was the second son of Sugimori Nobuyoshi, a samurai of minor rank; and that he was born in the province of Echizen and did not move to Kyoto until he was in his teens, when he became the page of a noble family.[78]

The legends generally had some basis in fact. The name Chikamatsu itself was the source of many of the unauthentic stories. Wondering why the dramatist should have chosen the pseudonym of Chikamatsu led scholars to seek some connection between the playwright and one of the Chikamatsu (or Kinshō,[79] an alternative reading) Temples in Japan. No documentary evidence is extant, if ever there were any such, that Chikamatsu had relations with one of the Chikamatsu Temples, but it was easy for his would-be biographers to leap from a first linking of the author with a temple to the conclusion that he had once been a monk there. The name Chikamatsu was not an uncommon one among actors, however, and it might be less fanciful to seek to establish connections between Chikamatsu and certain of the actors of his time than with any temple.[80]

Be that as it may, there is nothing to indicate that Chikamatsu ever led a clerical life. His biographers are fond of praising his vast store of knowledge —one of them claimed that in reading Chikamatsu's plays one learned all about Buddhism, Confucianism and Shinto[81]—but his learning is actually of no extraordinary quality, certainly not of a degree to suggest the product of monastic discipline. A less reverent critic likened Chikamatsu's mind "if not to a wastepaper basket filled with odd scraps, at least to a pawnbroker's office with tickets for a variety of articles."[82] There is no doubt but that Chikamatsu was very well read in the Nō drama—no less than eighty-two of them are quoted in his plays— and in such works as the *Analects* of Confucius and the *Lotus Sutra*, but his knowledge seems to have been gleaned chiefly from anthologies. His popularity was such, however, that some of his admirers described his learning in glowing terms: "The profundity of his learning was such that it would be no exaggeration to say that he is truly without example in all history".[83]

Chikamatsu stands out in an age which produced such men as the irrepressible novelist Ibara Saikaku as the one important fiction writer of samurai origin. Although Saikaku and other writers of humble origin were ill at ease in descriptions of life among the warrior class, Chikamatsu's samurai tales carry conviction.[84] He was famed for his ability to capture the speech of the different classes with accuracy. If there is little individual characterisation in Chikamatsu's plays, the personages all speak with fidelity to their particular station. Chikamatsu was particularly fortunate in that, having early become familiar with the speech and manners of the samurai, he was quick enough of ear and eye to catch those of the merchants and artisans with whom his work brought him into contact. This was one of the reasons for his success with all classes.

Little is known of Chikamatsu's youth. The only record to have survived from that period is the haiku he wrote, which was published in a collection along with similar poems by other members of his family in 1671 (when he was eighteen).

> Shirakumo ya   White clouds
> Hananaki yama no   Have covered the shame
> Haji kakushi   Of the flowerless mountain.[85]

Chikamatsu's career as an author was launched with this modest start.

The date of his first play is a matter of conjecture, but some scholars put it as early as 1673, the year of publication of the unsigned *The Quarrel of the Consorts of Kazan-in*.[86] A note in the Sugimori family annals tells us that Chikamatsu served Ichijō Zenkō Ekan.[87] It may have been shortly after the latter's death in 1672 that Chikamatsu began his dramatic career. The assumption of the pen name of Chikamatsu also seems to date from the period. Perhaps the playwright did pay a visit to the Kinshō Temple[88] in Ōmi after the death of his patron. In any case, he was soon turning out both *kabuki* and *jōruri* plays under his new name.

Unlike his forerunners, Chikamatsu felt no shame in attaching his name openly to his *kabuki* works. A critic, writing in 1687, declared:

> Someone said to me, "I find nothing to praise in a writer's being so pretentious as to write his name on a *jōruri* libretto, but nowadays they write the name of the author even on *kabuki* plays. The words 'written by Chikamatsu' appear even on the theatrical billboards at the crossways. How conceited this seems! If he were writing a book of poetry or a novel, should he call it *The Novel Written by Chikamatsu?*"
>
> I answered him "I quite agree with you; it *is* peculiar. However, the important thing here is the matter of a livelihood. In the old days it would have appeared in very bad taste, and there would have been some doubt as to whether they should write 'play by Chikamatsu'. Since he has succeeded in making a living out of the theatre, it is his intention to end his days in theatrical pursuits. This being the case, it is only fair that people should know his name."[89]

We learn from the same source that at one time Chikamatsu was a scene-shifter at the Miyako Mandayū Theatre. This experience may have been useful to the playwright in learning the techniques of the theatre.

Chikamatsu continued to write *kabuki* plays until as late as about 1704, principally for the actor Sakada Tōjūrō, but the most important, if not the most voluminous, part of his production was always his *jōruri* plays.[90] It was in 1686 that Chikamatsu met Takemoto Gidayū and wrote for him *Kagekiyo Victorious*. To what degree Chikamatsu must be considered to have been Gidayū's pupil we may never know, but the dramatist's later easy mastery of the medium presupposed careful training. At first Chikamatsu felt obliged to adhere to the old forms traditional to the *jōruri*, even in the use of the stereotyped phrases that introduced acts. As he became accustomed to Gidayū's style, however, he shows increasing boldness in his experimentations: "Those move easiest who have learned to dance".

Chikamatsu died on the twenty-second day of the eleventh lunar month of 1724, or 6th January, 1725 by Western reckoning. He had written, by Sonoda's calculation, 129 *jōruri* plays (of which 22 were domestic tragedies) and 31 *kabuki* plays. Eighteen of the total number of plays have not survived, and others are of disputed authorship.[91]

Critics have divided Chikamatsu's career into three or four phases, the number depending on whether a particular writer is interested in Chikamatsu's *kabuki* plays. For example, Sonoda Tamio proposed a three period division of the *jōruri* works: (1) 1673 to 1704—period of apprenticeship and development; (2) 1705-1714—period of maturation; (3) 1715 to 1724—period of full maturity.[92] Kuroki Kanzō preferred a four period division: (1) Old *jōruri* period—until 1686 when Chikamatsu wrote *Kagekiyo Victorious*; (2) *Kabuki* period—until 1692; (3) Domestic tragedy period—until 1714, when Gidayū died; (4) Period of full maturity—until 1724, the year of his death.[93] Serge Elisséev made a more subjective analysis of the periods of Chikamatsu's career: (1) 1678 to 1690—during which Chikamatsu was inspired almost exclusively by historical subjects borrowed from the Nō drama; (2) 1690 to 1703—in which Chikamatsu looked for the relations between the events and the acts of his heroes; (3) 1703 to 1713—a period beginning with *Love Suicides at Sonezaki* and marked by dramas which show Chikamatsu as a superior psychologist; (4) 1713 to 1724—in which Chikamatsu introduced into his historical dramas what he had studied in his survey of bourgeois life.[94]

Rather than attempt to make a new division of the periods of Chikamatsu's activity, or even to choose among the analyses of the distinguished scholars above mentioned, I should prefer to give what may be considered the three most important dates in the career of the dramatist: 1686—beginning of his association with Gidayū; 1703—production of *Love Suicides at Sonezaki*; and 1715—production of *The Battles of Coxinga*. The significance of the first date has been explained. The play *Love Suicides at Sonezaki* was important in itself, and was also the first of the domestic tragedies Chikamatsu wrote. *The Battles of Coxinga* was Chikamatsu's greatest success. It established him as supreme, not only among writers of *jōruri*, but among all those associated with the art, for it was his first major work produced without the collaboration of Gidayū, who had died the year before.

It may be that Chikamatsu's natural development would have led him to write plays in his last manner even had Gidayū not died. It seems more likely, however, that Chikamatsu, elevated by Gidayū's death from the role of chief assistant to the master chanter to the position of seniority in the company, felt at greater liberty to write as he chose. He was helped rather than hindered by the fact that Gidayū's successor, Masatayū, had a light voice more suited to passages of romantic or emotional colouring than to those of grand heroics. The final successes of Chikamatsu's career, including most of his masterpieces, were written for Masatayū. These included both domestic tragedies and historical plays, the latter so unlike works of Chikamatsu's earlier periods that they are sometimes called "historico-domestic plays".

The plays of Chikamatsu have been divided into two main categories—historical (*jidaimono*) and domestic (*sewamono*). Most of his *kabuki* and *jōruri* works belong to the former class, and it was to those plays that he devoted his greatest efforts. Modern critics generally tend to prefer Chikamatsu's domestic tragedies for various reasons. They are much closer to Western tragedies and demand no special indulgence on the part of the spectator or reader. Unlike the historical plays (which really require presentation as *jōruri* for full effect) the domestic tragedies may be performed equally well by actors; this has meant that critics outside Osaka, where the last important puppet *jōruri* theatre is located, have no ready chance to see the historical plays in their most favourable setting.

The historical plays, both by their number and quality, are no mean part of Chikamatsu's work, and merit more attention than some critics have given them. They treat a great variety of subjects, ranging in time from the ancient Japanese mythology (the age of the gods, told of in *The Beginning of Long Sleeves in Japan*)[95] to events which had taken place only a few months before the play (like the Chu I-kuei rebellion, treated in *The Chinese Boat: A Modern Coxinga*). Over thirty of the plays are set in the turbulent days at the end of the Heian Period, when the great clans of Taira and Minamoto were battling for supremacy. No real attempt was made to achieve historical accuracy. The characters, whatever the time of the play is supposed to be, are Japanese of the Genroku era. Sometimes Chikamatsu dealt with incidents which were too close to the time of writing to be passed by the censors. Such works as *The Thousand Dogs of the Priest of Sagami* (about the Genroku Shōgun Tsunayoshi), *The Battle of the Frogs at Shimabara* (about the Christian uprising at Shimabara) and *Goban Taiheiki* (about the revenge of the loyal retainers of Akō),[96] could escape official wrath by being dressed in the garb of hundreds of years before. It goes without saying that no one in Chikamatsu's audience was deceived when he called Tsunayoshi "Hōjō Takatoki", nor would Chikamatsu have been criticised for anachronisms in his text.

The grand theme of the historical and domestic plays alike is the conflict between love and duty. In this respect Chikamatsu recalls John Dryden, for the English heroic tragedies of the late seventeenth century bear many resemblances to Chikamatsu's historical plays. The quality of Chikamatsu's plays is aptly described by Mark van Doren in writing of the heroic tragedies of Dryden. "Some of his plays were largely dependent for their success on the quality of the meter, or perhaps the quantity. Writing them with a flesh-and-blood audience, an actually hearing audience in mind, he could not be inattentive to the claims of the ear. His dramatic triumph, such as it was, was a triumph chiefly of the ear...[97] The heroic plays were staged with an elaborate musical accompaniment, and it is certain that the audiences accepted the verse as only a portion of a greater ensemble."[98]

In the historical plays, even in such an unusual example of one as *The Battles of Coxinga*, duty (or honour) generally wins out over love. Kanki is willing to sacrifice his beloved spouse in order to maintain his honour; the wife, Kinshōjo, commits suicide for the same purpose. In the domestic plays, on the other hand, love is the victor, with disastrous results.

Chikamatsu's domestic tragedies often have titles prefixed with the word *shinjū* or "love suicide". The fashion for love suicides in Japan had its one flourishing period at the end of the seventeenth and beginning of the eighteenth centuries. Chikamatsu's historical plays dealt usually, though not always, with events of preceding centuries; his domestic tragedies were sometimes based on happenings of the week before. The actual love suicides at Sonezaki took place on the 27th day of the 4th moon, while Chikamatsu's puppet play was presented on the 7th day of the 5th moon. Love suicides were a conspicuous feature of the time, and it was inevitable that Chikamatsu chose to treat them in his plays. In a typical domestic tragedy the first act shows a young man beset by the need for money, demands for a marriage, or by rivalry in love. In the second act things seem to grow more cheerful, but just when we hope that all may be well, the villain puts in his appearance and forces the young man to choose between his love and his duty. Nothing remains for him but to make one final journey with his beloved to some quiet spot, there to stage a double suicide. This is the subject matter of the third and last act; the triumph of love over duty was likely always to end thus.

The characters in the domestic tragedies, unlike the famous personages of the historical dramas, are generally drawn from the lower middle class. The protagonists are often merchants—of saké, oil, paper. Aristotle would have found such men unworthy to be the heroes of tragedy, and we are not likely to be purged of pity and terror by one of Chikamatsu's domestic tragedies. They are pathetic, and we may well be moved by them to tears, but they lack the greatness of true tragedy. The domestic tragedy had many affinities with the *bunya-bushi* style of *jōruri*. *Bunya-bushi*, named after Okamoto Bunya, was a sentimental sort of *jōruri*, of a very lachrymose nature most of the time. The first domestic tragedy (1702) must be credited to Okamoto Bunya, and probably influenced Chikamatsu's writings.[99] But if Chikamatsu needed any defence against a charge of sentimentality in his tragedies, it could be found in the words of Lamartine:

> Le sublime lasse, le beau trompe, le pathétique seul est infaillible dans l'art. Celui qui sait attendrir sait tout. Il y a plus de génie dans une larme que dans tous les musées et dans toutes les bibliothèques de l'univers. L'homme est comme l'arbre qu'on secoue pour en faire tomber ses fruits: on n'ébranle jamais l'homme sans qu'il en tombe des pleurs.[100]

Apart from whatever influence there may have been from the *bunya-bushi*, Chikamatsu's domestic tragedy is almost entirely his own invention. The three-act, instead of five-act, form is new with him. It may have been derived from the three-play programme of the *kabuki* stage or, as has been suggested, an expansion of the third act of the historical *jōruri*.[101] Chikamatsu must have sensed that the tragic love of a paper dealer and a prostitute would be more effective if presented only in its moments of greatest dramatic intensity. The leisurely pace of the historical dramas would reduce the specific gravity of the often rather slight incidents of the domestic play to an insignificant figure. Chikamatsu retained certain features of the historical play without intrinsic dramatic value, such as the *michiyuki*, in his domestic tragedies, but he went as far in the direction of creating a new theatre as his public would permit.[102]

The success of Chikamatsu's domestic tragedies did not mean that he ceased to write historical dramas. On the contrary, he turned out three times as many historical as domestic plays in the years between the composition of *The Battles of Coxinga* and his death. The historical plays of this last period, as has been suggested, differ markedly from the earlier ones. Chikamatsu attempted to impart to the personages of his histories the psychological insights he had gained in his study of bourgeois life. Chikamatsu did not create memorable characters; his heroes and heroines cannot be conceived of as having an existence apart from the plays in which they figure. There is little characterisation. Most of the time, in the domestic plays at least, we have to do with a hard-pressed young hero, his virtuous but dull wife, and the passionate heroine, a prostitute, together with a number of older persons and villains. These were stock figures of the Japanese stage, and most of his characters would fit in one play quite as easily as in another.[103]

Chikamatsu's personages are types, but not in the manner of the humorous or eccentric types of Molière. They are types because the author was writing in the Japanese manner, the virtuoso manner, which seeks to render with peculiar excellence the familiar. The contrast between Chikamatsu and great Western dramatists may be brought out more strongly by examining the titles of typical plays: *Hamlet, Macbeth, King Lear*; *L'Avare, Les Femmes Savantes, Le Misanthrope*; *Love Suicides at Sonezaki, The Battles of Coxinga, Harakiri of the Woman from Nagamachi*. In the above plays by Shakespeare we are interested in a man, whose name is the title. In those of Molière, it is a type rather than a complex individual, who is the subject. Chikamatsu gives us a situation in which his types exist.

It is not intended to lay too much stress on the matter of the titles; others could be found in the works of Shakespeare, Molière, and Chikamatsu which would indicate quite the opposite. The distinction, however, is probably a fair one. Hamlet or Macbeth or Lear is a full tragic hero, good and bad by turns, great but foolish, impossible to define. He brings his doom upon himself, and it is a doom proportionate to his grandeur. The hero of a Molière comedy is not tragic, of course, although his obsession might so have been treated by other hands. Molière's hero is a type, the expansion of the play's title. Harpagon is *the* miser, an unadulterated essence of miserliness. We are not interested in how he came to be so miserly, or if he died without reforming; we want only to see how his miserliness will stand the test of new situations. Nothing which is not connected with his life as a miser is of importance. Indeed, his life and his miserliness are one for us. The characters in a tragedy by Chikamatsu are functions of their destinies—a love suicide if the title so indicates. In the domestic tragedies, especially, there is no swerving in the straightness of the road to the final solution. The characters are capable of making decisions, changing their minds, obtaining seeming reprieves from their fates, but there is never any real doubt what must happen. Even when nothing seems to stand in the way of happiness, there is an underlying, ever more intense current which, we sense, is dragging the principal characters into the inevitable whirlpool.

39

D

Shakespeare's tragedies usually have a beginning, a middle, and an end. Molière wrote comedies, and his plays are therefore all middle, with only the most arbitrary event, such as the sudden arrival of the sheriff, to terminate what might just as well go on forever. Chikamatsu's plays are all end, or rather, they seem to be written from a knowledge of what the end was to be. They betray their origins; knowing at all times what will happen in the play, we are interested in seeing *how* the author will arrive at the end. It is clear that Chikamatsu has taken the equivalent of a modern newspaper report, or perhaps a paragraph from an historical account, and expanded it into a full length play. In Shakespeare we often have the impression that the play has been cut down from a great deal more material, and that was actually the case. Only rarely, as in *All's Well That Ends Well*, do we experience the opposite sensation, that the play has been built up from an incident, a mere anecdote, but that is true of many of the best of Chikamatsu's plays.

To state the matter in a different way: a play of Shakespeare's or Molière's was written from beginning to end, while Chikamatsu's were written in the opposite direction so to speak. Shakespeare, though aware of course of the eventual resolution of this play, might have wondered, "Othello being the sort of person he is, what will he do when I have Desdemona plead her innocence?" Or Molière might have puzzled, "What would happen if at this point I make my miser meet a miser twice as stingy?" Chikamatsu started with the dead body of a young man and wondered, "How did he happen to die in this way?" When he found an answer, he would go on to, "But why did he become a pirate in the first place?" and so on.

Because he wrote in reverse, so to speak, Chikamatsu's plays have a certain inflexible cause and effect sequence, as though all the earlier events in a character's life must be interpreted in the light of actions leading to his fate. Juliet, Ophelia and Othello all commit suicide, but for entirely dissimilar reasons. Chikamatsu, starting with the fact of a love suicide, could summon only a limited variety of causes. The very limitation in theme possibilities may have appealed to Chikamatsu, for it enabled him to devote his talents to the virtuoso possibilities of a story in which no surprises were expected, as a Flemish painter undertook the familiar, prescribed, but eternally interesting subject of a Madonna and Child. It would never have occurred to Chikamatsu to wish to free himself of the conventional *michiyuki*. The last journey of the suicide-intent lovers might seem much the same from play to play, but to the connoisseur even a slight touch of novelty would be worthy of comment.

The Battles of Coxinga occupies a key place in the work of Chikamatsu. The play may seem curiously old-fashioned to a modern reader, or even nonsensical, but it is in many ways the high point of the Japanese theatre, leaving apart the short Nō dramas. There may not be many modern readers who can justify the great reputation of the play by their own response to it. Nevertheless, both by the judgment of critics and of the countless audiences which have applauded *The Battles of Coxinga* in the two hundred years and more since it was first written, it is a great play.[104]

The Battles of Coxinga is a classic of the modern Japanese language. The play is a catalogue of Japanese styles; almost every variety of expression of which the language is capable is here displayed. It is written chiefly in the alternating verses of seven and five syllables, the traditional Japanese form, but never so regularly as to become monotonous. The play opens with a scene at the Chinese court, and the style is appropriately a heavy Chinese-sounding one, of which an English equivalent might be poetry of the degree of Latinity of Milton's or Dr. Johnson's. The second act, set at a seaside village, enables Chikamatsu to show his mastery of the common colloquial, as well as to give exhibitions of punning and word-plays. The third act, at the Castle of the Lions, has scenes of varied emotional content, and Chikamatsu managed by his style as well as his words to convey the desired feelings. The fourth act, with its *michiyuki* and *keiji*, or scenic description, is a virtuoso performance. The *michiyuki*, if not so appealing emotionally as the famous one from *Love Suicides at Sonezaki*, is probably the best example of this form, and was recognised as such by Chikamatsu's early audiences. The Japanese weakness for place names has never been more sweetly indulged. The battle scenes are of an excitement and swiftness that tax the Japanese language to the last degree.

Two examples will suffice to show the range of Chikamatsu's poetry. The first passage is from the recognition scene in the third act, in which Lady Kinshōjo, on the castle wall, compares the image reflected in the mirror of the old man at the foot of the wall with the picture of her father as he was twenty years before.

E ni todomeshi wa	Caught in the picture
Inishie no	The old-time
Kao mo tsuya ari	Face was sleek
Midori no bin.	(With) glossy side-locks.
Kagami wa ima no	(In) the mirror, the present
Oi-yatsure	Old age and gauntness
Atama no yuki to	The head to snow
Kaware-domo	Had changed, but
Kawarade nokoru	Left unchanged
Omokage no	The face's
Memoto kuchimoto	Eyes and mouth,

Sono mama ni	As they had been,
Wa ga kage ni mo	To her own features also
Samo nitari	Bore close resemblance.

This passage, occurring in a scene of great dramatic power, is as direct as Japanese can be, and, astonishingly enough, considering the complete dissimilarity between English and Japanese, is intelligible even in a line for line literal translation. This is not significant in itself except that it shows Chikamatsu's ability to make his verse of great simplicity and beauty when he wanted nothing to stand between the listener and the ideas.

The second passage is from the *michiyuki* in the fourth act. This is the sort of poetry characteristic of the Nō dramas. It is compact, highly allusive, and usually yields several meanings for any line. Poetry of this type is not common in English plays because melody is not permitted to substitute for sense. In some modern English poetry, however, we are given lines of comparable difficulty and obscurity. We can appreciate such lines at first for their melody only; later, one or several meanings may disengage themselves for us.

Sasoe ya sasoe	Lead, oh lead
Wa ga tsuma mo	My husband too
Nijūgo suji no	The twenty-five corded
Koto no ito	Strings of the lute
Musubi chigirishi	Tied and pledged
Toshi no kazu	Number of years
Iza sugagakite	Come! play a lute
Hakozaki no	Hakozaki's
Matsu to shi kikaba	Pines, when I hear
Ware mo isogan	I too shall hurry

It is not likely that anyone reading the English text alone will be able to form any coherent idea of the full meaning of the Japanese. Here is a freer translation of these lines, "Lead me, lead me to my husband, whose years are twenty-five, like the strings of the Chinese lute, for we are joined together as lute strings are. Come, let us play our lutes, and when we hear the music among the pines of Hakozaki, we shall think of those who are pining for us, and hurry ahead."

In the translation it has been necessary to resort to double renderings of certain phrases in order to bring out the two meanings of a pun, for either half is incomplete. The most familiar Japanese pun, "matsu", meaning either the "pine tree" or the verb "to long after" (here translated by the verb "to pine"), is introduced by mention of the name Hakozaki, a place famous for its pines.

A commentator suggests that the word *suji*, or "cord", is a kind of play on the the word *sai*, or "years".[105] This may seem far-fetched, but when the manner of delivery of the *jōruri* chanter is taken into account, the nature of the ʃpun may be understood. The chanter says, "Wa ga tsuma mo nijūgo...", and the audience, hearing the initial "s" of the next word, which was probably prolonged before the vowel was pronounced, would assume the word was to be *sai*, only to be surprised by *suji*. The author assumes that *sai* will be understood; the thought, incompletely expressed in any case, is unintelligible without the word "years" —"My husband is twenty-five years old". The word is omitted because Chikamatsu wants to switch to another image, the Chinese lute of twenty-five strings. Thus we have two images linked by the word "twenty-five": "My husband is twenty-five", "Twenty-five stringed lute". The image is reversed in the next two lines. "Tied and pledged" (*musubi chigirishi*) refers to the manner in which lute strings are joined in one instrument, as husband and wife are joined. "Number of years" (*toshi no kazu*), which "tied and pledged" grammatically modifies, must be a return to the half-expressed mention of the husband's age, for context forbids the otherwise possible interpretation of "the number of years which we have been tied and pledged". [106]

The Battles of Coxinga is Chikamatsu's most important work, if not the most appealing to modern readers. It has been attempted to give some reasons why this is so: its popularity, its subject, its style. In making a translation of the play it was hoped that these things might be clear of themselves to any reader kind enough to overlook such awkwardnesses as a translator dealing with so dissimilar a language is likely to commit. It now seems less likely to me that, without a good deal of faith, many readers will accept on the basis of the translated work that Chikamatsu is one of the great dramatists of the world. The failure of Racine in English translation has been complete, and those English-speaking people unfamiliar with French must take on faith his greatness. How much more difficult it is to attempt to convey the qualities of Chikamatsu, yet, because of the unlikelihood that many in the English-speaking world will ever learn Japanese well enough to read Chikamatsu, how much more necessary! If only a part of Chikamatsu's power comes through in translation, the effort will not have been in vain.

III

A LITERARY HISTORY OF COXINGA'S LIFE

THE LIVES of few men in history are richer in dramatic possibilities than was Coxinga's. It is small wonder, then, that even those who have professed to be writing biographical accounts have been led into colourful tales which have every merit save that of truth. Such stories were not always the work of authors removed by many generations from the times of Coxinga, but were sometimes written while the unhappy hero was still warm in his grave, and while men still lived whose personal experience could have revealed the fictitious nature of the supposed facts. Chikamatsu's play *The Battles of Coxinga* cannot be taken seriously as history, nor was it meant so to be taken; bur in spite of its avowedly fictional nature, it is not much further from the facts than some of the "histories", and we may regard it as one work in the larger body of the legends of Coxinga.

. There is hardly a single fact in Coxinga's life which has not been questioned, denied, or contradicted in the years since his death. In the attempt to establish an authentic history of Coxinga, it is necessary to evaluate the various accounts and to check them against material in primary sources. It is relatively easy thus to dispose of most of the Coxinga legends, but this tends to leave us with great gaps in his life, rather than with a clear picture of the man. Of his death, for instance, there are at least a dozen accounts, some of them written within a few years of the event. If we discard all the unauthenticated versions, we are left with nothing but a date, and we have lost a number of picturesque stories as worthy of preservation, perhaps, as any of the historical facts. Some of these interesting tales will be cited, but in order to make an evaluation of Chikamatsu's and the other Coxinga legends, it will be necessary to attempt also to present the figure known to history, with as few embellishments as possible.

First of all, the name "Coxinga" must be explained. "Coxinga" is a Europeanised version of three Chinese words, *kuo-hsing-yeh* 國姓爺 or, in the Amoy dialect, which was Coxinga's own, *kok-seng-ya*. These words mean literally "Lord of the Imperial Surname." This curious appellation refers to a special honour conferred on Coxinga in his youth, when the Ming pretender to the throne, Lung Wu, bestowed on him the surname of Chu, that of the

44

imperial family. This distinction was not without precedent in Chinese history. In the Han Dynasty, for example, the imperial surname of Liu was given to Lou Ching for having conceived a successful plan with which to deal with the barbarians. Indeed, Coxinga's cousin, a youth of no subsequent fame, was given the imperial surname on the day before Coxinga.[1] Nevertheless, it is by the name of " Lord of the Imperial Surname" that he was later known in China, in Japan, and throughout Europe.

As far as the European spelling of "Coxinga" is concerned, it would seem to be of Dutch origin. Dutch records as early as 1653,[2] nine years before Coxinga's death, refer to " Cocksinja." The report of the Second and Third Dutch Embassies to China, published in 1670, refers to " Koxinga,"[3] and an English translation of the following year has "Coxinga."[4] Each nation that dealt with Coxinga felt privileged to spell his name as it chose, however, and the reader will soon identify with our hero such appellations as " Cogseng," " Con-seng," "Kuesim,""Cogsin,""Coseng,""Kue-sing,""Quoesing,""Coxiny,""Quesim," "Quesin," "Cocxima" and "Quesingus," as well as such puzzling names as "Maroto" and "Pompoan" (or "Pun Poin").[5]

Needless to say, our hero was born with none of these names, though, as a Chinese, he was certainly never in want of a new one. Coxinga was born in the seventh lunar month of 1624 in Hirado, a town near Nagasaki in Japan.[6] His father, Cheng Chih-lung, was also blessed with a variety of names, of which Nicholas Iquan, a name given him when he was baptized a Christian, was perhaps the most common in European works. Little is known of his mother's family beyond its name, Tagawa, although her partizans have attempted to prove that it belonged to the minor nobility. Others have declared that the mother was a courtesan.[7] It seems hardly likely that the young Cheng Chih-lung, a foreigner with neither fortune nor a promising future to recommend him, could have won a woman of any great birth. On the other hand, Coxinga was not the result of the chance union between a visiting Chinese sailor and a willing Japanese girl. Although the former Miss Tagawa was outranked by Cheng Chih-lung's second wife, a Chinese, the first marriage was a real one, and Chih-lung was anxious to have his Japanese family join him in China when he had established himself there. By 1627 he had a pirate fleet of one thousand sails, had captured Amoy and was undisputed master of the coast of China between the Yangtze and the Pearl Rivers.[8]

Coxinga's first name may have been a Japanese one, Fukumatsu,[9] but by the time of his trip to China in 1630 he was known as Cheng Sen. In that year Cheng Chih-lung, who had returned to China after a brief visit to Japan, sent for his family. His wife, apparently afraid to expose her second son, Shichizaemon, to the rigours of the journey, and unwilling to leave him behind alone,

45

chose to send the young Sen with an older companion to Chih-lung's residence at An-hai in Fukien, while she remained with Shichizaemon in Japan.[10] Little Sen was a clever lad, and great things were predicted for him by fortunetellers. At the age of fifteen he was entered in the Imperial Collegiate School at Nanking.[11] He called on the great scholar Ch'ien Ch'ien-i about this time, and was given the pen-name of Ta-mu.[11]

Sen was married about 1641 to a Miss Tung, and in 1642 his son and heir, Ching, was born.[12] Two years later the Manchus took possession of Peking, and the Ming sovereign, the seventeenth in his line, hanged himself in his palace.[13] In 1645 the Manchus extended their conquests to Nanking. The eighteenth Ming sovereign died, and Cheng Chih-lung was instrumental in having the Prince of T'ang proclaimed his successor, with the dynastic name of Lung Wu.[14] It was Lung Wu who, in the sixth moon of the same year, bestowed the "national surname" on Sen, henceforth to be known as "Kuo-hsing-yeh" or Coxinga. He also gave the young man the given name of Ch'eng-kung,[15] meaning "achievement", and, patting him on the back, declared that he regretted he had no daughter the boy might marry. He further appointed him a General in the Central Army of the Imperial Camp, to rank as an imperial son-in-law. In the twelfth moon of 1645 he was named Chairman of the Bureau of Imperial Clansmen, in keeping with his adoption into the imperial family.[16]

One more important event crowded the same year, 1645. This was the arrival of Coxinga's mother from Japan. His younger brother, Shichizaemon, was left behind in Nagasaki, where he assumed his mother's maiden name, a not infrequent Japanese practice when there are no other male heirs.[17] Although Coxinga had been separated from his mother for fifteen years, she had always been in his thoughts. A Chinese biographer wrote, "Every day he would face east and look towards his mother, hiding his tears".[18] Cheng Chih-lung's reception of his Japanese wife was less warm; he already had a large brood of offspring from his second spouse.

1646 was a year of disasters for Coxinga. The Emperor Lung Wu, disregarding Cheng Chih-lung's advice, decided to stage an active campaign against the Manchus. Had he elected instead to keep to his coastal holdings, where he was protected by Cheng Chih-lung's powerful fleet, he might have reigned to the end of his days, but by pitting his inadequate land forces against the superior Manchus, he invited the miserable fate he soon suffered.[19] The circumstances of the death of Lung Wu were never clear. In later years an imposter, pretending to be Lung Wu, returned from the land of the missing, sent an envoy to Coxinga to claim his sworn loyalty, but the latter was little inclined to believe him.[20] It is more likely that Lung Wu died at Foochow after his defeat near that place in the eighth moon of 1646, a suicide by starvation.[21]

The defeat of Lung Wu is often ascribed to the defection of Cheng Chih-lung, which occurred in the same year, 1646, but it is not sure to what extent this may be true. Chih-lung, sensing that Lung Wu's decision to fight would end in disaster, had made overtures to the Manchus, and encouraged dissatisfaction among the Ming forces, going so far as to neglect to supply his son's forces with food and equipment when Coxinga was defending a key pass.[22] Chih-lung's surrender did not take place, however, until after Lung Wu's death. Coxinga urged his father not to go over to the Manchus, but Chih-lung, attracted by the promises of high position made to him by the conquerors of China, went to Foochow, where he entered into negotiations with them. Chih-lung had been wary of his newly made friends, and was unwilling to place himself in their power even after his surrender, but the Manchus succeeded in tricking him into separation from his military strength, and he was sent as an honoured prisoner to Peking.[23]

The Manchu troops in their victorious sweep southwards captured the city of An-hai. Most of the defenders fled, but among those who did not leave the city was Coxinga's mother. The accounts of her death are so disparate as to afford no clear picture of what happened. Japanese sources, delighted at the opportunity to point out that the former Miss Tagawa, true to the Yamato spirit, preferred death to surrender, relate that she plunged a Japanese sword into herself, then leapt from the city wall. The Manchus, seeing this extraordinary exhibition of resolution, marvelled, "If the women of Japan are of such a sort, what must the men be like?"[24] An early Chinese version has it that Coxinga's mother was violated by Manchu soldiers, and then hanged herself. This account concludes with the description of Coxinga's rage on discovering the body of his mother. Then, "using the barbarian method, he cut open his mother's abdomen".[25] This statement must have caught the imagination of Chinese story-tellers, for the "cutting open of the mother's abdomen" became an established part of the Coxinga legend.[26]

Another episode in Coxinga's life which passed over into the story-teller's domain was that of the burning of his Confucian robes. After Coxinga learned of the death of his mother and of his father's intention of deserting the Ming partisans, he decided to give up his career as a scholar and to become a soldier. He went to a Confucian temple and there burned his scholar's robes. Looking up to Heaven, he declared, "The former Confucian scholar is now an unfortunate subject. My every action must have a purpose, whether I serve or oppose, stay or go. I now bid farewell to my Confucian attire. Will the Master please take cognizance of the fact."[27]

After this momentous happening, Coxinga joined forces with a group of other Ming patriots, forming a band of a little over ninety men. This small body developed into a force that eventually served as the chief Ming army, and reached the very gate of success in the struggle against the Manchus.

During the ten years that followed Coxinga's burning of his Confucian robes, he won significant victories at a number of places in South China, but the narration of the particular triumphs or defeats, for there were many of the latter as well, would add little to our understanding of the man. Coxinga continued to correspond with his father in Peking. Some of his letters have been preserved in a journal written by one of his officials.[28] The Manchus had thought that Cheng Chih-lung would be able to persuade his son to yield to them, and had treated the father royally so that Coxinga would have no apprehensions about his fate once he had surrendered. The conquerors chose not to take official cognizance of his open state of rebellion, and even granted him additional patents of nobility. To these courtesies they added messages promising great rewards if he would but co-operate.

Coxinga did not ignore the letters the Manchus sent him. Although his naval forces were the match of and even superior to the Manchus', he was not in a secure position. Four times, in 1648, 1652, 1658 and 1660, he sent embassies to Japan requesting assistance.[29] Sympathy for his cause was so strong in Japan that he was almost successful in spite of the strongly isolationist policy followed by the Shogunate government.[30] His appeals for help betrayed his weakness no more than did his negotiations with the Manchus. In 1653 he was created Duke of Hai-ch'eng by the Manchus and letters were sent to him by his father urging surrender. Coxinga must have given a deceptively favourable answer, but he wrote privately to his father in the eighth moon, "The Manchu court has already broken faith with you. How could I accept your words for the truth? . . . When you surrendered to the Manchus you were not the last to do so, were you? If you, who were one of the earliest to go to them, have been so treated, what can I expect when I must be one of the last to do so? Perhaps, since they baited you with the empty promise of the three provinces, they will now bait me. I, your son, do not want to distrust my father's words, but it is really very difficult for me to do otherwise."[31]

Coxinga's peace negotiations with the Manchus were a delaying tactic, intended to give him time for the major struggle which he foresaw.[32] Between 1652 and 1659 much correspondence was exchanged on the subject between Coxinga and his father. That this pretence continued into 1659, the year of Coxinga's attack on Nanking, cannot fail to surprise us, for his expedition had already set out in 1658, and would then have pressed its attack on the great city had it not met with a crippling storm at sea.

The campaign at Nanking was the high point of Coxinga's career. It seemed as though nothing could halt his onrushing troops. The following account is by Huang Tsung-hsi (1610-1695), a celebrated philosopher and loyal Ming adherent, found in his work *The Story of Coxinga*.

In the fifth moon of 1659 the entire force headed north. Chang Huang-yen, with a vanguard composed of volunteers, headed toward the Yangtze River, and reached Kua-chou. The next day Coxinga arrived. The Manchus came out to resist and over a thousand Manchus and Chinese in their army perished. Coxinga's army profited by the victory to seize the city.

Coxinga crossed the river to the south and attacked Chen-chiang. Chang went up the Yangtze. When he was within fifty *li* of I-chen, the officials and the people of the city came out to surrender and to welcome him. On the twenty-eighth day of the sixth moon Chang reached the Kuan-yin Gate of Nanking. Coxinga had already taken Chen-chiang, and his naval forces had all arrived. On the first day of the seventh moon seven scouts raided Chiang-p'u and occupied it.

On the fifth day a document of surrender arrived from Wu-hu. Coxinga said to Chang, "Wu-hu is the gateway to all the regions up the river. If Nanking does not fall quickly, relief forces will come every day from Hunan and Hupei. You must stop them at that strategic point." Chang reached Wu-hu and despatched military orders to the prefectures, districts and villages. Cities and villages to the north and south of the river went over to his side one after another . . . Moreover, the permanent garrisons and all subordinate districts on the lower reaches of the river were also all awaiting the opportunity to surrender . . . Nanking also wished to discuss surrender.

While the issue was still not settled, the Manchus spied on the island-ers'[33] forces. They observed them to be unguarded: the soldiers were out in the four directions gathering firewood: the trenches were all deserted; and the troops had left their weapons and were amusing themselves. The Manchus attacked and took the front encampment with their light cavalry. Coxinga hastily moved his tent . . . The Manchus poured from the city and came out to do battle. Coxinga's soldiers were without fighting spirit and suffered a great defeat. Commanders such as Kan Hui died there. Coxinga then followed the receding tide and sailed. He also withdrew his troops at Chen-chiang. Chang went to T'ung-ling and encountered the army of Hupei. His troops were annihilated.[34]

A French account written some ten years after the events, gives us a better picture of the effect of Coxinga's campaign on the Manchus.

Quoysim (*Coxinga*) estant entré dans la Province de Nankim (*Nanking*), avec une Armée navalle composée de mille vaisseaux pour le moins, &

environ cinquante mille hommes, assiégea par terre et par eau la Ville Capitale qu'on appelle du mesme nom. Il envoya aussi-tost des Deputez aux principaux Mandarins non seulement de cette Province, mais encore des Provinces voisines, pour les engager à prendre le party d'un Prince Chinois de la Maison Royale, dont il disoit qu'il vouloit maintenir le droit contre les Tartares. Plusieurs Mandarins trompez par un pretexte si specieux, estoient déja fort ébranlez, & n'attendoient pour se rendre que le succés du siege de Nankim, qui ne pouvoit pas resister long-temps a une Armée si puissante.

La consternation estoit si grande dans Pekim, que les Tartares traitoient déja d'abandonner la Chine & de s'en retourner en Tartarie.[35]

The Manchus in Nanking were just as frightened as those in Peking. François de Rougemont, a Belgian Jesuit priest described conditions within the city.

When the city had been besieged only twenty days, even though much rice had been brought in those three gates [*i.e. those Coxinga had failed to cut off*], a large number of inhabitants died of hunger every day, and many, despairing, hanged themselves . . . In one day in one ward of the city alone, the names of two hundred persons were reported to the magistrate as individuals having been brought to death by hunger or despair. The troops of the Tartar garrison were in fear because of the great numbers of the inhabitants, as they were aware of their own smallness of numbers. It is almost incredible, but there were only 500 real Tartar troops in the garrison of so immense a city; the other members of the garrison were Chinese fighting under the Tartars. Their commander was a Tartar himself, a cruel man of inhuman disposition, who was discouraged because of the small numbers of his own men, and who thought that he could never be secure so long as the townspeople were alive. He therefore thought it was necessary to kill them all, and thus protect the interests of the state. The supreme viceroy of the province, when he heard this, was strongly opposed to such savage cruelty and said, "If you have decided to ensure the security of yourself and the state, come kill me first, for while I am alive so cruel a slaughter of so many innocents will never be brought about". The courage of so pious a prince prevented the impious cruelty of the Tartar, and the voice of one saved the lives of very many. It is not to be wondered at that at the time he was much loved by all the Chinese. As he had governed Nanking for many years, he was treated as the father of his country. He himself was a Chinese by birth, but because he was born within the borders of Tartary and had been raised from childhood among the Tartars, the Emperor Xunchi (*Shun-chih*) entrusted his empire to him . . .

About that time the birthday of Quesingus had come. This day the Chinese think is solemn and holy, so that even when they are under arms they frequently are accustomed to pass it in festivals and rituals . . . Quesingus could have refrained from so inappropriate a ceremony in that time and place, or could have put it off until victory, which he hoped was near, but whether he did it through contempt of his enemy, or whether he was influenced by some empty superstition, he permitted his birthday to be celebrated throughout the entire camp until late at night. After all his troops were careless with sleep and wine, the Tartars, informed of all this by their scouts, were not at all asleep to this fine occasion for advancing their own cause. It was night. They gathered together their troops silently and swiftly, and drew up their ranks within the gates of the city . . .[36]

The battle, which Rougemont went on to describe, was a complete débâcle for Coxinga's forces. Whether because of the debilitating effect of the birthday celebration, or because of contempt for the enemy, or because of the inherent superiority of the Manchu cavalry,[37] Coxinga's forces suffered a defeat of the first magnitude. Coxinga himself was probably in large part to blame for the disaster. One of his lieutenants, Kan Hui (the Kanki of the play), had proposed to Coxinga that Nanking be stormed in one powerful assault,[38] claiming that Coxinga lacked sufficient forces to maintain an effective siege. If Rougemont's figure of 500 Manchus represented only the fiftieth part of the whole garrison, the great body of troops that filled the 3,000 junks[39] of Coxinga's armada would still have had no great trouble in overcoming the defenders of Nanking.[40] As it was, some of the gates of the city were left accessible to the Manchus for supplying and reinforcing the besieged garrison. A large number of Manchu cavalry came down from Peking. It was probably these troops who where responsible for Coxinga's defeat.[41]

Flight was the only possibility left Coxinga's forces after the Manchu triumph. It is not recorded how many troops were able to retreat to Amoy, Coxinga's base, but he probably saved a major part. The success of the retreat by sea could have afforded Coxinga little comfort, for he must have been thinking of the empire that might have been his had he but acted sooner.

The Manchus, elated over their triumph at Nanking, attempted to follow up their land victory with one on the sea, and thus complete the destruction of the adherents of Coxinga. To this end they mustered a large fleet, about 800 vessels. Coxinga's battered navy numbered only half so many fighting ships, but his sailors were veteran seamen, and the Manchus were novices on the water.[42]

Kue-sing, more familiar with sea warfare than his adversaries, did not fear the numerical superiority of their junks, but assumed position to begin the combat. It was the 17th of June of 1660 when, the two enemy squadrons advancing abreast, the cannons roared out simultaneously up and down the entire line . . .

Victory was uncertain from dawn until sunset, but finally the skill and indomitable valour of the corsair prevailed over the numerical superiority of his enemy, and he then caught them between two wings of fire, which entirely destroyed the powerful Tartar fleet. For many weeks after this terrible catastrophe the beaches of Hiamuen (*Amoy*) were covered with rotting bodies and naval spoils that the flux and surge of the sea would daily cast on the shores . . . Not one man lived to tell the tale.[43]

There is a French embellishment of the account of the victory, which tells how Coxinga addressed 4,000 Manchu prisoners who were brought before him on the day after the triumph.

Après une petite remontrance sur le tort qu'avoient les Mancheoux de vouloir usurper l'Empire, & de retenir à Pekin son pere Chinchilong, il déclara à ces malheureux qu'ils auroient la vie sauve & une liberté entière de s'en retourner chacun chez soi: "Cependant", ajoûta-t-il, "ce sera à condition que vous voudrez bien vous charger de porter mes plaintes à votre Maître. Peut-être seriez-vous tentés d'oublier ma commission; mais voici un gage de ma part, qui sûrement vous en fera souvenir." A ces mots on saisit ces pauvres gens, & leur ayant coupé le nez et les oreilles, on alla les exposer ce jour-là même sur une des côtes du Foukien.[44]

If Coxinga's vengeance was extreme, the Manchus would have been no less severe. Vittorio Ricci, an Italian Dominican monk who was associated with Coxinga from 1655 until the latter's death in 1662, was in the city of Amoy at the time of the sea battle with the Manchus.

There he raised his hands and his heart to God, asking him to deign to concede the honour of the victory to the arms of Kuesing, so as to save the city from the horrible vengeance of the Tartars, who had sworn to destroy it with blood and fire, and to fling its ashes to the wind like criminal dust.[45]

After the victory of Chin-men Bay (off Amoy), Coxinga was left in approximately the same position he had been in some fifteen years before, when he had succeeded to his father's naval might. He had proved that he was still supreme on the sea, but his armies had been unequal to the task of wresting China back from the Manchus. He must have realised that the vow he had

once made of restoring the Ming emperors to the throne of China was never
to be accomplished.

After the death of Lung Wu, under the circumstances already mentioned,
the Prince of Kuei, Chu Yu-lang, had been proclaimed regent on 20th November
1646 at Chao-ch'ing in Kuangtung.[46] This prince ascended the throne on
24th December of the same year and assumed the reign name of Yung Li.
During all the time that Coxinga served Yung Li, he was never to have the
opportunity of entering his presence, for the Ming sovereign, after a brief
period of prosperity from 1648-1650 in Kuangtung, was in perpetual flight
before the Manchu conquerors, always in the direction away from Coxinga's
bases. In 1659, the year of Coxinga's defeat at Nanking, the hard-pressed
Yung Li took refuge in Burma. Three years later, on 11th June, 1662, he was
executed by the Chinese, to whom he had been delivered by the Burmese, in
the market-place of Yunnan-fu.[47] With him perished his young son Constantine.
The boy had been baptised a Christian, along with his mother and grandmother,
by an Austrian priest attached to the exiled court. It had been hoped by some
that he would be the first of a long line of Christian emperors of China.[48]

In 1660, after the naval victory, there were still some in Coxinga's entourage
who thought that his duty lay with the Emperor Yung Li, and that he should
continue his efforts to restore the late dynasty. Some, like Chang Huang-yen,
even thought that chances were better than ever of overthrowing the Manchus.[49]
Coxinga chose, however, to direct his attention toward the island of Formosa,
and the rest of that year was spent in preparation for the assault of April, 1661.

Coxinga's father, Cheng Chih-lung (or Iquan), had served at one time as
interpreter of sorts for the Dutch forces on Formosa.[50] Certain Chinese sources
state that he was instrumental in the colonisation of the island by the Fukienese.[51]
Be that as it may, Coxinga lent a ready ear to the plans of Ho T'ing-pin when
the latter proposed to him that the Dutch strongholds on Formosa be taken.
He had been an interpreter, had rendered considerable services to the Dutch,
and had amassed a fortune. Whether because of the discovery of his embezzle-
ment, as Chinese writers believed, or of his fraudulent practices, as stated
in Dutch works,[52] Ho decided to quit Formosa and join Coxinga in Amoy.
There he presented the general with a map of the island and with various
items of strategic information. On 25th October, 1660, a Chinese merchant
from Formosa called on Ho in Amoy. "In the course of conversation, the interpreter said that there was not the slightest chance for Tayouan [*the island
on which Castle Zeelandia was located*]. He also produced a model in wood
of Fort Provintia, and emphatically declared that Koxinga had intended to
arrive in Formosa during the eighth moon, but that . . . [*for various reasons*]
the expedition should be postponed till one month before harvest."[53]

This was not the first intimation to the Dutch of the forthcoming Chinese attack on their Formosan possessions. As early as 1646 warning had come from the factory at Nagasaki of possible trouble from the Chinese. The Minute-book of the factory contains the following entry for 11th November, 1646.

> Yesterday a junk arrived here from Hokchiu (*Foochow*) with a few slaves and a cargo of sugar, half of which had been rendered useless. It became known through the interpreter that the Tartars had been very fortunate in their war in the Empire of China. They continued their victories with so great success that the king had been driven out of Hokchiu by I-quan . . . It also became known that the escaping Chinese, who would not surrender, had been warned to have regard to the Fort of Tayouan, as it was possible they might succeed in strongly entrenching themselves there. We hope and trust that the good God will never permit this to happen, although the island of Formosa would afford a splendid retreat for the Chinese fugitives.[54]

The Directors of the Dutch East India Company in Holland had decided in 1650 that Fort Zeelandia should have not fewer than 1,200 men even in time of peace, and their decision seemed a wise one when, in 1652, a Jesuit father arrived in Batavia from China with news that Coxinga had roused an agitation in his favour among the Chinese colonists on Formosa. There was indeed a revolt in that year on the part of the settlers, but they were virtually unarmed, and the Dutch had no trouble in putting a speedy if sanguinary end to the disturbance.[55]

Frederic Coyett was appointed Governor of Formosa in 1656. He was to be the chief figure in the subsequent Dutch misfortunes on Formosa. Coyett was desirous of promoting friendship with Coxinga, hoping perhaps to stave off a Chinese attack in that way. In 1657 he had sent Ho T'ing-pin as envoy to Coxinga.[56] While Ho was in Amoy he formed a liaison with a certain Chinese known to the Dutch as Sangae, and together they fostered a scheme whereby the excise duties levied on goods from Formosa bound for Coxinga's territory were collected in Formosa rather than at Amoy, as had been done previously.[57] The collection of duties always having been a profitable pursuit for those thereby engaged, it was natural that Sangae and Ho should have waxed rich. It was not until February of 1659 that the Dutch learned of the agreement and issued a warrant against Ho. The latter, suddenly deprived of his fortune, fled Formosa (under cover of a spectacular fireworks display, according to certain writers),[58] and took refuge in Amoy with his old friend Sangae, who recommended him to Coxinga.

There was an invasion scare in March, 1660, and some influential Chinese were kept prisoner by the Dutch in the castle, to serve as hostages. Inflammatory rumours were circulated among the Chinese in the Formosan villages about the might of Coxinga's armies, and for a few months there existed a state of extreme tension.[59] Coyett was always worried about the possibility of an attack, but the other high Dutch civil and military officials (most of whom were ill disposed toward Coyett) made light of the threat to the island. In October Coyett sent a message to Coxinga asking if he harboured any hostile intentions, to which Coxinga returned a scornful reply:—

> Certainly, I have now for many years waged war for the recovery of my own territories, and have been so fully occupied in this way, that there was no opportunity for taking hostile action against such a small grass-producing country as Formosa.[60]

To confirm the absence of hostile aims, he reopened trade with Formosa.

Coyett was not reassured by Coxinga's friendly gesture. Terrible portents had been seen. A story was circulated that a mermaid had shown herself in the Canal and "on the Execution ground between the Castle and the City, a woeful groaning was heard, as of dying people—the voices of the Hollanders being distinguishable from those of the Chinese; and the water of the Canal was once seen changing into fire and flames. There were said to be many more such fearful premonitions . . . "[61] Just before the invasion Coyett was himself to see even stranger manifestations.

> At daylight the Prince (*Coyett*) and his officers mounted the city wall to reconnoitre, and on looking seaward they observed a whale swimming to and fro with a human figure seated on his back. The figure was clad in red garments, and its locks were dishevelled.
>
> From Luh-urh-mun the fish started, and, after indulging in a variety of gambols, finally passed Chi-khan city and disappeared. The Prince and his staff stood staring at one another, until, finding their tongues, they concluded that they had either been in a trance or had seen a vision.[62]

Whenever it was that Coxinga originally intended to stage his invasion of Formosa, it was not until the first moon of 1661 that any definite plans were made.[63] At that time he summoned his generals and told them in secret conference, "On the map of Formosa that Ho T'ing-pin presented to me the year before last, there were 10,000 *ch'ing* [1 *ch'ing equals* 15·1 *acres*] of cultivated lands and 1,000 *li* [1 *li equals* 1890 *feet*] of rich land. The revenues amount to several hundred thousands. There are shipbuilding facilities. If my forces were to be marshalled against the Dutch, mine would be superior. The number of foreigners in the forts the Dutch occupy has in recent times

E

not exceeded 1,000 men. If we attack these forts, they will prove no trouble at all to take. I want to conquer Formosa and make it my base of operations."[64] There was some difference of opinion among Coxinga's generals, for the reasons already mentioned, but Coxinga had his way.[65]

Coxinga's forces left Amoy in the second moon of 1661, but unfavourable weather prevented their departure from the continent until the 23rd day of the third moon. After seizing without resistance the Pescadores on the 24th day of the third moon, the expedition was again delayed, and did not arrive off Formosa until the first day of the fourth moon, or 30th April.[66] On that day a few thousand soldiers were disembarked within a few hours. How great a surprise Coxinga's arrival was to the Dutch may be gathered from the account of a German mercenary serving in the Dutch forces.

> On the morning of 30th April 1661 there was a very thick fog, as there had been during the whole night previous, so that one could not see any distance. As soon as the fog had lifted we perceived such a fleet of ships, Chinese junks lying in the sea before Boxamboy, that we could not even estimate their numbers, much less count them. There were so many masts that it was as if a thick wood had appeared. We beheld this sight as if overcome with astonishment, for no one, not even the Governor himself, could have expected this, and no one knew whether they had come as friend or enemy.[67]

Coxinga's first objective was the smaller of the two Dutch forts, Fort Provintia. This fort was quite without means of defence, being particularly vulnerable in that its water supply lay in an exposed place soon captured by Coxinga. He demanded the surrender of the fort. On 2nd May 1661 delegates were appointed to discuss capitulation with him,[68] and the following day surrender was effected.

The Fort of Tayouan (Castle Zeelandia), on a little island off the coast of Formosa, was much better equipped to deal with the invaders. Within the fort were about 1140 fully armed men. In 1652 two or three hundred Dutch soldiers quite overwhelmed seven or eight thousand armed Chinese. "Since that time, the Chinese in Formosa were regarded by the Hollanders as insignificant, and in warfare as cowardly and effeminate. It was reckoned that twenty-five of them put together would barely equal one Dutch soldier, and the whole Chinese race was regarded in the same way, no distinction being made between Chinese peasants and soldiers; if he was but a native of China, then he was cowardly and had no stamina."[69]

If the defenders of Castle Zeelandia had been comforting themselves with such thoughts, their first contact with Coxinga's men must have come as a rude surprise, for in that engagement the Chinese clearly got the better of the Dutch, who ran in terror from them, abandoning their weapons. Governor Coyett, who had all along realised the weakness of the Dutch forces, and whose repeated warnings and pleas for reinforcements had been decried by his numerous enemies, still hoped that some agreement could be reached with Coxinga. In a letter addressed to the "Serene and renowned Prince", he wrote

> We are to request that Your Highness will be good enough to make known the reasons and motives of your displeasure against the Company, and the satisfaction demanded; so that, after investigation, such terms may be arranged, that the old friendship between the Company and Your Highness may again be speedily restored.[70]

Coxinga's reply took the form of an ultimatum, in which he offered the Dutch the choice of surrendering and being permitted to embark their goods and effects, as well as the armament of their forts, in his ships, or of facing the consequences. He declared that it was his intention to take possession of Formosa, an island which had always been a Chinese possession, in order to facilitate the prosecution of the war with the Manchus. Castle Zeelandia flew the "blood-flag" the next day as sign that no surrender was forthcoming.[71]

On the 24th May there came a delegation from Coxinga, composed of the venerable preacher Anthonius Hambroeck, another Dutchman who had fallen into Coxinga's hands, a Chinese mandarin named Sangae,[72] and two interpreters. When asked their business they produced the following letter from Coxinga.

> Translation of the Letter sent by Heer Pompoan to Heer Frederick Coyett, Governor in Tayouan
>
> Teybingh, Syautoo, Teysiankon, Koxsin[73] sends this letter to the Governor Coyett in Tayouan
>
> You Dutch, scarcely a hundred in number, how can you war against us, who are so mighty? Surely you must be wandering out of your senses and deprived of reason.
>
> I, Pompoan, declare that it is the will of God that all things live and be preserved from destruction. I am therefore disposed that you people remain alive; it is for this reason that I have sent you my letters at various times. You should consider well, as a matter of the greatest importance, the preservation from harm of your wives, your children, and all your possessions.
>
> I send to you my mandarin, Sanquae by name, and in addition the preacher Hambroeck, the interpreters Ouhincko and Joucko, to greet the Governor and to ask your surrender on such conditions as hereafter follow: consider them well, you people.

First: If you hand over the fortress before my artillery has displayed its might against it, I shall treat you in the same way I treated the Commandant of Fort Provintia and his people; if you desire anything and request it, you will receive it in the same way. I tell the truth and shall not deceive you.

Furthermore: Even when my artillery has already displayed its might, I shall order cease fire at once if the Governor, together with some other persons of great and small degree, raise the white flag, come out to me, and ask for peace. That should be sufficient for you to have confidence in my words. When high and low commanders come out to welcome me with their wives and children, I shall at once order all my artillery to be silenced. When I am made aware that you seriously mean peace, I shall give the Governor and his men such additional proofs that they will trust me all the more.

One other word: When you will have made peace, your soldiers must march out immediately. I shall despatch some of my troops inside to guard the fort and the houses within, and to establish order, so that your property will not be made the less by the least blade of grass or hair. I shall also give permission for some male and female slaves to remain within these houses to look after them. I shall also permit those of you who want to live at Saccam (Provintia) or Tayouan, either at your own homes or at the homes of others, to do so, and you may take then all the money and goods you possess there.

Still another word: It is the Chinese custom to grant everything which is requested save possession of the fortress; we place much importance on that. All other things that you people want you may have, but you will not have the two days time to salvage your goods and march out with them that the people at Saccam had. You will not have this time because you have delayed, while the people of Saccam surrendered before they tasted our gunfire. But if you people wait so long that you desire peace only when our guns have opened breeches in your walls, you will not have a single hour's respite, but will have to march out at once.

Furthermore: I realise that since the Dutch have come here from so great a distance to carry on trade it is their duty and obligation to do whatever they can to preserve their fortress. This devotion pleases me, and I see no guilt or misdeed in it; I hope that you will not be afraid for that cause.

When I say something the whole world has confidence in me, and knows that I shall keep my word. I am inclined neither to lie nor deceive. Preserve this letter, all you Hollanders. Everything in it is just and certain.

The point has been reached where we can take or save your lives. You must therefore decide at once. To let your thoughts wander is to long after death. Mr. Coyett has indicated to this writer that he does not understand Chinese, and I have thus often written him letters which he has not comprehended. Now I send a letter to him with interpreters who have read and translated the same. Valentyn has had it written in Dutch so that nothing will be left to be desired. You people must understand my intentions.

Indick,[74] fifteenth year, 26th day of fourth moon. Translated by J. Valentyn 24th May 1661, to the best of my capability.

The following day Coyett sent his reply, a refusal, as he had already done two weeks before. Fighting continued in the months that succeeded, with neither side being able to win a clear victory. The heads of the Company in Batavia, finally aroused to action, decided to send a relief force for Formosa. Typically enough, the Company chose to command the expedition one Jacob Caeuw who, by his own confession, "had no other experience in warfare than of having, when in the Academy at Leyden, often run his sword through the stones in the streets or through the windows of decent people's houses".[75] On 30th July Hermanus Clenk, the governor sent to replace the supposedly culpable Coyett, arrived in Formosa, stayed just long enough to observe the blood-flag flying over Fort Zeelandia, and then headed for Japan, never to put into Formosan waters again. The Company rewarded Clenk in its own manner, by returning him to Holland as Admiral of the home-bound fleet.[76] Coyett remained governor, for want of a replacement.

If the Dutch within Fort Zeelandia were having a hard time of it, Coxinga's forces were also in considerable difficulty. From the first there had been trouble about provisions. It was about this time that the effects of the drastic Manchu order of 1660 to evacuate the coast of southern China to a depth of some fifteen miles first began to affect Coxinga. The purpose of the order had been to deprive Coxinga of help from the coastal population, but its effects went far beyond his lifetime, and caused immense suffering to the people forcibly removed from their homes and work. Coxinga had not worried much about provisions, for he had been led to believe by the over-sanguine Ho T'ing-pin that food was to be had for the asking in Formosa, but the delay in the Pescadores had depleted the rations, and it was necessary even at the outset to take special measures to ensure a supply of food.[77] By October the situation of the Chinese was very poor. The Dutch even had word of desertions on the part of Coxinga's ships and soldiers. On 6th November Coyett received a letter from the Manchu Governor of Fukien promising assistance against the common enemy. Two Manchu ships were supposed to be sent, but the valorous General Jacob Caeuw, who had arrived in Formosa with reinforcements at the beginning of September and who was to have gone to accept the Manchu offer, retreated instead to safer waters in Siam, and the plan of assistance fell through.[78]

Chinese sources state that the fall of Fort Provintia had been facilitated by a "native of Formosa".[79] It seems unlikely that Coxinga would have needed such help in the case of tiny Provintia, but treachery may have played a greater part in the capture of Fort Zeelandia. We read in Dutch books of the desertion of one Hans Jurgen Radis of Stockaert, a German mercenary by one account,[80] who revealed to Coxinga the desperate position of the defenders of Zeelandia, and showed him how the capture of the weakly held Utrecht Redoubt would place the Dutch virtually at the mercy of the besiegers. Credit for this piece of treachery was given to a Frenchman, Abraham Dupuis of Rouen, by Tavernier,[81] whose hatred for the Dutch was such that any action hostile to them was perforce praiseworthy. He tells how Dupuis, whose term of service was up, asked permission to leave. The Governor said to him "brutally" that he would have to wait until the fortress sailed out to sea. During the siege there was a great flood, and Dupuis thought the time for desertion had come. A sergeant sent after him also deserted. They reached the camp of General Coxinga and were led before him.

> Ce General qui estoit homme d'esprit, les caressa fort, & s'informa d'eux de l'estat où estoit la Forteresse: ce qu'ayant sceu, il prit ses mesures sur ce que ces deux hommes luy dirent, qu'il n'étoit pas bien posté pour prendre la Forteresse, pour ce qu'il la battoit du costé qui estoit le plus fort, & où estoit le plus de deffense; mais que s'il la vouloit attaquer du costé qu'ils luy diroient, ils consentoient qu'il les fist mourir s'il n'emportoit la Place dans huit ou dix jours.[82]

The final surrender did not take place until 1st February 1662, [83] after a siege of nine months. Coyett had been in favour of holding out until reinforcements would arrive from Batavia. As usual, he seems to have been right; Coxinga's army was gravely short of provisions and ammunition, and might easily have abandoned the venture, while the Dutch had supplies for another four or five months. As usual, too, Coyett was overridden, in this instance by the Council, which all but unanimously favoured capitulation.[84]

Coxinga's terms of surrender were most generous, considering the length of the siege. Each of the twenty-eight councillors could take with him two hundred rijksdaalders,[85] and twenty chosen civilians an aggregate sum of one thousand rijksdaalders. The act of surrender stated, "After inspection, the Dutch soldiers may come forth with flying banners, burning fusees, loaded rifles, and beating drums, marching thus for embarkation under command of the Governor". A total of about nine hundred men, sound and sick, came forth. All goods, however, were left in the fortress for the Chinese; these had a value of some 471,000 guilders.[86]

Those who had been captured by Coxinga previous to the fall of Castle Zeelandia did not participate in the repatriation. Some of them had to wait until 1683, when Formosa was captured by the Manchus, for liberation;[87] many others died in captivity. Among the Dutch who perished at the hands of Coxinga's forces, none was more celebrated than the Reverend Anthonius Hambroeck, who had served as envoy for Coxinga, as related above. He had promised to return to Coxinga's camp with the Dutch reply and, though he knew that return meant death, he rejected the pleadings of his two daughters within the city to remain, and went back to his wife and other children, who were in Coxinga's hands. He was later beheaded for his failure to gain the surrender of Castle Zeelandia, and so passed into the ranks of the heroes of Dutch poetry.

> Hij komt!—hij drukt zijn kroost in de armen!
> Hij spreekt: geeft nooit de vesting op!
>   Wat zucht gij op mijn' grijzen kop?
> Uw pligt is 't Neerland te beschermen.—
>   Hij zwijgt:—daar alles schreit en beeft,
> Sterkt hij elks moed, verzacht elks smarte,
> Klemt zeegnend gade en kroost aan 't harte,
>   Keert—bidt—stijgt op 't schavot—en sneeft.
>
> Hij sneeft!—neen! neen! dit is geen sneven,
>   't Is de overgang tot eedler' stand!
>   Zijn naam blijft in elks hart geplant,
> Blijft eeuwig in elks boezem leven!
>   Zijn voorbeeld is een heilige schat,
> Dien nooit zich Holland laat ontrooven. . . .
>
> He comes!—he presses his brood in his arms!
> He speaks: Never surrender the fortress!
>   What! You sigh for my gray head?
> Your duty is to protect the Netherlands.—
>   He is silent:—then all weep and tremble;
> He fortifies every heart, softens every grief,
> Clasps in blessing his wife and children to his heart,
>   Returns, prays, climbs the scaffold and dies.

He dies! No! No! This is not dying,
   'Tis a transformation to a nobler state!
His name is planted in every heart,
Lives eternally in every breast!
   His example is a sacred treasure
That Holland never shall abandon. . . .[88]

Hambroeck was also made the hero of a tragedy presented in Amsterdam in 1775. The cast of characters included the Governor (here called Frederik Cajet), his son, young Frederik, Hambroeck's daughter Cornelia, and an emissary of Coxinga's with the extraordinary name of Xamti, which was the Portuguese transcription of a Chinese word for God. The play concluded with a scene in which Cornelia, on the wall of Castle Zeelandia, witnessed the execution of her father.

Cornelia: Genade, Coxinga!
   Kom dat uw beul terstond dit hoofd van't ligchaam sla!
   Bevry my van den moord mijns vaders te overleven!
   Wat zie ik, Hemel! Ach! ik zie mijn moeder beven:
   Zy moet het moorden zien! . . . o Wee! het is gedaan;
   Daar stort het hoofd in 't zand! . . . 't ziet noch mijn moeder aan!
   Het spalkt noch de ooren op, om haar gekerm te vangen;
   De mond tracht haar en my noch troost te doen erlangen! . . .
(ter aarde stortende)
   Wraak, Hemel! voor zyn bloed! . . . en 't myne![89]

Cornelia: Mercy, Coxinga.
   Come, let your headsman chop off this head from my body!
   Spare me from living past my father's murder!
   What do I see? Heavens! Oh! I see my mother tremble:
   She has to see the murder! . . . Oh, woe! It is done;
   His head falls there in the sand! . . . It looks at my mother yet!
   It still bends its ears to catch her moans;
   The mouth tries to give her and me comfort. . . .
(leaping from the wall)
   Vengeance, Heaven! for his blood! . . . and mine!

A contemporary writer estimated that the Dutch had lost 1600 men in the campaign.[90]Although Coyett was one of the few to have recognised from the start the menace Coxinga represented, although he had also led a valiant struggle against the Chinese when the anticipated invasion finally materialised (and sought to carry on the fight when the other councillors declared for peace), the Dutch East India Company was so infuriated at the loss of property at Zeelandia (if not at the loss of lives), that it had Coyett banished to the tiny island of Ay in the Indies. He might have remained there for the rest of his days had it not been for the personal intervention of the Prince of Orange, who allowed Coyett to return home.[91]

So much for the Dutch, although they were later to cause trouble for Coxinga's son, Cheng Ching, when he succeeded in 1662 to his father's position.

One other event of the year 1661 must be described here: the death in the tenth moon of old Iquan, Coxinga's father, in Peking. It had not been until 1654 that Iquan was actually imprisoned by the Manchus. Until that year he had led an extremely comfortable life in the mildest of political custody because the Manchus hoped thereby to induce Coxinga to submit to their rule. Under Manchu guidance Iquan wrote Coxinga a number of letters pointing out the advantages of yielding to the conquerors of China. One of Coxinga's answers, dated the eighth moon of 1653, has already been quoted. There must also have been a number of letters smuggled out without official sanction. Huang Wu, an officer of Coxinga's who had gone over to the Manchus, included in his five proposals for "pacifying the sea" one designed to cut off such clandestine correspondence. "His father, Chih-lung, is imprisoned in the capital. Ch'eng-kung [Coxinga] has been bribing merchants who travel north and south on business to carry messages for him at times. Such persons should be investigated at once, severely punished, and their merchandise confiscated. Then their communication can be cut off.[92]

It was an intercepted letter that ended Iquan's period of luxurious life in Peking. The Spanish priest Antonio de Santa Maria wrote on 12 January, 1660[93] of the cause of Iquan's imprisonment.

> The said Chinchillon [Cheng Chih-lung, *i.e.* Iquan] used to write letters to his son Kuesim in which he would tell of his obedience to the new Tartar king, sending his letters by the royal register. One letter was discovered that had not been registered, for whatever disloyal reason it may have been, upon which the new king put in prison the said Chinchillon, a brother of his, and another son of his, a minor, and the three are now held in Pequin, each in his separate prison.

Iquan's friends who had been supplying him with every comfort, melted away in face of the severe disfavour into which he had now fallen, and he began to feel the rigours of imprisonment. A Dutch account gives a rather lurid description of Iquan's condition at that time.

Since his arrival in Peking he has been kept in a solidly built prison, and the doors of his house, or prison, have been walled up; in addition, he has been chained about the neck and feet. On account of some new difficulties his son caused the Court in Peking during the year 1657, when we had an embassy there, the chains were increased to fifteen.[94]

Unexpected help was given Iquan at this time by the Jesuit fathers. Iquan, who had been baptised a Christian during his early days in Macao, and whose daughter had married a Portuguese,[95] had always maintained some interest in his adopted faith. "The Portuguezes observed that Icoan had a very curious Oratory, in which they remarked amongst other things, the Statues of our Saviour and the Virgin Mary, and of divers other Saints; but it must not be imagined that these were any Marks of Christian piety . . . The Portuguezes could never observe that he ever rendered more honour to Jesus Christ that he did to his idols."[96] Iquan's personal bodyguard in the days when he was the chief Ming military leader had been composed of Portuguese-speaking Negro Christians, who were led to battle with the traditional religious cry of "Santiago'.[97] His contacts with Christians had continued during his early stay in Peking. "In 1648 the Portuguese Gabriel de Magalhaes and the Italian Luis Buglio were brought to Peking from Szechuan. Iquan took a fancy to the Fathers and often visited them, erecting a house and chapel for their use, and supplied them with money, servants and household goods."[98] After his fall from favour with the Manchus he remembered the fathers.

The wretched man, in such great solitude, began to feel want, which indeed was so great that he did not hesitate to ask, through an intermediary who was faithful to him, two or three gold pieces from our Fathers, in the name of charity. To such circumstances was he then reduced, to whom the riches of the whole East had formerly not sufficed. This charity was not without its perils, nor indeed were those most friendly to him afraid without cause, but the Fathers could not bear not to help him, especially as he had asked it of them. They hoped that when he had seen the courageous charity of our Fathers and how great the contrast was between the Gentiles and the Christians, he would be aroused from that lethargy of soul in which he had lain dormant and oppressed for many years. Therefore, they sent very friendly messages to him, and about ten gold pieces, which was surely a great gift, considering the poverty of the senders.

Nicolaus was amazed and moved to tears. "Who would expect", he said, "such faith from foreigners? But if it is granted to me to be restored to my former fortunes, I shall not be ungrateful." His prayers were too late. For, after a little time, whether indeed he was convicted of plotting, or whether the Tartars were exacerbated by the very great amount of serious harm which Quaesingus had repeatedly done them and were avenging their grief on the father since they had no power over the son (that suspicion of conspiracies of which I have spoken always persisting)—for whatever reason it was—he was condemned by the sentence of the judges to death, and that with great torture. His life was to be taken away while he was still alive and breathing by very small mutilations of his body, beginning with the ends of his limbs, a kind of torture which, as it is lingering and slow, is by far the most painful to the bodily senses. The Four Regents, moderating the rigour of the sentence, finally decided on a milder punishment; namely, that his head be struck off. But the poor man did not thus escape from torture, for he had as companions of his punishment his two small sons, of whom one he had begotten in the prison itself. Who would deny that for the death of such innocents to befall a father is more bitter than any death or than any torture? And this was the end of Nicolaus.[99]

Accounts of the last days of Iquan vary so considerably as to afford only a dim picture of what actually took place. The *Sheng-wu-chi* (or *Chronicles of Holy Wars*) by Wei Yüan (1794-1856) credits the interception of the clandestine letter to the governor of the province and places the event in early 1655.[100] According to the same work, Huang Wu addressed a memorial to the Throne in 1657 asking for the death of Iquan, but the emperor exiled him instead to Manchuria, the death penalty not being meted out until the winter of 1661, when Iquan and three sons perished.[101] A Spanish work of 1676 stated Iquan was killed by a sabre blow.[102] Later Spanish books tended to insist that Iquan and the others were "placed on a great mount of gunpowder" and blown up "to the clouds".[103] According to the report of the First Dutch Embassy, Iquan was "finally poisoned to death secretly".[104]

Such a great variety of resolutions to Iquan's life furnish the literary historian with an illustration of the ease with which imaginative minds distort facts. What is noteworthy here, apart from the one fact that Iquan, or Cheng Chihlung, was put to death by the Manchus in 1661 after a long imprisonment is that the person of Iquan, like that of his more famous son, was of such interest that people chose to invent incidents rather than state the insufficient facts known to them. Thus we find even in the histories of conscientious chroniclers pieces of dramatic fiction which have no justification save as poetic truth: we might almost hear some pious old priest saying, "This is what should have happened". The actual falsifications might have had their genesis then, or perhaps they gained currency through the fault of some interpreter, or perhaps some Chinese, with the barest trace of a smile of amusement, made up for the benefit of the credulous foreigners as wild a story as he thought they would accept.

One distortion of fact which gained particularly wide circulation appears to stem from the *Histoire des Deux Conquérans Tartares qui ont subjugué la Chine*, by Father Pierre Joseph d'Orléans, published in 1688. We are told how the Manchu ministers first thought that they could catch Coxinga by treating Iquan well.

> Mais ils changerent de conduite, quant ils virent qu'ils perdoient leur peine, & que Quesin ne plioit point. Ils luy osterent d'abord ses appointemens, & le reduisirent à une si grande pauvreté, qu'il subsista longtems par les secours que luy donnerent les Jesuites de Pekin, qu'il avoit toujours favorisez, quoyque tout occupé de son ambition, il fust assez mauvais Chrestien. L'exil et la prison suivirent la pauvreté, & enfin une mort violente finit ses malheurs avec sa vie.
>
> Quesin, qui avoit pour son pere les sentimens que la morale Chinoise inspire aux enfans pour leurs parens, chercha à vanger sa mort par toutes sortes de voyes; & ce fut la guerre qu'il fit pour cela, que le Prince, devenu majeur, eut à soutenir contre luy.[105]

The mistaken idea that Coxinga first began his opposition to the Manchus as a means of avenging his father's death appears constantly in European literature from that date on, an echo of it finding expression in an article in a publication of as recently as 1930.[106] What Coxinga's public emotions were when he learned of his father's death, probably late in 1661 or early in 1662, we have not much difficulty in imagining. There was undoubtedly much filial weeping and wailing and self-reviling for failure to deliver Iquan from the hands of the invaders.

But Coxinga could not have had much time for such lamentations. Barely had he consolidated his hold on Formosa than he began to look farther afield. The Philippine Islands next attracted his interest. In January of 1661[107] Father de Santa Maria had warned the Governor General of the Philippines of the possibility of an attack by Coxinga, and had urged that a treaty of commerce and friendship be made with the Manchus, but apparently nothing came of his words.[108] If more heed had been paid to his warning, consternation might not have been so great when, on 18th May 1662, an embassy arrived in Manila from Coxinga, and it was discovered that it had come to demand the surrender of the Spaniards. In a letter written on 21st April 1662, Coxinga declared,

> It has been the practice from all antiquity—and is still the custom to-day—that every foreign nation recognise celebrated princes chosen by Heaven, and that it pay them tribute. The mad Dutch, not understanding

the decrees of Heaven, conducted themselves with neither fear nor shame, and tyrannised over my subjects . . . Now your little kingdom has oppressed my subjects, and has done wrong to my commercial shipping, in more or less the same manner as did the Dutch, by provoking discord and stirring up by your present outrages the desire for vengeance. Matters in the island of Formosa have all been concluded in accordance with my wishes. I have hundreds of thousands of good soldiers, and a large number of war and merchant ships at this island. The distance which separates us from your kingdom is not great; indeed, if we set sail in the morning we could arrive there in the evening. I have thought of going there in person with my fleet to punish your crimes and your presumption . . .[109]

The anger of the proud Spaniards on receiving this message, and the various threats which it goes on to enumerate, may well be imagined. Many were in favour of putting to death at once all the Sangleys (Chinese)[110] in the Philippines, so as to reduce the danger of having to cope with enemies within as well as without. More than patriotism may have been involved in the anxiety of many Spaniards to get rid of the Chinese:

> One seldom finds a person who is not interested in the ruin of the Sangley—some on account of the loot [*that may be obtained from them*]; the rest, because there are few persons who do not hold property of the Sangleys in trust, or else owe for much merchandise which they have bought on credit.[111]

The panic of the Chinese grew with each hour, and with each new measure designed to strengthen the defences of the islands.

> Their desperation was completed by the interpretation which the common people gave to everything—irresponsible soldiers with mestizos, mulattoes, and blacks, telling the Sangleys that they were to have their heads cut off, as if they were men already sentenced to death; and inflicting on them many injuries and uttering a thousand insults.[112]

Two Spaniards were killed by a Chinese mob in the district of Parian. The party which favoured massacre of all Chinese demanded vengeance, but the more moderate governor sent instead a delegation, which included Vittorio Ricci, the Dominican priest who headed Coxinga's embassy, and Fr. Jose de Madrid, who could speak Chinese fluently. The Chinese, who had heard rumours that the Chinese members of Coxinga's embassy, actually living comfortably in Manila, had been put to death, were in a hostile mood, and refused to listen to the well-intentioned priests. Finally, after Ricci had left, they killed Fr. Jose de Madrid.[113] Apparently the Chinese repented immediately afterwards, for they tracked down the persons believed to be guilty of the deed, but the killing of the priest so infuriated the most influential personages and military leaders in Manila that it was only the governor's determined stand that prevented a mass decapitation of all Chinese. Instead, they were ordered to come to the Parian, under penalty of execution if they failed to obey. Some Chinese convinced that only death awaited them in the Parian if they proceeded there, chose to flee to the mountains. There they were hunted by the Spanish troops who drove them into the jungles, where hunger and the cruelty of the savages caused the death of most of them. Those Chinese who were caught outside the Parian were decapitated, while those who there took refuge were herded together until such time as they might board the junks that were to evacuate them.[114]

The junks departed one after another, so heavily loaded with passengers— one alone took 1,300 of them—that there was scarcely room enough for the unhappy refugees to sit down. On 10th July, the day on which the last three junks sailed, to impress the departing Chinese, the governor deliberately ordered that church bells be rung as a token of rejoicing over supposed news of the arrival of ships from Nueva Espana.[115] To the departing ambassador, Ricci, the governor delivered a reply to Coxinga's demands.

> Don Sabiniano Manrique de Lara, Caballero de la Orden de Calatrava, del Consejo de Su Magestad Catholica del Rey N. Senor Don Phelipe IV, gran Monarca de las Espanas y de las Indias Orientales y Occidentales, Yslas y Tierra firme del mar Occeano: su Gouernador y Capitan General en las Filipinas y Presidente de la Audiencia y Chancilleria Real donde reside, &. Al Kuesing, que rige, y govierna las costas maritimas del Reyno de China.

> No nation is unaware that the Spaniards obey only their king, acknowledging and worshipping God, the all-powerful Creator of heaven and earth, cause of all causes, without beginning, middle or end; and that they live in his holy law, and die in his defence, and that his treatment is just, praiseworthy and constant, as has been seen in what has been done for many years in these parts with the natives of the Kingdom of China, who have transacted business to the sum of millions, by which they have been enriched, and have acquired innumerable treasures from reciprocal trade secured by promises, gaining our care and help by the friendship which they professed . . .[116]

It is impossible that Coxinga ever read these high-sounding words, or any other part of the governor's rejection of his demands, for the Spaniards state that he was already dead when the message arrived from the Philippines.[117] Other suggested causes and manners of the death of Coxinga will presently be listed, but for the moment the chief Spanish accounts will be pursued. According to these sources, there was a certain Chinese captain named Nachiu who, on the first day of the Chinese uprising in the Parian, set sail in his junk for Formosa with a number of Chinese refugees. When he arrived in Formosa he threw himself at Coxinga's feet "weeping and with a thousand demonstrations of sentiment", and related to him how the Spaniards, with inhuman barbarity, had put to the sword all the Chinese in the Philippines.

The false messenger informed Kuesing of all the circumstances of the country and of Manila. When the latter heard these things, he roared like a goaded bull, and the saliva dropped from his mouth. He was furious that he had adopted so politic a counsel as to send threats before putting deeds into execution. He threatened to reduce to ashes the ambassador and all the Spaniards, and, if it were necessary, the whole world, to avenge his offended sense of honour. He declared he would secure a truce with the Tartars, and would have at his control a greater military machine than the one he displayed against Nan-king, junks, arms, soldiers, munitions, and pieces of artillery, threatening to come in person to destroy the island of Luzon, without leaving one stone on another in all its breadth, and declaring that he sought a war of blood and fire. But Divine pity again looked favourably on its little flock of Manila, and thus it was that one day when Kuesing had gone out by way of diversion to inspect the military preparations that were being made, he returned to his house in a state of great melancholy which turned that night into a fever and a loss of reason, with such violence that he clawed his face, bit his hands, and kicked at all those who approached him, without ceasing to utter cries that the whole world be killed, and in particular the Spaniards. When he was answered that his wish had already been executed, he calmed down a little, but then began again to repeat his frantic actions, which finally took from him his life that same night, as he was making frightful faces and movements.[118]

Another Spanish version adds other gruesome details, in the national manner.

When he learned these terrible tidings, the proud pirate became furious; the pupils of his eyes turned into fierce balls of fire; convulsively seizing his sabre, he swore by the infernal regions that he would reduce to powder the Spaniards and would sweep them from the surface of the sea. He ordered that his fleet be ready to set sail for the Philippines. But God, who has always watched over the independence of these Spanish provinces, foiled these plans and upset his impious oath. This sudden burst of terrible wrath had so affected the robust constitution of the pirate, that he was attacked a few hours afterwards by a frightful madness. In his horrible frenzy he tore his flesh, bit his lips and tongue until they bled, furiously attacked anyone who approached him, and passed a sentence of death on the king and the governors of Spain. These terrible paroxysms lasted five whole days; finally, suffocated by rage, he delivered up his perverted soul to the demons. Thus died the Attila of the East, the second of July 1662, in his thirty-ninth year... He who could defy with a bold countenance the fury and the power of the angry elements; he who, in his horrible impiety feared neither God nor men, nor the very powers of hell, succumbed at the thought of seeing himself conquered and humiliated by the high dignity of the Spanish nation, even before he had recourse to the barbarous action of warfare.[119]

In reading these Spanish accounts one cannot help feeling that the true facts of the death of Coxinga, whatever they may have been, have somehow been translated into the Spanish mould; that Coxinga, dying of rage because of wounded pride seems less the half-Chinese, half-Japanese adventurer we know him to be, than some hero (or villain) of old Spain.

The account of the Belgian priest, Rougemont, written in Latin, has a definitely classical flavour.

His death was undoubtedly a working of divine vengeance and justice, God demanding punishment for his pride and his cruelty. The very nature and form of his death, of a type never before known, were proof of this. At one and the same time, messengers arrived with most grievous tidings from the islands of the Philippines and from the city where his son was staying; none of all the projects which he had been planning was succeeding as he had hoped, but on the contrary, things had turned out most unfortunately at both places, and had inflicted an almost irreparable harm on his fortunes. It was reported that the Dutch were again attacking with an armed fleet and had concluded an alliance of war with the Tartars. Already they were besieging the lesser islands and castles closest to the part of the continent held by his garrisons. The wretch, stunned by these tidings, as I have mentioned above, was agitated by the opposing motions like waves of his soul powerless to control itself, and at once fell into a grave illness.

After a few days, when the strength of his disease had waned a little, he wished to go outdoors and walk with his friends to dispel the heavy sadness that held him in its grip. He happened to be standing on a certain rather lofty tower of the castle, whence a view spread out over the sea and the land, when, suddenly crying out with a fearful shout, he covered both his eyes with his hands and said, "Take at once from my sight those men whose heads have been cut off! Do you not see them? There, see there, they lie prostrate!"(Saying this he stretched out his fingers towards a certain place visible to them all.) "Do you not hear them? To me they cry out, to me. They are looking for me, and they say, 'You, cruel man, have killed us, who were guilty of no crime'." While he was thus crying out, his companions caught him as he fell, and, grieving and astonished, carried him back to the palace . . . He lay thus ill for three days with this sickness of mind and body. Finally, driven mad, he wounded his fingers with repeated bites, and died the image of utter madness. His death fell on the twenty-third day of June of 1662.[120]

The Italian, Careri, apparently writing with a knowledge of Rougemont's text, describes how Ricci returned from the Philippines to find

the Tyrant, through the just Judgments of God, had dy'd with Rage, having first gnaw'd off his Fingers with his Teeth, upon hearing of the League concluded against him between the Tartars and the Dutch; and that the Governor had discover'd his Conspiracy in the Philippine Islands and put to Death several thousands of Chineses; as also that his Son had committed Incest with one of his Wives.[121]

Careri repeats the combination of three events mentioned by Rougemont, but the first French account exercises a Gallic prerogative in reducing the three to one, the one which had to do with the ever important theme of love.

Dans une Isle de la Province de Fokien, où son pere avoit fait bastir une Forteresse, il avoit laissé un fils qu'il avoit, nommé Chin, avec ses femmes. Ce fils s'étoit si fort oublié du respect qu'il devoit à son pere, qu'il en avoit osé aimer une, & par malheur il ne l'avoit pas trouvée insensible à sa passion. Cette injure piqua si vivement Quesin, qui en fut averti, qu'il resolut de s'en vanger; & sa colere le porta jusqu'à vouloir faire mourir son fils. Le jeune homme fut averti aussi, & avec l'aide de sa mere, qui demeuroit dans la mesme Forteresse, & qui estoit une femme de teste, il s'estoit mis en disposition de traiter avec le Tartare, aprés avoir prévenu celuy que son père envoyait pour le tuer, lorsqu'il apprit que le dépit, que Quesin avoit conceu de sa revolte, l'avoit luy-mesme fait mourir.[122]

Later French writers usually continued the tradition of "l'amour toujours l'amour" to the exclusion of other possible causes of Coxinga's death. The

F

account by the Dutch ambassador to the court of Muscovy is noteworthy in that it combines the author's native interest in financial matters with his acquired Russian taste for despair. He tells us that Coxinga was defeated at Nanking after his disastrous birthday party. His original quarrel with the Manchus had stemmed from the theft of "three Ships freighted with Silver", and he was bitterly chagrined that he had failed to recoup his losses.

> The Prince with his small Remainder returns to his Island, and is reported to be so much affected with this scandalous loss, that running distracted he bit off a piece of his Tongue, which occasioned such a Flux of Blood, as could not timely be staunched, so that he died of it.[123]

However curious and agreeably shocking a seventeenth-century reader may have found such a description, it was scarcely tolerable for a nineteenth-century Englishman or American, and thus a new and more suitable death had to be culled from Chinese sources.

> On May 1st, 1662, Koxinga was suffering from a severe cold. Nevertheless he ascended the stairs to the upper balcony of his palace and there with a glass searched the seas towards the Pescadores looking for the arrival of some vessels expected. Eight days later he again ascended the stairs and as before made careful observations with his glass. With the help of his faithful aides he then descended to his study. His cold had now developed into a disease,... and Koxinga was much weakened by its ravages. Here he changed his dress for his ceremonial robes, and then with much solemnity he took up the sacred testament of the first Ming Emperor and bowing reverently before it, sat down with the precious document in his hands. His grief now overpowered him, and looking towards his courtiers he cried, "How can I meet my Emperor in Heaven with my mission unfulfilled?" Then bowing forward and covering his face with his hands the defender of the Mings breathed his last . . .
> Koxinga was not a vulgar pirate.[124]

If an Englishman or American was satisfied with Coxinga's dying the victim of a bad cold, a Scot had to add a moral note. After relating the indiscretion of Coxinga's son, and Coxinga's consequent rage, he states

> On hearing of this unexpected issue, Chunggoong (*Ch'eng-kung*) was so wild in his rage that he became mad; he gnashed his teeth, bit his own finger, and, as his powerful constitution was probably ruined by his indulgence with wine and women, he died, aged thirty-eight.[125]

These are not the only variants by any means. A recent American encyclopædia article, for example, declared that "he was killed in an engagement with the Dutch",[126] while a nineteenth-century Japanese account says that Coxinga died of illness brought on by "rage and grief" over the news of the death of the Ming pretender, Yung Li.[127]

The question must certainly arise, "What, then, is the truth?" No account is indisputably accurate, but it seems likely that Rougemont's came closest to the facts. The European who was best prepared to report on the manner of Coxinga's death was Vittorio Ricci. Although his ship was forced by storms to proceed to Amoy from Manila, instead of returning to Formosa where he might have obtained first-hand information about Coxinga's death,[128] Ricci's position as ambassador entitled him to an accurate report on the subject. When Ricci returned to Manila in April, 1663, as ambassador for Coxinga's son, he would undoubtedly have informed the Spaniards of the circumstances of the death of a person so important to them. Before that time even, Ricci may have been in touch with his fellow missionaries, including the Jesuit Rougemont, reporting the events in Formosa. It is probable, then, that both Rougemont's account and the Spanish ones were derived from a common source, Ricci, but independently. The details of the madness were modified by the Spaniards in their national manner, but the madness (as opposed, say, to a bad cold or death by enemy action) is probably a fact.[129]

Chinese sources offer us little help on the matter. Some give the account already quoted in translation of Coxinga bewailing his failure to restore the Ming. Others cite his wrath when he heard of his son's misbehaviour. One states that he "died from the fatigue of his military service in Formosa",[130] and still another that he was killed by his son,[131] surely a theme as typical of Chinese history as amorous intrigue is of French. The account of Coxinga's campaigns by his officer Yang Ying, who may have been an eye witness, does not specify the manner of his death.[132]

But even if some document were to be discovered which would give indisputable testimony as to the death of Coxinga, would it be advisable to condemn to oblivion the false and contradictory evidence of the seventeenth-century writers that have been quoted? However these writings may have been intended, they usually proved to be works of dramatic fiction, guided by the individual or national taste of the author. The matter of Coxinga's death has been examined at length in order to show how accounts may vary, but the circumstances of his birth, his upbringing and education, his motivation for opposing the Manchus, his acquisition of the imperial surname, his various battles (particularly that of Nanking), and his campaign on Formosa are among the points at which a multiplicity of traditions exists. The reason why the facts are so difficult to come by is clear : the life and death of Coxinga so stirred the imaginations of the writers of the seventeenth century (and later) that consciously or otherwise an attempt was almost invariably made to give a dramatic unity and integrity to narratives of them.

It is obviously of prime importance for the serious biographer to chronicle the authenticated facts of the life of his subject. For a full understanding of the subject's importance in his time and afterwards, however, this is not enough. If the subject is a dramatic hero, as Coxinga certainly was, there will be created an aura and a myth, which may at times supersede in cultural importance the actual facts.[133] Coxinga survives to-day not in the treasures he once piled up, nor in the noses and ears he may once have caused to be cut off, nor even in the documents he addressed to his friends or enemies, but in the legends, the myths, and the works of artistry that have grown over his grave. If we prove that Coxinga never burnt his Confucian robes, the story-tellers in Fukien will not cease to mention this deed in their tales. If we prove that he died of a bad cold and not of madness, we shall not have unsaid the pious reflections on divine retribution that the Spanish priests must have addressed to their congregations. If our investigations lead us to conclude that Coxinga was not a "vulgar pirate", we shall have to cross out every mention of him in European books until most recent times.[134] If, on the other hand, we decide that he was a cruel and stupid man, more obstinate than talented, we shall not have convinced the Chinese or Japanese who pray at his shrines, for he has been deified in both countries, that they pray in vain; an Emperor of China once bore witness that Coxinga "has given ear to supplications whenever addressed to him in times of flood or drought, thus adding to the benefits for which Formosa has to thank him".[135]

In Japan the tradition has been shaped largely by Chikamatsu's play *The Battles of Coxinga*. When, as in the case of serious modern articles, the fantastic elements of Chikamatsu's invention are left out of descriptions of the life of Coxinga, the central theme of the marriage of Japan and China is never neglected; Coxinga is always portrayed as a Japanese with a Chinese father.[136] Japanese scholars will go to great pains to uncover proofs of Coxinga's interest in and fondness for things Japanese. It goes without saying that in works of a less scholarly nature Chikamatsu's plays have been used as virtually unquestioned source material.

The cultural historian who attempts to give a complete picture of Coxinga's life will thus have to take into account all that grew up around the man. This will still not be enough if he wishes to make of the subject a living creature so that the moment when Coxinga learned of the defection of his father, or the hour when, outside Nanking, he realised that his long-planned campaign was ended and forever lost, will seem more than sententious statement in neatly turned Chinese phrases. But there the historian will run the risk of turning dramatist, in the manner of his seventeenth-century predecessors. Then probably we shall have a Coxinga as distinctly for our age as Chikamatsu's was for his.

IV

SOURCES AND INFLUENCES OF
CHIKAMATSU'S PLAY

(a) Sources

THE SLIGHT relationship which Chikamatsu's play bears to historical fact may be inferred from the previous chapter. However, it is not a pure fantasy on the life of some person from a distant and exotic land, as was the tragedy of the little-known English dramatist, Aaron Hill, entitled *The Fatal Vision: or, the Fall of Siam*.[1] Hill, in his preface, described his reasons for having chosen an oriental subject.

That I might be at liberty to form the proper incidents with less confinement to my fancy, I resolved to choose no noted character of History. Our distance from, and dark ideas of, the Chinese nation, and her borders, tempted me to fix my scene in so remote a situation. The fable is fictitious; and the characters are all imaginary, even to the very names, excepting only Umcham, common to the Emperors of China, as at Rome, the Cæsars.[2]

The play by Chikamatsu's predecessor, Nishiki Bunryū,[3] on the subject of Coxinga had no more connection with historical truth than had Hill's on Siam, but Chikamatsu preferred to elaborate on what he considered to be the facts.[4] It is possible to ascertain some of the sources to which he had access concerning the life of the famous Ming loyalist.[5] Although historical authenticity was not his intention, he desired to write a work that would bear some relationship to the truth.

Chikamatsu could have obtained information about Coxinga from one of several Chinese accounts written by his time,[6] but his primary interest was in Coxinga's connections with Japan, and for this purpose a Chinese history would not be suited. Instead, the book he used for reference was the *Minshin Tōki* (*Account of the Battles of the Ming and Ch'ing*), a work written by Maezono Jinzaemon about 1665.[7] Many of the distortions of historical fact and otherwise inexplicable embellishments of Chikamatsu's drama may be traced to incidents in the *Minshin Tōki*. Such episodes in the play as the battle between the shrike and the clam, the game of *go*, and the prophecies of the spirits on the mountain were originally found in Maezono's work and were freely adapted by Chikamatsu for his dramatic purposes.

In any case, Chikamatsu's almost exclusive concern was to write a good play. For this reason, in writing a play on Coxinga's life he did not include all of the facts even as known to him from the inaccurate *Minshin Tōki*. Since a complete account of Coxinga from his boyhood to his death would not make for a dramatically unified work, he chose to treat only that part of Coxinga's life from the time when he decided to go to China until the battle of Nanking. Coxinga actually left for China as a boy in his seventh year,[8] but some accounts that Chikamatsu may have read give other figures for his age. For example, it is stated in a book by Nishikawa Joken (1648-1724) that Coxinga was seventeen when he made the journey to China.[9] However, as Chikamatsu wished Coxinga's connections with Japan to be as strong as possible, Coxinga is married to a Japanese wife. It was probably for this reason that Chikamatsu added a few years of age to Nishikawa's seventeen.

The play ends with the battle of Nanking; because of this fact, Chikamatsu changes the defeat into a great triumph for Coxinga. If Coxinga had died gallantly at Nanking the play might have been written as an inspiring tragedy, but a despondent Coxinga gazing at the ruins of his army and of his work of many years would not fit the Japanese pattern at all. The only possible way for the play to end if the earlier auspicious incidents were to be retained was with the complete triumph of Coxinga.

The beginning and end of the biography of his hero having been determined, Chikamatsu had to look for the usual accessories to a drama, a villain and love interest. Probably the most conspicuous evil-doer of the end of the Ming dynasty was Li Tzu-ch'eng, the famous bandit leader.[10] Chikamatsu's attention may have been drawn to him by the *Minshin Tōki* in which he figures prominently. Rather than call him Ri Jisei, the normal Japanese rendering of Li Tzu-ch'eng, however, he named him Ri Tōten, possibly because the latter name was more suited to declamation.[11] There is very little to link Ri Tōten with the historical character on whom he is based. The fact that Li Tzu-ch'eng lost his left eye in fighting[12] may have been responsible for the scene in the first act in which Ri Tōten gouges out his left eye, as a warrant to the Tartars that he will join them in the attack on the Mings. That is the only direct point of resemblance in the play. The other wicked characters of the play are entirely fictitious; their villainy usually consists in the fact that they oppose Coxinga's forces, not in any inherent wickedness.

As for a love interest, Chikamatsu appears to have felt that Coxinga should remain faithful to his Japanese wife. Thus it was that the *michiyuki*, which almost always is a journey of lovers, had to be modified in this instance; *faute de mieux*, we have Komutsu dressed as a man accompanying the Princess Sendan. In place of the usual love interest Chikamatsu described Coxinga's relationship with three women, Komutsu, Sendan and Kinshōjo. Komutsu seems to have been entirely a creation of Chikamatsu's invention.[13] Sendan was apparently derived from the Princess Sendara in Nishiki's play.[14] Kinshōjo, the most appealing of the three women, was also original with Chikamatsu.

The other men in the play of importance, Go Sankei and Kanki, are both historical. Go Sankei is derived from Wu San-kuei (1612-1678), one of the chief figures of the early Manchu dynasty. When Li Tzu-ch'eng was pressing on Peking in 1644, the Emperor ordered Wu to return to the capital. He delayed so long in doing so that before he reached Peking he learned of its fall to Li Tzu-ch'eng. His father was held hostage by the bandit and Wu might have yielded to Li in order to save his father's life, but Li so offended him by taking his favourite concubine that Wu preferred to negotiate with the Manchus. When the latter refused to bargain with him over the spoils of the Ming empire, he surrendered to them. He was granted positions of high responsibility by the Manchus and remained a loyal soldier to them until 1673 when he revolted. He later proclaimed himself emperor of a new dynasty, but his revolt was eventually put down.[15]

That Chikamatsu could make of this man the model of loyalty that Go Sankei becomes in the play should serve as adequate testimonial of the strange uses to which history was sometimes put by him. However, Chikamatsu's interpretation of the man may have been influenced by such a description of him as one finds in Nishikawa Joken's *Night Tales of Nagasaki*.[16]

> The father of Coxinga was called Tei Shiryū, and had the appellation of Ikkanrō. He was from Fukien. When the Ming Dynasty reached a time of troubles, he . . . did not submit to Tartary, but communicated with Go Sankei . . .
>
> [*Later, in describing Coxinga's grandson, who surrendered Formosa to the Manchus.*] However, he was far from resembling his father and grandfather in his abilities. He was at a loss what to do; he had no supporters in the fifteen provinces. Go Sankei was dead and his survivors scattered. He therefore surrendered to the Manchus.[17]

If Chikamatsu read some work of similar content, he would have been given the impression that Wu San-kuei (like Coxinga's father) was loyal to the Ming. This was enough knowledge of the man for Chikamatsu to possess. He needed a loyal minister to counterbalance the wicked Ri Tōten, and such an account of Wu San-kuei could have supplied him with the man. Once Chikamatsu had his loyal minister, a stock character of Chinese history, he used him throughout the play whenever needed.[18]

Very little else in the play is even remotely related to history, although Chikamatsu may actually have regarded details derived from the *Minshin Tōki* as documentation for his work. For example, the lecture on the significance of ideographs delivered by Go Sankei to the Emperor in the first act comes directly from the *Minshin Tōki*. In the first volume of the work, under the heading of the "Emperor's Dream", we are told of an incident said to have occurred on the ninth day of the ninth moon of 1635. The interpretations offered by a soothsayer to the emperor concerning his dream about an ideograph correspond exactly to Go Sankei's explanations in the first act.[19]

Similarly, the fight between the shrike and the clam in the second act is also found in the *Minshin Tōki*. If the scene is not very convincing in Chikamatsu's play, it is partially because the moral of the incident does not apply. The moral would seem to be that when two parties are fighting bitterly they will not have time to look out for an enemy with designs on both of them, and thus will fall easy prey to a clever outsider. But it is not Watōnai's ambition to conquer both the Manchus and the Ming adherents. He intends instead to help the latter against the former. In the *Minshin Tōki* the moral actually applies. The story serves to describe how the Manchus were able to take Peking without effort while the Mings and the bandit forces of Li Tzu-ch'eng were fighting one another.[20] Chikamatsu adopted the image for his play without considering its inappropriateness.

A better piece of adaptation was done by Chikamatsu in the case of the scene of the Mountain of the Nine Immortals. This story is originally scattered in different parts of the *Minshin Tōki*. In the latter work it is Kanki who visits the mountain. There he bows before a temple of the immortals and prays that he be granted a divine message telling of his future. He falls asleep and in a dream an old man comes to deliver a prophecy. Chikamatsu substituted Go Sankei for Kanki, and the first Ming emperor and Liu Po-wen for the nameless prophetic old man of the original. These two men figure in the first book of the *Minshin Tōki* in connection with other prophecies. Another legend which is treated in the scene on the mountain is that of Wang Chih, the man who became so absorbed in a game of *go* that he lost all sense of time. Go Sankei also is substituted for Wang Chih. From these scattered pieces in the *Minshin Tōki* and from various bits from other works he built the famous mountain scene.[21]

One other major borrowing from the *Minshin Tōki* was the group of stratagems suggested by Go Sankei and Kanki in the final act. The concealed hornets in bamboo tubes advocated by Go had been used in the theatre before, notably in Nishiki's play on Coxinga.[22] It may have been to discredit the device his predecessor used that Chikamatsu rejected the plan. It is more likely, however, that Chikamatsu found it in the sixth volume of the *Minshin Tōki*. In the seventh volume of the same book is found Kanki's plan of poisoned baskets of fruit, there described as an invention of Coxinga's.[23]

To summarise, it may be said that *The Battles of Coxinga* owes less to history than it does to the *Minshin Tōki*, and less to the *Minshin Tōki* than it does to Chikamatsu's imagination. The plot was nevertheless regarded as historical by many people of Chikamatsu's time and for years afterwards. Of this fact one soon becomes aware in examining the works written under the influence of the *Battles of Coxinga*.

(b) Influences of the Play

It is interesting to learn of the sources of the *Battles of Coxinga*, but the influences of Chikamatsu's play are of far greater significance in Japanese literary history. In addition to the various versions of the *Battles of Coxinga* itself that have been made to suit the demands of theatres of later times, there exist numerous works which are based entirely or in part on the play. Some of these works have been lost or are now difficult to obtain, but a number have become famous in their own right and are included in collections of Japanese literature.

A typical work derived from *The Battles of Coxinga* is the play by Ki no Kaion, Chikamatsu's rival dramatist. It is entitled *Keisei Kokusenya*.[24] *Keisei*, meaning "courtesan", is a word found at the head of the titles of many plays of the Tokugawa period, serving to show that the protagonists will be creatures of the demi-monde. Ki no Kaion's play was a demi-monde version of *The Battles of Coxinga*, written about a year after Chikamatsu's play in order to profit by its popularity.

Although the change of milieu necessitated many revisions in the structure of the original, there still remains a number of striking resemblances to Chikamatsu's work. For example, in the second act there is a scene in which the hero is pursued while carrying the heroine, Kaguyama, on his back. By showing the pursuers a chart of Kaguyama's pedigree, he makes them his followers, the *keisei* equivalent of the scene in the bamboo forest.

Again, in the third act, we have a close adaptation of the original. The hero and heroine, together with a friend, appear before the house of a wealthy man, Iwabuchi Sazen, the husband of Kaguyama's elder sister. Kaguyama, who was separated from her sister when a child, comes to seek her help in raising funds for redeeming her from the brothel in which Kaguyama works. She raps on the garden gate and asks to speak with her sister. The sister then appears at a window in the tower. Kaguyama shows her an image of Buddha with a broken left arm, a souvenir of their childhood, and calls her sister by name. The husband, Sazen, is absent, but the sister lets Kaguyama in. She is about to hand over the necessary sum of money when Sazen returns. He declares that he intends to kill the courtesan. He puts down his sword for a moment and Kaguyama snatches it up. Her sister rushes to stop her. At that moment, Kaguyama's companions, who have been waiting impatiently outside the house, burst into the room. But all are too late; Kaguyama opens her robe to disclose that she has already stabbed herself.

Ki no Kaion's play was highly regarded by certain critics, but it never enjoyed much success. Some *kabuki* versions of *The Battles of Coxinga* achieved more popularity, usually because of the actor who played the role of Coxinga. *Kokusenya Takenuki Gorō* (1727), for instance, was successful because the adaptor, Ichikawa Danjūrō, was the most famous actor of his day. In his version the characters were all given Japanese names (Coxinga became Soga Gorō) and the "rough business" of the original was emphasised to such an extent that the play was popularly called "Oshimodoshi" or "Pushing Back", referring to the hero's energetic behaviour in the last act.[26]

One unusual adaptation of Chikamatsu's play was the Nō drama *Watōnai*, written by Hara Kanchiku in 1756. Many *jōruri* plays by Chikamatsu and other dramatists were derived from the Nō, but this is probably the only case of a Nō drama having been inspired by a *jōruri*. *Watōnai* is based on the beginning of the second act of *The Battles of Coxinga*.[27]

Other imitations of the play were produced through the eighteenth and well into the nineteenth centuries.[28] The last of the line, *The Magic Lantern Picture of Coxinga* (1872), is one of the most interesting. This work by the dramatist Kawatake Mokuami (1804-1893) was designed as a farewell piece for the retiring actor, Sawamura Tanosuke. Frankly intended to excite the tears of the audience, it incorporated one of the most touching scenes of Chikamatsu's play in new and even more exotic surroundings. Kokin, a geisha, is shipwrecked off Naruto in a storm, and is rescued by a foreign ship. In the course of time she becomes the mistress of one Kankisu, an Englishman, and lives with him for seven years in London. Her husband, Hikosō, journeys all the way from Japan to see her again. They speak to one another, she up in a tower and he down on the ground. Kokin declares that she is unable to return to Japan with Hikosō because of the illness of her benefactor, Kankisu. Hikosō has just been informed that his father is critically ill and cannot tarry any longer in England. The two part, accompanied in all likelihood by the sighs and tears of the audience which was moved equally by the sorrow of the spectacle of husband and wife parting forever and by the knowledge that it was seeing its favourite actor play for the last time. The play was never repeated.[29]

Apart from such direct imitations as the ones above cited, there are numerous instances of indirect borrowing from *The Battles of Coxinga*. In the celebrated *Chūshingura* by Takeda Izumo, for example, we find a number of such passages, although the plays have no similarity of plot. Most striking is the scene in which Oboshi Yuranosuke reads a long scroll. At the same time Okaru is reading it by its reflection in her mirror, and the villain Kudayu, who is under the verandah, reads it by the light of the moon as it unrolls. The passage is derived from the third act scene in Chikamatsu's play in which Kinshōjo on the wall sees the moonlit reflection of her father in her mirror.[30]

The influence of *The Battles of Coxinga* was not restricted to plays. As early as 1716 there was the novel *Military Tales of Coxinga*, a work in five books that are slavishly modelled on the acts of the play.[31] *Keiseiya Gundan* (1717) by Andō Jishō (*c.* 1660-1745) goes to the opposite extreme in that it preserves of the original only a few similarities in the names of the characters.[32]

Probably the best work which was inspired chiefly by Chikamatsu's play was the novel *Kokusenya Minchō Taiheiki* (1717) by Ejima Kiseki (1667-1736).[33]   The author retained the main outlines of Chikamatsu's plot, but expanded it into a novel of complexity and humour. A comparison of the extracts below with their originals in the first act of *The Battles of Coxinga* may best show Kiseki's technique.

Women's long tongues are the source of all evil. Misfortunes do not originate in Heaven but with women. All disturbances in the nation, all derelictions in the administration, have their sources in women: of this there are many examples both ancient and modern.

Now, he who was called the Emperor Shisōretsu, the seventeenth sovereign of the Ming, was the second son of the Emperor Kōsō. When he first ascended the throne the world was at peace, and thus is was that he devoted himself to his revels and did not stint himself in his luxuries. He gave himself to sensual pleasure and drinking parties. On spring days before the flowers had come out, rare incense was buried in the ground to scent the shoes of the passers-by. On summer nights when there was no moon over the palace, fireflies were massed together to serve as lanterns. Yet, though one day of sensual pleasure succeeded another without pause, his corrupt ministers still flattered the emperor, and did not admonish him. The emperor in his besotted state, seemed to have forgotten everything.

Now, of the many consorts who were favoured by him, the Lady Kasei and the Lady Rishi surpassed all the others of the three thousand court-ladies, being gentle and elegant in their figures and faces. They were his two hands, and he bestowed on them his favours, alike in the season of spring flowers and in that of autumn leaves; thus it was his years were spent in deep delight.

The Lady Kasei had conceived in the autumn of the previous year, and the imperial birth was to occur in the following month. Her ladies-in-waiting, and all the others of the court down to the lowly attendants, prayed that a crown prince would be born as heir to the throne. There had been a sudden change in the language used toward the Lady Kasei, and she was already addressed with reverence as "Her Majesty, the Empress-Mother".

Now, there was an eldest son of an old minister named Ri Chin, whose name was Ri Tōten. When he had grown to manhood, his behaviour was so cruel that his father Ri Chin had turned his back on him, disinherited him, and had him driven from his doors. Ri Tōten was not permitted to remain in Nanking, and, having nowhere to turn, had gone to Tartary. For over ten years he had lived in friendship with the people of that land. However, as his father Ri Chin was growing old and weak, his mind dwelt more and more on Ri Tōten, and he longed for the son he had once cast forth. He pardoned Ri Tōten his past misdeeds and called him back. Later, he presented him with a house, and made him the successor to the family name. He also found for him an official position in the palace.

Ri Tōten was by nature of surpassing cunning. A wily person, with a talent for fabrication as his birthright, he soon won over people's affections. Frequenting both the mighty and those of low degree, he ingratiated himself with all. He was lionised by those close to the throne, and even the emperor wondered, "What would we do without him?" Thus it was that he gradually rose to eminence, even surpassing his father in the official emoluments he was granted. His power grew with each day. Those who did not meet with his favour, even if they were loyal ministers, were slandered and driven from the court. Everything was done as he desired.

Now, when he had been in Tartary he had promised that if he returned to China he would destroy the Ming dynasty, and would divide the capital city of Nanking in two, sharing rule with the Tartars. It was his plan to wait for something exceptional to occur, and then to take advantage of it to throw the country into agitation. Then he would raise a rebellion in the midst of the resulting confusion. To this end he watched with unremitting attention. When he heard that the Lady Kasei was with child, he thought that this would prove a splendid opening for the disasters he was plotting, and his heart was suffused with smiles.

He hurried with all speed to the Lady Rishi and whispered to her, "Do you not feel aggrieved? Of all the many court ladies, you and Kasei are the ones who have enjoyed the warmest favours of his Majesty. Neither one is inferior or superior to the other; the emperor considers you his two hands. The court ladies and all the others who frequent the palace treat you two consorts with equal and profound respect. But now, if the Lady Kasei is delivered safely, and an imperial prince is born, no words will suffice to describe the awe in which she, as Her Majesty, the Empress-Mother, will be held by subjects and ministers alike. Your own prestige will sink day by day, and finally no one will know if you are here or gone, and you will be relegated to some distant quarter of the palace. You will feel as do those court ladies who have been forgotten. Until your hair has turned white, yours will be the life of a widow, and you will learn to lament the length of autumn nights. If this should come to pass your state will be most pitiable".[34]

Ri Tōten goes on to suggest means whereby Lady Rishi can prevent this melancholy situation from arriving; his plans finally succeed in wrecking the dynasty. The amplifications of Kiseki are often very good. For example, there are several amusing episodes arising from the troubles of the Japanese Komutsu and the Chinese Sendan in understanding one another.

(*One day*) Komutsu's father, who claimed to be an authority on language matters, caught the family tortoiseshell cat and put it on the chopping board. As he stood there, butcher's cleaver in hand, about to cut the cat up into cutlets, Komutsu cried in astonishment, "Hey! Why are you trying to kill our dear little kitty?" And she snatched the cat away. Her father, pretending to understand Chinese, said, "Just now when the princess was chattering, she was saying, 'Let's eat the cat fried in sesame oil'. You wouldn't know about such things. Chinese are meat-eaters, and they put anything at all into their dishes, even cats and rats."[35]

In the field of "history", *The Life of Coxinga* (1855) by Kanagaki Robun (1829-1894) may be mentioned.[36] The author attempted to combine historical facts with Chikamatsu's invention. This may be seen in the names used for the characters of his history. We are told of "Watōnai, the only son of Tei Shiryū Ikkan", following Chikamatsu's appellation, but the Ri Tōten of the play is here called Ri Jisei (Li Tzu-ch'eng), showing the author's superior knowledge of Chinese history.[36] *The Life of Coxinga* cannot be taken seriously by a Westerner as an historical work, but the distinction between fact and legend is much less clear in Japanese minds, and most of the book's readers must have believed it to be factual.

The popularity of Coxinga in Japan continued to grow as a result of the continued successes of the play when revived, and of the imitations and adaptations, some of which have been described. It could not have come as a shock to Japanese, then, when in 1898, at the time of the cession of Formosa to Japan, the first Governor-General of the island, Admiral Count Kabayama, at once proceeded to Coxinga's temple in the city of Tainan, and recommended that it be known henceforth as a *jinja* (or Shinto shrine) instead of as a *miao* (or Chinese temple).[37] The request was granted and Coxinga took his place among the other Japanese immortals. The move was undoubtedly politically inspired, serving to stress the half-Japanese, half-Chinese parentage of the hero, but even if it is admitted that Coxinga, as a loyal defender of the Ming, was entitled to veneration by the Chinese, it is difficult to see why Japanese should have wanted to worship at his shrine. Yet already in the late eighteenth century there was a shrine to him in Kyoto,[38] and none expressed surprise at his deification a hundred years later. By what means was it that Coxinga, the son of a prostitute by some accounts, a man who left Japan in his seventh year and never returned, was enabled to scale the Japanese heaven? Is it not likely that Chikamatsu's *Battles of Coxinga* was responsible for elevating a rather dubious half-breed, the "Attila of the East" for some, to the status of a Japanese hero, and even a Japanese god?

V

LITERARY ANALYSIS OF
"THE BATTLES OF COXINGA"

HE FIRST question a European is likely to ask about a play with which he is unfamiliar, is whether it is a comedy or a tragedy. This is a traditional and useful way of dividing works for the theatre, but at times it has been found that a given play does not fit easily into either category. The history plays of Shakespeare, for example, are usually not classified under either heading, but form a group of their own. Even in the case of the history plays, a prevailing tone generally leads the reader or spectator to consider the play as comedy or tragedy, in spite of contrary incidents that may occur in the work. That is to say, neither the death of Falstaff nor the massacre of the boys in the English camp, tragic though they are, disturbs the essentially comical and high-spirited tone of the play *Henry V*, nor, for that matter, do Faulconbridge's banterings make *King John* seem the less a tragedy. In the case of *The Battles of Coxinga*, however, we have a play in which the tone itself is constantly changing. We may decide on the basis of the happy ending that the play is a comedy, but its most memorable incidents are pathetic if not tragic. This strange ambivalence might appear a fault to Westerners, but it is precisely the quality that Japanese critics have most often praised in the play, and was certainly an important reason for its success.

It has previously been mentioned that the five acts of the *jōruri* play are believed to have been imitated from the five Nō plays customarily presented at one theatrical performance. It was also noted that in between the individual Nō plays there were short comic interludes called *kyōgen*. These interlude-plays were often parodies of the pieces they followed; a Nō play about a devoted priest might be followed by a *kyōgen* about a roguish one. It might seem that this alternation of mood from the tragic tone of the Nō to the broad farce of the *kyōgen* and back again would be too great a wrench for the sensibilities of the audience, especially when presented in roughly equal amounts. On the contrary, the *kyōgen* were considered a highly important part of a day's entertainment, and appear to have responded to some need felt at a certain stage of development of the theatre in every country. We find a curious parallel, for example, in the theatre of Italy during the eighteenth century.

86

Metastasio wrote not only the tragic play itself but wrote also two little comic interludes, according to that illogical jumbling fashion which prevails whenever an art is adolescent. After the curtain had fallen upon the intensely tragic Dido upbraiding the stately and statuesque Aeneas, it rose upon Signorina Santa Marchesini, as a prima donna, quarrelling with the stage tailors about the length of her train, and interrupted by the arrival of a famous buffo as Nibbio, a ridiculous manager from the Canary Islands . . . These interludes are droll enough—caricatures of the very tragedy they relieve, caricatures of the wrath and faintings of just such a queen as Dido, caricatures of just such airs, with tremendous nautical, botanical, meteorological similes . . . [It was the] turning of everything into ridicule fearlessly, from the certainty that as soon as the tragedy was resumed people would weep as much at the originals of the caricature as they had laughed at the caricature itself.[1]

It was just about the time of *The Battles of Coxinga* that the Japanese puppet theatre began to emerge from its "adolescence"; or, rather, it would be more accurate to say that it was at this time that Chikamatsu was lifting it to a level of maturity. His domestic tragedies, for example, have a uniform tone, and there is no catering to the public craving for low comedy. But one may find in any country a certain reluctance to give up old forms, and Japan, of all countries, is the one which preserves the things of the past the longest. It was thus that, even after the new stage represented by the three-act domestic tragedies was attained, a demand continued to exist for the older style of plays, plays which still preserved the heterogeneous elements of a programme of Nō tragedies and *kyōgen*. In *The Battles of Coxinga* Chikamatsu offered an excellent example of this mixture. To appreciate the play as a Japanese can, we must be able to admit the possibility of sandwiching regularly in one theatrical piece scenes of solemn spendour, low comedy, pathos, poetic description divorced from plot, fantasy and rough action. This is not the same as the inclusion of short comic scenes in Western tragedies; the play is in a composite form, of which we should have more examples in the West had the Italian entertainment described above been fused into one drama, instead of remaining three acts of a play and two comic interludes.[2]

The similarities that may be noted between the structure of *The Battles of Coxinga* and the order of a programme of Nō and *kyōgen* are not exact, but they are striking enough to afford us insight into the form of Chikamatsu's play. The five Nō plays that were offered at one performance were in a traditional order, which was a fixed one except for some accepted alternatives. The normal order was (1) the gods (2) men (3) women (4) mad people and (5) demons, but in place of (4) mad people, it was possible to have a dramatic realistic piece, and in place of (5) demons, a congratulatory piece. Much leeway was permitted in the interpretation of these categories, and certain Nō plays have been assigned at different times to one or another of them. The third, or "woman" play, was the high point of the programme, and most of the best dramas belong to this group. In between the Nō plays were presented *kyōgen*. Sometimes there would also be short interpolated *kyōgen* episodes even within the Nō play itself; these, however, were generally pertinent to the plot, unlike the interlude-plays, and have some correspondence with the "comic relief" found in Western plays.

The first act of *The Battles of Coxinga* has nothing to do with the gods, but it does treat of the court of the Chinese emperor, an exalted subject. The effect of this act on the audience must have been to inspire awe by the loftiness of its diction and the splendour of its décor and costumes.[3] This, presumably, should have been the effect of the first of a Nō series. It is the only act of the play which has this effect, although the mood is not maintained to its conclusion, but breaks up into scenes of battles between the Chinese and the Tartars.

The second act opens with a very different setting. Instead of the Chinese emperor and his glorious court, we have two simple Japanese fisherfolk wandering along the beach. This first part of the second act seems to me to correspond in effect to a *kyōgen* interlude. It is not farcical, but in the abruptness and violence of the change of mood, we have a parallel to the effect of a *kyōgen* after a Nō.

There is another quick shift of mood in the second part of the act. The audience, which has been listening with amusement to Komutsu's shrewish comments and to Sendan's nonsensical Chinese, is told that the bizarre stranger in bedraggled clothes is the princess last seen leaving China in her little boat. A link is then established with the serious business of the first act. The next of the Nō series now begins, the "man" play. The "man" in question is, of course, Watōnai, the future Coxinga, and his mighty deeds are the subject of the act. Watōnai realises that he is a man of destiny, and that he is to be the agent for the restoration of the Ming. He crosses over to China with his mother, overcomes a tiger with divine help, and then, with the aid of the now friendly tiger, defeats a hostile Chinese force, recruiting its members as his own followers. The second act ends in farce, with Watōnai and his mother shaving the heads of the Chinese soldiers in the Japanese manner. The Chinese soldiers, bereft of their locks, catch cold and sneeze, while their "noses ran and eyes watered like the showers of summer". The followers are required to assume comical names denoting their places of origin, and the whole happy troupe rides off.

The third act, like the third of the Nō play series, is easily the most important, and contains the chief elements that were retained in later performances of the plays as well as in imitations and adaptations. The third is the "woman" play, and the woman is Kinshōjo, Ikkan's daughter. She figures in all of the famous scenes of the act—the recognition between father and daughter, Kanki's various changes of decision, the "flowing rouge" and her suicide. The third is the one act without any sharp changes of mood. There is comic relief in the conversation of Kinshōjo's maids, but it is slight and not sustained. There is also a little "rough business" when Watōnai breaks into the castle, but it is over in a sentence, and is not the swinging, crashing, slaughtering of a real "rough business" scene.

The third act develops to its lyrical conclusion with no break, but the fourth act is divided into two parts. The first of these is composed of two rather light-hearted episodes, Komutsu's fencing practice and the *michiyuki* of Princess Sendan. The second part of the act is in an entirely different mood, describing the adventures that befell Go Sankei on the Mountain of the Nine Immortals and afterwards. He is shown in a vision the various triumphs won by Coxinga. As he watches time passes rapidly, and five years have already elapsed by the time the vision comes to an end. He then meets his old friend Ikkan, who is with a party of the Ming adherents. The Tartars spot them, and they are able to escape only by means of a miraculous cloud bridge supplied by the god Sumiyoshi. This bridge is the source of the undoing of the Tartar troops and the act ends with a Ming victory.

The fourth act of the Nō series was usually the "mad person" play. One Japanese critic felt that the effect of the *michiyuki* and of the scene on the Mountain of the Nine Immortals was that of fantasy and illogicality, which represented an equivalent of the madness of the Nō series.[4] It may also be that the scenes of battle are realistic enough for this fourth act to be likened to the dramatic realistic piece that was a permitted substitute for the "mad person" play, but in either case the parallel is not as close as elsewhere. The first part of the act may be considered a *kyōgen*-like episode, as may be the high-spirited closing moments.

As we have seen, a Nō programme was generally concluded with a "devil" piece, but a congratulatory play could take its place. The last act of *The Battles of Coxinga* is of the latter sort, ending as it does with the complete triumph of Coxinga's forces, and with prayers for the continued happiness of China under Japanese auspices.

When we examine the structure of the individual acts of the play, we are struck by their self-sufficiency. That is to say, each act virtually stands on its own; this would be explained, of course, by the fact that the play's structure was influenced by the tradition of the performance of a series of self-contained Nō plays. An act usually ends in such a manner as to give us an effect of completion, and not of leading us on to the following act.[5] The first act ends with an encomium of Lady Ryūka, the second with a description of Watōnai's triumphal parade of his new followers, the third with praise of Watōnai (now Coxinga), the fourth with the victorious entry into Foochow, and the last with the final successes of Coxinga and the praise of Japan. Only at the end of the fourth act is there any suggestion of action to come. The following is a typical act ending of *The Battles of Coxinga.*

> That he was the most wonderful of men from Japan, where such heroes are born, where the land is as land should be, and the sovereign is a true sovereign, he showed by illuminating a foreign country with the brilliance of his martial talents.

(Act III)

Contrast with this a typical act ending from Shakespeare.

> Two things are to be done,—
> My wife must move for Cassio to her mistress;
> I'll set her on;
> And bring him jump when he may Cassio find
> Soliciting his wife:—ay, that's the way;
> Dull not device by coldness and delay.

(*Othello*, Act II, Scene 3.)

In *Othello* we are led on to the next act by Iago's revelation of his plans. He tells us that the play is not ended, and even specifies what action is to come. In Chikamatsu's play the incompleteness of the action is implicit and not explicit; we expect that the hero will restore the Ming dynasty, but Chikamatsu does not promise us this, much less give us any detailed plans. If the play had ended after the third-act lines quoted above, one would not have been quite satisfied perhaps, but the eventual success of the hero Coxinga could be inferred. Certainly had the story of Coxinga been as well known to a Japanese audience as that of the Soga brothers, for example, Chikamatsu would not have hesitated to end his play at that point, knowing that the audience would supply the eventual resolution. In the case of the comparatively unknown Coxinga, Chikamatsu had to present a more complete picture. Although the audience could have been quite certain that the plea of Coxinga's mother for vengeance on the Tartars would not go unanswered, it wanted to know how the triumph was effected. When, in later years, the story of Coxinga became thoroughly familiar to Japanese playgoers, it became possible to stage only one act of *The Battles of Coxinga* without fear that the audience would be unable to understand what was going on.[6]

The acts of the play also show an individual development corresponding to the similar development in a Nō drama. Japanese critics, using the terminology first applied to the Nō, distinguish three phases of action in each of the acts of a *jōruri*. These are called *jo*, *ha* and *kyū*[7] in Japanese, corresponding roughly in speed, if not in mood, to an andante, allegro and presto. Where the line of demarcation between the sections is to be drawn rests largely with the particular critic, but a shift from one tempo to another is readily observable in each act. A Western play, on the other hand, is usually treated as a unity, and the acts may or may not embody any particular mood. In the case of the fourth act of *Macbeth*, for example, we have an interlude of the relative calm of England, to contrast with the terrible doings in Scotland that have preceded and are to culminate in the following act. More often, however, there will be no divisions corresponding to the formal structure of the play; the graph of the action will show a continued rise to the climax and then a falling off to the denouement. Seldom will each act show a rise and fall of its own. In many cases, indeed, the end of an act will be purely formal; modern revivals of Shakespeare which present an entire play in two acts do not suffer on that account.

The acts of *The Battles of Coxinga* are joined only in a rather loose federal union, but the union exists. A graph of the action of the entire play might also be made, and divisions of *jo*, *ha* and *kyū* sections established. This second graph is more difficult to draw than one for an individual act, partly because the fourth act, which was the high point of the original *jōruri* performances,[8] is probably less interesting for a reader than the third act, thus throwing off balance for him the development Chikamatsu may have intended.

At this point we touch on a most difficult and delicate matter: to what degree may a *jōruri* be judged on the basis of a reading knowledge of it, divorced as it then is from the accompanying music and spectacle? Chikamatsu was considered to have been the first Japanese dramatist whose writings were of sufficient literary quality to make them worth reading,[9] but the neglect from which he suffered until the search was begun for a Japanese Shakespeare[10] was probably due to the feeling that his works could be appreciated only in performance.

The text of a *jōruri* has been compared to that of a motion picture script.[11] Very seldom is it possible for one to read a script with pleasure because it is usually not much more than the outline of the unspoken action. It is in the nature of the motion picture medium to exploit the possibilities of chases across the house-tops, charges of soldiers, and the excitement of inarticulate crowds. It is difficult to realise such scenes on the stage, and they are likely to embarrass us when attempted; words alone must bear the action. A *jōruri* is somewhere in between the two. The narrator describes the action as it occurs, but however skilful the words of the dramatist, hearing or reading the description will not be the equal of seeing the action. For example, there is the sentence recited by the narrator, " When suddenly they lift together their thousands of paper lanterns on poles, it is just like seeing the thousand suns and moons of a thousands worlds at the same instant, and the soldiers of the castle, dumbfounded, stand in utter bewilderment". This is Chikamatsu at his best, but the words still do not have the startling power that the sudden brilliant flash of light must have had on the audiences. The wild battles, which are the chief feature of the *kyū* sections of four of the acts, are relatively uninteresting to read, but must have been fascinating to view. Chikamatsu was, of course, counting on such effects.

Of the two elements, music and spectacle, the reader probably loses most by the absence of the latter. Japanese music, while often capable of expressing great pathos, is not able to afford a very wide range of emotions. The music of *The Battles of Coxinga* was not composed afresh for the play, but had been used years before by Takemoto Gidayū, who composed it.[12] The relationship between Chikamatsu's text and the music was one of form, rather than of emotion, as would be true of a Western opera. That is to say, if the music called for a series of low notes, Chikamasu's text could not demand at that point sounds that were necessarily, or at least more comfortably, sung in a high voice. Nor, of course, could he write more sounds than the music would accommodate. On the other hand, there was no correspondence between the words and the music that accompanied them; the same music might be used in different plays for dissimilar emotions. There was also nothing in the music to distinguish any of the characters. It is even impossible to tell from the music whether a man or a woman is supposed to be singing.[13] The music was necessary to a *jōruri* if only because it helped to avoid monotony in the recitation of the narrator. It occupies a place of about the importance of music in a motion picture, rather than in an opera or a stage play. In an opera the music can make us accept a ridiculous plot told in clumsy words. In a stage play, on the other hand, no music, however beautiful, must ever be permitted to interfere with the intelligibility of a single word. In the motion picture or the *jōruri* it can heighten the effect of the words and sometimes even take their place, but the music is always subservient to the spectacle.[14]

A Westerner who has never seen a *jōruri* performance, but only photographs of the expressionless-faced operators in their elaborate dress standing beside the puppets, which are about two-thirds as tall as the operators, may doubt that any convincing spectacle is likely to be seen in the *jōruri* theatre. Yet the *jōruri* is still capable of exerting a powerful appeal, as the following statement by the French poet Paul Claudel would indicate.

> L'acteur vivant, quel que soit son talent, nous gêne toujours en mêlant au drame fictif qu'il incorpore un élément intrus, quelque chose d'actuel et de quotidien, il reste toujours un *déguisé*. La marionette au contraire n'a de vie et de mouvement que celui qu'elle tire de l'action. Elle s'anime sous le récit, c'est comme une ombre qu'on ressucite en lui racontant tout ce qu'elle a fait et qui peu à peu de souvenir devient présence. Ce n'est pas un acteur qui parle, c'est une parole qui agit. Le personnage de bois incarne la prosopopée. Il nage sur la frontière indécise entre le fait et le récit. L'assistance en lui voit tout ce que le vociférateur à son pupitre raconte, soutenu par le shamisen, cet instrument qui donne la vibration des nerfs pincés, et par ce camarade à son coté qui par ses cris inarticulés et ses grognements traduit non seulement l'émotion de la scène, mais le désir d'exister, l'effort pour revivre de l'être imaginaire. La marionette est comme un fantôme. Elle ne pose pas les pieds à terre. On ne la touche pas et elle ne sait pas toucher. Toute sa vie, tout son mouvement lui vient du cœur—et de ce conciliabule mystérieux derrière elle d'animateurs masqués ou non, de cette fatalité collective dont elle est l'expression. La réalité a été si habilement divisée que l'histoire se passe entièrement dans l'imagination et le rêve, sans le support d'aucune matérialité désobligeante. Par d'autres moyens, le Jōruri arrive au même résultat que le No.[15]

Certain of Claudel's remarks show that he was familiar with the preface to *Naniwa Miyage* by Hozumi Ikan, written in 1738.[16] In the second part of the preface Hozumi relates a conversation he once had with Chikamatsu.

> This is what Chikamatsu told me when I visited him many years ago. "*Jōruri* differs from other forms of fiction in that, since it is primarily concerned with puppets, the words should all be living things in which action is the most important feature. Because *jōruri* is performed in theatres that operate in close competition with those of the *kabuki*, which is the art of living actors, the author must impart to lifeless wooden puppets a variety of emotions, and attempt in this way to capture the interest of the audience. It is thus generally very difficult to write a work of great distinction.

> "Once, when I was young and reading a story about the court, I came across a passage which told how, on the occasion of a festival, the snow had fallen heavily and piled up. An order was then given to a guard to clear away the snow from an orange tree. When this happened, the pine tree next to it, apparently resentful that its boughs were bent with snow, recoiled its

branches. This was a stroke of the pen which gave life to the inanimate tree. It did so because the spectacle of the pine tree, resentful that the snow has been cleared from the orange tree, recoiling its branches itself and shaking off the snow which bends it down, is one which creates the feeling of a living, moving thing. Is that not so?

"From this model I learned how to put life into my *jōruri*. Thus, even descriptive passages like the *michiyuki*, to say nothing of the narrative phrases and dialogue, must be charged with feeling or they will be greeted with scant applause. This is the same thing as is called evocative power in poets. For example, if a poet should fail to bring emotion to his praise of even the superb scenery of Matsushima or Miyajima in his poem, it would be like looking at the carelessly drawn picture of a beautiful woman. For this reason, it should be borne in mind that feeling is the basis of writing.

"When a composition is filled with particles, its literary quality is somehow lowered. Authors of no merit invariably try to cast their writings exactly in the form of *waka* or *haikai*,[17] stringing together alternating lines of five and seven syllables. This naturally results in the use of many unnecessary particles. For example, when one should say, 'Toshi mo yukanu musume wo', they say such things as, 'Toshiha mo yukanu musume wo ba'. This comes from concerning oneself with the syllable count, and naturally causes the language to sound vulgar. Thus, while verse is generally written by arranging long and short lines in order, the *jōruri* is basically a musical form, and the length of the lines recited is therefore determined by the melody. Thus, if an author adheres implicitly to the rules of metrics, his lines may prove to be awkward to recite. For this reason I am not concerned with metrics in my writings and I use few particles.

"The old *jōruri* was just like our modern street story-telling[18] and was without either flower or fruit. From the time that I began to write *jōruri*, first for Kaga-no-jō and then for Chikugo-no-jō,[19] I have used care in my writing, which was not true of the old *jōruri*. As a result, the medium was raised one level. For example, inasmuch as the nobility, the samurai and the lower classes all have different social stations, it is essential that they be distinguished in their representation from their appearance down to their speech. Similarly, even within the same samurai class, there are both daimyō and retainers, as well as others of lower rank, each rank possessed of distinct qualities; such differences must be established. This is because it is essential that they be well pictured in the emotions of the reader.

"In writing *jōruri*, one attempts first to describe facts as they really are, but in so doing one writes things which are not true, in the interest of art. To be precise, many things are said by the female characters which real women could not utter. Such things fall under the heading of art; it is because they say what could not come from a real woman's lips that their true emotions are disclosed. If in such cases the author were to model his character on the ways of a real woman and conceal her feelings, such realism, far from being admired, would permit no pleasure in the work. Thus, if one examines a play without paying attention to the question of art, one will probably criticise it on the grounds that it contains many unpleasant words which are not suitable for women. But such things should be considered as art. In addition, there are numerous instances in the portrayal of a villain as excessively cowardly, or of a clown as being funny, which are outside the truth and which must be regarded as art. The spectator must bear this consideration in mind.

"There are some who, thinking that pathos is essential to a *jōruri*, make frequent use of such expressions as 'it was touching' in their writing, or who when chanting do so in voices thick with tears, in the manner of the *Bunya-bushi*.[20] This is foreign to my style. I take pathos to be entirely a matter of restraint.[21] Since it is moving when all parts of the art[22] are controlled by restraint, the stronger and firmer the melody and words are, the sadder will be the impression created. For this reason, when one says of something which is sad that it is sad, one loses the implications, and in the end, even the impression of sadness is slight. It is essential that one not say of a thing that 'it is sad', but that it be sad of itself. For example, when one praises a place renowned for its scenery such as Matsushima by saying, 'Ah, what a fine view!' one has said in one phrase all that one can about the sight, but without effect. If one wishes to praise the view, and one says numerous things indirectly about its appearance, the quality of the view may be known of itself, without one's having to say, 'It is a fine view'. This is true of everything of its kind.

"Someone said, 'People nowadays will not accept plays unless they are realistic and well reasoned out. There are many things in the old stories which people will not now tolerate. It is thus that such people as *kabuki* actors are considered skilful to the degree that their acting resembles reality. The first consideration is to have the chief retainer in the play resemble a real chief retainer, and to have the daimyō look like a real daimyō. People will not stand for the childish nonsense they did in the past.' Chikamatsu answered, 'Your view seems like a plausible one, but it is a theory which does not take into account the real methods of art. Art is something which lies in the slender margin between the real and the unreal. Of course it seems desirable, in view of the current taste for realism, to have the chief retainer in the play copy the gestures and speech of a real retainer, but in that case should a real chief retainer of a daimyō put rouge and powder on his face like an actor? Or, would it prove entertaining if an actor, on the grounds that real chief retainers do not make up their faces, were to appear on the stage and perform, with his beard growing wild and his head shaven? This is what I mean by the slender margin between the real and the unreal. It is unreal, and yet it is not unreal; it is real, and yet it is not real. Entertainment lies between the two.

"In this connection, there is the story of a certain court lady who had a lover. The two loved each other very passionately, but the lady lived far deep in the women's palace, and the man could not visit her quarters. She could see him therefore only very rarely, from between the cracks of her screen of state at the court. She longed for him so desperately that she had a wooden image carved of the man. Its appearance was not like that of any ordinary doll, but did not differ in any particle from the man. It goes without saying that the colour of his complexion was perfectly rendered; even the pores of his skin were delineated. The openings in his ears and nostrils were fashioned, and there was no discrepancy even in the number of teeth in the mouth. Since it was made with the man posing beside it, the only difference between the man and this doll was the presence in one, and the absence in the other, of a soul. However, when the lady drew the doll close to her and looked at it, the exactness of the reproduction of the living man chilled her, and she felt unpleasant and rather frightened. Court lady that she was, her love was also chilled, and as she found it distressing to have the doll by her side, she soon threw it away.

"In view of this we can see that if one makes an exact copy of a living being, even if it happend to be Yang Kuei-fei,[23] one will become disgusted with it. Thus, if when one paints an image or carves it of wood there are, in the name of artistic licence, some stylised parts in a work otherwise resembling the real form; this is, after all, what people love in art. The same is true of literary composition. While bearing resemblance to the original, it should have stylisation; this makes it art, and is what delights men's minds. Theatrical dialogue written with this in mind is apt to be worthwhile."[24]

These remarks by Chikamatsu are of paramount importance in understanding all of his writings in general, and *The Battles of Coxinga* in particular. We must first note Chikamatsu's insistence on the special demands of the puppet *jōruri*. Many of the features which may puzzle us as we read *The Battles of Coxinga* become clear when we realise that Chikamatsu was consciously attempting to "impart to lifeless wooden puppets a variety of emotions". The effects an actor can achieve by his facial expression, the modulations of his voice, and the general manner in which he moves about, are almost impossible to duplicate in the puppet theatre. The puppet, as Claudel stated, is the incarnation of the dramatist's words, incapable of expressing more than has been written. To aid the puppets there is the narrator, who can inform us, in case we were not sure, that the speech we have just heard was delivered in anger or in jest, but by and large the life of the play must come from within the words.

A certain amount of exaggeration and emphasis is required if the puppet's actions are to acquire any of the force of an actor's. But beyond the exaggerations required to give the semblance of life to the puppets, there are those which are permissible solely because the work is conceived for the puppet stage and not for actors. However skilful an author may be in imparting life to the puppets, however cleverly they are manipulated by the operators, the audience can never forget that they are not human beings. Because the structure of a *jōruri* play is thus built on a basis of unreality, the audience will accept exaggerations and fantasy such as would be intolerable in an ordinary stage presentation. In a somewhat similar fashion, the unreality of a Wagnerian opera will permit dragons and giants to people its stage. The audience will accept not only such curiosities, but even the spectacle of a stout middle-aged woman playing the part of a radiant young goddess, because of the initial suspension of disbelief in a world where people sing instead of talk.

Many of the scenes in *The Battles of Coxinga* which appear fantastic and foolish to the reader relied for their effect on a similar suspension of disbelief on the part of the *jōruri* audience. For example, the battle between Watōnai and the tiger in the Bamboo Forest of Senri would be ludicrous on the stage, for the spectator would be conscious of the two men inside the tiger skin, and could not take seriously Watōnai's wrestling with so unwieldy a creature. Only a very generous spectator would suspend disbelief at that point. A reader of the play is in a similar position. In the puppet theatre, on the other hand, the tiger is no less realistic than Watōnai, and there is no reason why a spectator who accepts the initial unreality of a puppet performing as a man should be unable to accept a puppet tiger. The *jōruri* dramatist is thus at liberty to write scenes of great extravagance of language and action whenever they suit his purpose.

The purpose of Chikamatsu in writing the story of the battle between Watōnai and the tiger is made apparent by his remarks on the importance of having sadness in a play felt of itself without recourse to expressions like "it is sad". In a similar way, when Chikamatsu wanted to show the audience how brave his young hero was, he chose to give an example which would show Watōnai's courage better than any statement about it the author could make, Instead of saying, "Watōnai was not afraid to pit his strength against a tiger",

Chikamatsu gave the audience a few minutes of exciting battle which would convince it most effectively of the fact. Later, to show the power of the Japanese gods he has Watōnai's mother subdue the tiger with the aid of a charm from the Great Shrine of Ise, which was the dramatic way of saying, "Even though Watōnai was the most powerful of men he could still not overcome the tiger, but this was no difficult matter for the gods".

If the effect on the reader of the battle in the Bamboo Forest of Senri or of the miraculous cloud bridge in the fourth act is not entirely convincing, it is further proof of the importance of seeing the play performed by puppets, for the requirements of the puppet theatre were Chikamatsu's first consideration. Other scenes, such as the one in which Kinshōjo on the wall recognises her father down below, may exert a more powerful appeal on the reader, but even in them the element of the unreal is never absent. It was impossible, for example, that the image in Kinshōjo's mirror would have been clear enough for her to make out her father's features, yet we are willing to allow this unreality in the interests of the story.[25]

In his attempt to make the puppets live and to make their qualities apparent of themselves, Chikamatsu was forced to sacrifice any subtlety of portrayal that would have been possible with actors. Chikamatsu declared, as we have seen, that it was important that the different social stations be distinguished in performance by their appearance and their speech. He did not add that it was important that different members of the same social class be differentiated. This may have been because the concept of the individual was still not sufficiently developed in Japan for individual traits to be studied, or it may have been because the puppets were incapable of detailed character portrayal. The personages of *The Battles of Coxinga* are types, and even extreme types. Watōnai is brave beyond all human bravery, Ri Tōten is the complete villain, and all the other characters are almost as quickly recognisable by their types as by their names. Chikamatsu is careful to distinguish between the countrified Komutsu and the lady-like Kinshōjo in their speech and attitudes, but he did not attempt to make either one of them come alive for us as a person. He might have regarded the reduction of the characters to their outstanding features as "stylisation" which he favoured. There is one important element yet to be mentioned in connection with the structure of *The Battles of Coxinga*, the element of surprise. Surprise is almost the governing factor of the play, whether it is surprise on the lowest level, where it takes the form of puns and plays on words, or surprise of a major nature over developments in the plot. The great danger of a play in which the recitation is done by one narrator at a time is that it will become monotonous, and to avoid this danger Chikamatsu filled his *jōruri* with surprises.

The action of *The Battles of Coxinga* may be traced in terms of its surprises, which are so frequent as to be the rule. Each act is composed of passages of varying length linked or separated by surprises, and the individual acts form a pattern of surprises and contrasts. There are also little surprises in the sentiments themselves, for those familiar with traditional Japanese usage. For example, when Go Sankei tells his infant son whom he is about to kill not to regret leaving his parents "in this world of illusion" we are surprised, because we would expect at this point some expression by Go Sankei of his sorrow, and the surprise makes the scene more touching.[26]

Any attempt to make a full literary analysis of the play, however, must be hindered by the non-literary elements. A *jōruri* text has been compared to a motion picture script; it might also be likened to the piano score of an opera. All the themes of the play and all the turns of phrases are apparent from the text, but we miss the accompaniment—the actions of the puppets, the music and the decor, as a piano version of the *Miserere* would communicate only a fraction of its power. A person endowed with an especially vigorous imagination might be able to restore to the text, even in translation, some of the elements that have been lost. It is the hope that, even for those not so gifted, at least the minimum fraction of the excitement and colour that made *The Battles of Coxinga* the most famous play of its day will make itself felt across the many obstacles.

VI

THE BATTLES OF COXINGA (*translation*)

TRANSLATOR'S NOTE

WHEN ONE looks at *The Battles of Coxinga* (*Kokusenya Kassen*) in a Japanese edition, it does not seem like a play at all. The speeches of the various characters are sometimes not indicated as such, and one has the impression that the whole is one long narrative. This, of course, was because in the *jōruri* theatre the chanter not only spoke for all the puppets, but also described their actions and thoughts. In the translation I have divided the speeches in the customary Western way, and have added the personage of the narrator. His words are those the chanter recited when not speaking for one of the puppets. I have often been tempted to leave out comments by the narrator in the interests of the dramatic continuity of the play, but have in practice only suppressed occasional words like "thus he spoke".

My first version of the translation was purely literal, and it has been from this initial draft that I have made a more polished version. Other changes might well be made to improve the play for Western readers, but I believe there is considerable value in presenting the play as it stands.

The transcription of the names has been a problem. In general, I have given Chinese names in their Japanese renderings when the name is of a person or place important to the play, and in their Chinese renderings when used in allusions to ancient times. I have called the hero Coxinga, rather than Kokusenya or any Chinese version, because I so call him elsewhere in this study. Kanki might better be rendered as Kan Ki, but I have preferred the former for typographical reasons.

ACT ONE

NARRATOR: Flowers fell and butterflies took fright at signs that spring was passing, but within the palace there were none dismayed. There, within the Water Pavilion and the Cloud Gallery, a special spring had been created. Early in the morning a thousand painted and powdered equestriennes showed the glossy black of their brows above the red of their lips;[1] even the earth was scented with the fragrance of plum blossoms like rare incense.[2]

The times were glorious, at the height of their brilliance, in Nanking, where the peach and the cherry bloomed forever.

Now, he who was styled Shi-sōretsutei,[3] the seventeenth sovereign of the Ming Dynasty, was the second son of the Emperor Kōsō. The thread of succession had passed unbroken and untangled from generation to generation. The lands to the four directions bowed in submission before him like a green willow swept by the wind, and he had amassed treasures in tribute. He delighted in singing, dancing, and carousing. In his palace were three consorts, nine spouses of the second rank, twenty-seven of the third rank, and eighty-one concubines.[4] Some three thousand beauties brought him delight by the loveliness of their faces. His ministers and nobles vied in flattering him; he was presented with rare and strange gifts, and was offered summer melons even in February.[5] Such was the luxury of his court.

Now, the Lady Kasei, the one among the three thousand beauties the Emperor most favoured,[6] had conceived in the autumn of the previous year, and this was the month that the imperial birth was due. Great was the pleasure of the emperor and the joy of his court, for though he had reached the age of forty, there was as yet no crown prince to carry on the succession. The previous prayers to heaven and earth had this time had their effect. When it was certain that a royal child would be born the lying-in chamber was decked with pearls and jade. Swaddling clothes were sewn of Yüeh gauze and Shu brocade, and all preparations were completed for the birth that might come at any moment. It was just at this time that Lady Ryūka, wife of Go Sankei,[7] the President of the Council of War, was safely delivered of her first child. Especially as her milk was for a boy, she was designated chief of the imperial wet-nurses. Other wet-nurses, serving-maids, house-keepers, and all ranks of ladies-in-waiting attended Kasei, and took care of her as though she were a precious jewel in their hands.

Early in the fourth moon of the seventeenth year of Ch'ung-chen,[8] Junji,[9] the Great King of Tartary, sent an envoy to present the emperor with tiger-skins, leopard-skins, cloth from the South Seas that was washed in fire,[10] horse-liver stones from Ceylon, and treasures from remote kingdoms and islands. The envoy, Prince Bairoku,[11] respectfully addressed the throne.

BAIROKU: From ancient times Tartary and China have fought for supremacy. Our countries have quarrelled over territory, raised armies, hurled spears at one another, and formed mutual enmities. This has been both contrary to the friendship that should prevail between neighbouring countries, and a source of affliction to the people. Our land of Tartary is a big country and, I may say, we are not wanting in the seven precious things or the ten thousand treasures,[12] but our women are inferior in appearance to those of other lands. Our Great King, hearing that Lady Kasei, the consort of the Ming emperor, is a peerless beauty, has become enamoured of her, and deeply desires her. It was for this reason that he sent these tributary offerings, as sign of his wish to honour her as his consort, to establish a future bond like that of parent and child between China and Tartary,[13] and to bring about a lasting peace. I, Guardian General Prince Bairoku, insignificant though I am, have come to your court to call for the consort.

NARRATOR: The emperor and the nobles, great and small, were much disturbed by this unreasonable Tartar proposal, the like of which had never been heard before, and the emperor wondered uneasily if it might lead to war. Just then, the first of his vassals, the General of the Right Ri Tōten[14], came forward and reported to the throne.

RI TŌTEN: Until now I have kept hidden our country's shame. In 1641, the Year of the Serpent, the five grains did not ripen at Peking. The people were on the verge of starvation when I secretly requested Tartary to supply us with some ten million bushels of rice and millet in aid. I thereby saved the people. In return, I solemnly promised that if the Tartars desired anything, whatever it might be, it would be granted to them without fail on one occasion. It is because of the kindness of Tartary at that time that your majesty possesses the land within the four seas and rules the people. Only devils and animals are unacquainted with gratitude. Though you may experience a certain regret in doing so, you must send off your consort at once.

NARRATOR: President of the Council of War Go Sankei, who had been listening attentively in the antechamber, leapt up the stairs and over the balustrade, and sat himself abruptly alongside Ri Tōten.

GO SANKEI: Heartless creature! Since when have you become the slave of the barbarians? China has produced the three emperors and the five rulers,[15] and devised the arts of etiquette and music. Here the philosophy of Confucius and Mencius has been passed down, and the teachings of the five constant virtues and the five human relationships are still flourishing.[16] In India Buddha taught the principle of *karma*, and there is the teaching of eschewing evil and cultivating virtue. In Japan there is honesty, and the Way of the eternal gods. In Tartary they are well fed and warmly clothed but have neither teachings nor laws.[17] The strong stand on top and the weak are pushed below. They make no differentiation between good and bad men, or between wise and foolish. They are northern barbarians who are just like beasts, and their country is commonly called the Land of Animals. However much you may have requested it of them, it is very suspicious that they should have furnished the ten million bushels of rice and saved this country. Why is it the people were exhausted and reduced to famine? It was because you encouraged senseless extravagance in the court, expended the treasury in feasting, and afflicted the people. If you had ceased these expenditures with which you indulged your extravagance, our country would not have lacked the wealth to feed the people for five or even ten years. Now, disregarding the wishes of the emperor, and without even consulting the nobles, you want, without further ado, to turn over our empress, who is with child, to the hands of the barbarians. I cannot in the slightest understand a mind that can think that way. The agreement was between you and them. The emperor knew nothing of it. The tribute-offerings of that beast-country are a defilement to the palace. Officials! Take them and throw them away!

NARRATOR: The manner in which he made light of the northern barbarians and showed the power of his country recalled the ninefold summoning of the feudal lords by Kuan Chung.[18] The Tartar envoy was enraged.

BAIROKU: Let us leave out of consideration the size of our countries. Because she is not grateful for having received help and enabled to take care of her people, and because she has broken her promises, it is China who has shown herself to be the Land of Animals, a country without teachings and without laws, and no match for us. You have only to count the days until we shall attack you with our troops, take your emperor and your empress both, and make them the lowly shoe-bearers of our Great King!

NARRATOR: He kicked aside his seat and rose to depart. Ri Tōten stopped him.

RI TŌTEN: Just a moment! Just a moment! Your indignation is entirely justified. I acted as a loyal minister should when I accepted your country's help a few years ago and, not taking a grain of rice for myself, I saved my nation. It is a disgrace to the dynasty and a disgrace to the country that promises should now be broken and war invited, that our emperor should be troubled and the people afflicted, and, what is worse, that our country should be called a Land of Animals that does not know gratitude. It is now the task of a loyal minister to sacrifice himself, to calm the emperor, and to wipe out our country's shame. Behold what I do!

NARRATOR: Grasping a knife point downwards, he drove it into his left eye, then turned it round along his eyelids. He drew out the crimsoned eyeball, and, placing it on a ceremonial baton, offered it to the envoy.

RI TŌTEN: Envoy! A man's two eyes are his sun and moon. The left eye belongs to the *yang* principle and is his sun. Now that I have only one eye, I have become deformed. I have gouged out an eye and offered it up to the King of Tartary. This is the way a loyal minister of the Ming emperor behaves, one who repays his country's obligations and who preserves his righteousness by respecting the Way.

H

NARRATOR: Prince Bairoku accepted it reverently.

BAIROKU: What splendid devotion ! Just when, as a result of Go Sankei's words, our two countries were quarrelling over authority and on the verge of war, unwillingly though it might have been, you have settled the issue by sacrificing yourself on behalf of your country. Magnificent! Words cannot describe how loyal and wise a minister you have shown yourself. The matter of calling for the consort has been settled. The Great King will approve, and I, who have served as his envoy, must not, for my reputation's sake, press the point any further. I hastily take my leave.

NARRATOR: The Emperor was highly pleased.

EMPEROR: Ri Tōten's gouging out of his eye is reminiscent of Wu Tzu-hsü and Go Sankei's far-reaching plans have the quality of those of Fan Li.[19] With two such ministers regulating the government, our rule will endure without change for a thousand generations, for ten thousand generations. Send the Tartar envoy back to his country at once!

NARRATOR: With these words he entered the Pavilion of Revels. Indeed it is true that wicked and loyal ministers resemble one another on the surface and may be confused. The extravagance of the Lord of Nanking, who was without judgment of men, knew no example.

Now, the Princess Sendan,[20] the younger sister of the emperor, was a maiden of not yet sixteen years, who in her beauty suggested she might be a child of the goddess of the moon, come down to earth with the dew.[21] She could play flutes and strings, was skilled in literary composition, and sang the poems that she wrote. In Japan it is said that poetry makes sweet the ties between men and women.[22] Here too, in China, they recited poetry in the same way, as go-betweens in love. In her mind she was older than her years.

To show her disapproval of the extravagance of her brother, the emperor, of his indulgence in sensual pleasures, his pride in his carousals, and his failure to hold morning levees, she conducted herself with the utmost decorum. The attendant ladies she gathered about herself might listen with longing ears to whispers of worldly gossip, but their eyes would flash disapproval. In their hearts smouldered buried thoughts of love, like burning aloes-wood.

From the Pavilion of Long Life came the cry, "The Emperor is coming!" and he entered, accompanied on either side by two hundred consorts, none of whom was more than twenty years of age. They carried and waved artificial branches, half of them with plum blossoms, and half with cherry blossoms.

EMPEROR: My lady sister. Since I succeeded to the imperial throne, of all my many ministers, Ri Tōten has been the one who has never disobeyed my commands. When I heard that this first of my loyal ministers, who has brought me comfort day and night, had fallen in love with you, I thought how happy I would be to have him as your husband, but you have to this day constantly refused him. To-day, however, an outrageous proposal was made by Tartary, and we were already on the point of war. When it seemed as though our country might be plunged into disorder, Go Sankei, with the look of a loyal minister on his face, reasoned with his tongue, as anyone might, but it was because Ri Tōten gouged out his left eye and appeased the envoy that he returned to his country. For the sake of his nation, for the sake of his emperor, he sacrificed and deformed himself. This minister, whose loyalty will stand unrivalled throughout all the ages, must be rewarded. I had promised him that I would without fail hand over to him, as husband of my sister, the capital of Peking, but you are probably unwilling to accept him. I have therefore staged a flower tournament. The virtuous ladies standing there will represent your unfeeling heart. The plum-blossom has been allotted to your side.[23] My side will have the cherry-blossoms. The ladies will contest together. If the cherry-blossoms scatter and the plum triumphs, you will have your way. If the cherry wins and the plum-blossoms are scattered, your defeat will be decided, and you will become the wife of Ri Tōten. Let the marriage be decided as heaven wills it! Whoever wins, whoever loses, we shall have a tournament like that of old.[24] Lay on! Lay on!

NARRATOR: The plum and the cherry, obeying the imperial command, divided into two sides and stood ready. Since this was an edict, even the princess, delicate though she was, had no choice but to take part and oppose a match that so went against her heart. With her flowers and her person to the fore she proclaimed, " I shall be the chief general in the battle to decide the marriage of Princess Sendan, sister to the emperor". No sooner had she spoken than somebody's sleeve brushed the plum-blossoms she carried. There was a fluttering sound along the branch, as though the wings of a swarm of orioles were scattering the petals, and the perfume of the plum-blossoms was fragrantly dispersed. Thus they fought, parrying and thrusting. The princess gave orders.

SENDAN: In the shadow of the willow that is whirled around you can tell that there must be a wind.[25] Against their weak branches lean your straight young shoots. Against their strong ones, make the flowers of your achievements bloom. Change your faded branches for fresh ones, and join forces with each other!

NARRATOR: When, shouting, they began to do battle in keeping with her flower-wise commands, they trampled on blossoms, and on both sides there was regret for the fallen flowers.[26] Some held their branches horizontally above their heads, and the blossoms scattered like the snows of February.[27] Flowers fell to the ground in confused fashion; the battle scattered the flowers.

The court ladies, acting in accordance with the previous orders of the emperor, with one accord purposely allowed the plum-blossom side to be defeated. Their branches and their flowers were broken and scattered. When they retreated in clusters in disorderly fashion, the cherry-blossoms with a look of triumph cried, "The marriage between the princess and Ri Tōten has been decided", and the kalavinka-like[28] voices of the many court ladies all raised at once in a cry of victory, resounded through the palace, so that one might have thought them the twittering of a thousand orioles or a hundred plovers.

President of the Council of War Go Sankei clad in shining armour and with his helmet on his head, burst in without ceremony, and, waving his crescent-topped spear, recklessly cut down the plum and cherry blossoms before him, and bowed before the emperor.

GO SANKEI: Just now I heard that there was a battle going on near the throne, and war cries echoed through the palace. Since this was a most unusual disturbance for a palace, I armed myself with my weapons and came rushing here. But what senseless thing do I find! I have never heard of an example of such a thing in all of history since the world was created, a flower tournament to decide the marriage of your sister and Ri Tōten! Does your majesty not know that if there is one loving family, the country will become loving, and if one man is greedy, the country will be in turmoil?[29] It is the custom of the people to follow the preferences of the upper classes. When they hear of this incident, there will be flower tournaments held in this place and that by woodsmen and peasants who are taking daughters or sons-in-law, and these will develop into quarrels and fights. When the flowers scatter they will have recourse to their swords, and real battles will occur. This is as clear as looking into a mirror. If, moreover, a disloyal subject just now burst into the palace shouting, people would think it was just another flower tournament, even if his cries had been heard, and no one would come rushing to your aid. Then, if your august person were suddenly put to the sword by the treacherous subject, however impious it would be, however ignoble, would there be any use in regretting it? That treacherous subject, that false minister of whom I speak is Ri Tōten. Has your majesty forgotten? When you were young there was a man named Tei Shiryū[30] who incurred your wrath by advising you to drive out the false courtiers. Tei Shiryū was exiled. I hear that he has now changed his name to Rōikkan, and is living in

Japan at a place called Hirado, or some such, in the province of Hizen. Will not the shame of China be communicated by Tei Shiryū to Japan? When, a few years ago, China was suffering from famine, Ri Tōten wickedly stole the rice from the treasuries throughout the country. He accepted the help of Tartary because he has no feeling for your majesty. Claiming to be saving the people, he scattered his largesse throughout the country. He ingratiated himself with the masses and strengthened the axis of sedition. How foolish of you not to be aware of these things!

When he gouged out his eye, it was a signal to his Tartar allies. Behold the plaque in the Southern Pavilion! The words *Ta Ming* mean "great" and "bright".[31] "Bright" is written by placing the symbols for sun and moon side by side. This Great Bright country is a southern *yang* land, a country of the sun. Tartary is a northern *yin* land, and a country of the moon.[32] For him to have gouged out his left eye, which belongs to *yang* and corresponds to the sun, was a warrant that he would deliver this Great Bright country into the hands of the Tartars. The envoy quickly understood what was meant, and returned joyfully to Tartary. Unless the evil counsellor, guilty of accumulated wickedness and villainy, is at once subjected to the five punishments,[33] this land, that has given birth to the sages, will fall under the yoke of the Mongols, and we shall become their slaves, differing from animals only in that we do not wag tails or have our bodies covered with fur. If heaven and earth are wroth, and the gods of our ancestral halls place curses upon us, the fault will all revert to the emperor. Doubt rather that I should miss the earth when striking at it with my fist, than that these words of Go Sankei are mistaken. How unfortunate your attitude is!

NARRATOR: Weeping and raging, using all of his reasoning and all of his words, he thus addressed the emperor. The emperor was exceedingly angry.

EMPEROR: Enough of your lectures on ideographs with that smug look on your face! With such reasoning you could prove that snow was actually black![34] Everything you said comes from the fact that you are jealous of Ri Tōten. You, who for no reason at all have approached my presence in your helmet and armour, are the treacherous minister!

NARRATOR: Standing up, he kicked Go Sankei in the forehead with his foot. Just then, strange to relate, there was a repeated rumbling in the palace, and the plaque written in the imperial hand began to shake. The golden-sword stroke in "Great"[35] and the symbol for "sun" in "Bright" crumbled into powder, a fearsome augury from heaven. Go Sankei, still feeling no concern for his person, cried out:

GO SANKEI: How heartless you are! Have your eyes been blinded? Have your ears become deaf? The ideograph for "Great" 大 is written by combining "one" — and "man" 人. The "one man" refers to the Son of Heaven, the Emperor. If one stroke is taken away from the "one man", the emperor becomes only half a man. If, in the ideograph "Bright" 明 the sun element is removed, the country is deprived of the light of the sun and becomes a land of eternal darkness. That plaque was written by your ancestor, the first emperor of the Ming, with the thought of the eternal prosperity of his descendants. Reflect how terrible is the wrath of the gods of your ancestral temple! Mend your ways, correct your injustices, and preserve your dynasty! Then, though the life of Go Sankei, whom you spurn before you, be trampled out or kicked out, he will not care. Though I be reduced to earth, though I be reduced to ashes, I shall not deviate from the way of a loyal subject.

NARRATOR: Clinging to the emperor's robe, he cried out in a loud voice, and weeping remonstrated with him. This would serve as a model of devotion for all ages to come.

At this point, there came from all directions the noises of men and horses. Horns and gongs were sounded, and drums beaten. War cries shook the earth, loud enough to tilt the very heavens. Go Sankei, who had been expecting this, raced up to an observation tower. When he looked out, the mountains and the villages were filled with the Tartar hordes. Waving their banners, and shooting their bows and muskets, they circled and stormed at the palace like the onrushing tide. Prince Bairoku, the general of the attacking force, rode into the garden, and shouted in a great voice.

BAIROKU: Hear ye! Hear ye! The story that the lord of our country, the Great King of Tartary Junji, had fallen in love with the empress of this country, Lady Kasei, was a scheme to seize the pregnant empress and cut off the seed of the Chinese emperor. Because Ri Tōten gouged out his eye and showed the signal to us, we have attacked without delay. You are no match for us, Go Sankei. We will seize the emperor and the empress. They will bow before us and squat in the kitchen of the Tartar king, sustaining their lives by drinking refuse water from our rice.

GO SANKEI: What nonsense! For you to attack the Ming court, where not even the plants or trees have shaken for 180 years, is just like an ant stalking a whale whose bulk stretches out over the ocean. Drive them back! Drive them back!

NARRATOR: Racing about, he gave orders, but his own forces did not exceed a hundred foot-soldiers. There was no one among the nobility or the warrior families who would join forces with him. As he stood there with his fists clenched, his wife, Lady Ryūka, holding her baby in her arms, led the empress by the hand to him. Gnashing her teeth, she cried.

RYUKA: Most miserable of days! The imperial fortunes are at an end. Everyone, from the aristocracy and the ministers down to the lowly servants, has sided with Ri Tōten. We are the only partisans of the imperial cause. Most mortifying of days!

GO SANKEI: Cease your lamenting. It will do no good. Since the emperor's seed is lodged in the empress's womb, she is the most important person. I shall cut open a way of escape, and will escort her and the emperor to safety. Leave the child with me too. You, for the time being, will look after the Princess Sendan. Go from here and head for the harbour of Kaidō.[36]

RYUKA: I shall do as you say.

NARRATOR: With this brave reply, she took the Princess Sendan by the hand. Together they slipped out along the narrow path through the Golden Stream Gate.

GO SANKEI: Now I shall engage the enemy at the front gate, disperse them and lead you safely to escape. Please do not leave this spot.

NARRATOR: Barely had he finished these words than he set off. Proclaiming himself "President of the Council of War, Go Sankei, first of the subjects of the Ming court", he and his force of less than a hundred drove into the millions of Mongol troops, and pushed them back. As they slashed in recklessly, the Tartars cried "Kill them all", and their muskets and catapults were fired incessantly. Amid flying arrows and bullets they fought.

At this time Ri Tōten and his younger brother Ri Kaihō wantonly burst in on the imperial presence and seized the emperor from both sides by the arms. The empress could not tell if this were a nightmare, but clinging to them, cried.

EMPRESS: You most wicked of men who know nothing of the punishment of heaven! Have you forgotten about your obligation to the emperor and about the divinity that protects him?

RI TOTEN: You won't escape either!

NARRATOR: He thrust her aside and touched his icy blade against the emperor's chest. The emperor had tears in his angry dragon eyes.

EMPEROR: It is true indeed that the rust on a blade comes from the blade itself and rots it. The fire in the cypress forest comes from the cypresses and consumes them. Now, for the first time, I realise that the enmity or kindness one is shown comes from oneself. I did not heed the advice of Tei Shiryū or Go Sankei, but was deceived by the flattery of you and your kind. I have lost my country and lost my life, and shall leave behind that reputation for all time to come. How foolish I was not to have known that food sweet to the taste proves harmful in the stomach!

As you know, my consort bears in her womb my child, which is now in its ninth month and will be born at any moment. I pray you, as the one kindness I ask, that you let it see the light of the sun and the moon.

NARRATOR: This was all that he said, and then was overwhelmed by tears.

RI TOTEN: Nɔ, that may never be! Why do you suppose I gouged out my precious eye? It wasn't on account of loyalty or duty. It was to put you off your guard, and to ally myself with the Tartars. My eye has won me an estate. Your head will get me a kingdom.

NARRATOR: Drawing the emperor's head toward him, he cut it off with one stroke.

RI TOTEN: Now, Ri Kaihō, I shall present this head to the King of Tartary. Tie up the empress and bring her along.

NARRATOR: With these words he rushed off to the camp of the invaders. President of the Council of War, Go Sankei, having slain many of the enemy, had without trouble opened a path of escape. When he returned to lead their majesties to safety, what was his horror to behold the headless body of the emperor lying there, bathed in crimson, and Ri Kaihō about to lead off the empress he had bound!

GO SANKEI: I have arrived at the moment of your success, haven't I? In my fight of vengeance for my dead sovereign, I have missed lunch and must content myself with tea![37]

NARRATOR: Flying at him, he split Ri Kaihō's skull through the middle. He then cut the empress's bonds. When, with tears in his eyes, he straightened up the body of the emperor, he found lying next to the imperial skin the sash and seal,[38] the symbol of enthronement passed from generation to generation. He thrust it into his armour next to his body.

GO SANKEI: Good! As long as he has this, the little prince to be born will have no worries about the succession. Now, shall I first escort the empress to safety or hide the body of the emperor?

NARRATOR: His problem was twofold, but he had only one body. Just then the enemy forces burst in on them seeking to kill them. Go Sankei cried, "I am ready for you!" and slew and scattered them. When they drew close, he struck back at them. He knocked them down, swept them down, and rolled them back. Then he ran back to the empress.

GO SANKEI: Now we must hurry. Whatever becomes of the emperor's body, the important thing is the succession.

NARRATOR: Taking the empress by the hand he started off, when his own child, longing for its mother's breast, began to howl.

GO SANKEI: What a nuisance you are! However, you *are* my heir.

NARRATOR: He picked him up and fastened him securely to the shaft of his spear.

GO SANKEI: If your father is killed, you must grow up and become a loyal support to the young prince. You are the last of our family.[39]

NARRRATOR: With these words he lifted up the baby. When the enemy soldiers came pressing forwards, seeking to stop the fugitives, he halted and fought with them. He slashed and beat them, and left them dead. At last they reached the harbour of Kaidō as the tide was receding. From there they wished to cross to Taisufu,[40] but there was no boat to be seen anywhere at the time. When they started to follow along the edge of the water, musket-fire from the mountains on all sides and from the cover of the woods swept down on them like a driving rain. Go Sankei was shielding the empress, taking bullet after bullet on his stoutly-fashioned armour, but as a stroke of misfortune, she was wounded in the breast. The jewelled thread of her life was cut and she breathed her last. Go Sankei stood at a loss what to do, then said:

GO SANKEI: Nothing more may be done for the empress-mother, but there is no reason why the imperial seed should perish darkly within the womb.

NARRATOR: He unsheathed his sword and cut open the empress's clothes to her skin, and then drove his sword into the side of her abdomen. When he had made an incision in the shape of a cross, a first cry from within the blood told that a jewel-like prince had been born. The occasion was happy, and yet it was not; it was tragic, and yet it was not. No more could be done, so, in tears, he tore off the empress's sleeve and wrapped the prince in it. He held him in his arms.

GO SANKEI: But wait! If the enemy who surrounds us should discover the dead body, they would know that the prince had been spirited away, and would keep searching until they found him. I would have no way of raising the prince.

NARRATOR: He thought earnestly for a while, then drew his child to him. Taking off its clothing, he put it on the prince. He raised his sword again and drove it through his baby's chest, then pushed him into the abdomen of the empress.

GO SANKEI: Admirable child! You have been blessed by fortune. You were born at just the right time, and have taken the place of the emperor.[41] You have done well; you have succeeded. Do not grieve for your parents left behind in this world of delusion. Your parents will not grieve for you.

NARRATOR: Though he thus spoke, the sorrow of parting clung to his heart, and he wrapped the baby prince in the sleeve of his armour as he choked in tears. And how sad it was for him then to go off and leave his son!

Lady Ryūka, knowing nothing of this, was leading Princess Sendan.
They had fled as far as the mouth of the harbour, but the enemy was everywhere about them in great numbers.

RYUKA: This is as far as we can go.

NARRATOR: Pushing aside the reeds that grew thickly there, they hid themselves. An Taijin, a subordinate general of Ri Tōten's, suddenly rushed up
close to them with a force of men.

AN: I feel certain that last burst of gun-fire hit either the empress or Go Sankei.

NARRATOR: They searched in all directions.

AN: Look here! The empress has been killed! Her belly has been split open,
and the prince she bore within her is dead. Go Sankei, who acted in so
loyal a fashion, has abandoned his sovereign and cast away his fair name.
Was he afraid for his life? That rogue has lost his honour. Now the only
thing left to do is to look for his wife, Lady Ryūka, and Princess Sendan.
Keep a sharp lookout, and gain glory!

NARRATOR: They spread out in all directions. Among them there was a knave
called Gōdatsu who, thinking to himself, "I'll capture Princess Sendan and
get all the glory for myself," threw a straw raincoat over his armour, and
poled a little fishing boat from inlet to inlet. "Now let me see behind these
reeds" he thought, and flattened them down with the end of his oar. Lady
Ryūka seized it tightly, and pushed back with all her might. He lost his
balance over the edge of the boat, and sank with a splash face down into
the water. When he tried to rise to the surface, she would beat him over
and over with the oar, as though she were trying to break it. When she
struck he would sink, and when he rose, she would strike again. She did
not give him a moment's respite, and he was like a great snapping-turtle
swimming in the mud. Finally he dived to the bottom and made his escape.

RYUKA: That was a useless stolen march! All the more so, since you've furnished
us with a boat. This is a case of finding a boat when one comes to a crossing![42]

NARRATOR: She picked up a sword that lay concealed in the boat, and girded
it at her side. She had Princess Sendan board the boat, and was about
to do so herself, when Gōdatsu crawled up from somewhere with his armour
dripping wet. He and some twenty others were carrying spears, and came
in pursuit, determined to kill both of them.

RYUKA: How occupied I am! Look! The enemy has come after us in terrible
pursuit. Please hide in the bottom of the boat for a few minutes while I defend us.

NARRATOR: She waited for them to come, waving her two swords, the one
she had found, and the one she wore at her side. Gōdatsu soon rushed up
to them.

GODATSU: You loathsome woman! I'll pay you back for hitting me with an oar!

NARRATOR: He thrust at her with his long-handled spear extended.

RYUKA: And I will pay you back for the sword you gave me!

NARRATOR: Slashing and turning, she began the combat, one woman against over twenty men. She struck down some of the seagulls,[43] creatures of the reeds that are at loss on shore, before they could even flap their wings; others escaped with severe wounds. Lady Ryūka and Gōdatsu were both badly wounded in several places and covered with blood. They pushed into a clump of reeds, charging back and forth, and blood streamed into the eyes of both of them. They fought blindly, without knowing where they aimed, and their swords struck sparks from the corners of the rocks of the cliffs, sparks as brief as human life. This was a most perilous spectacle.

Gōdatsu's spear was broken, and he hobbled forward to grapple with Lady Ryūka, hoping to wrest away the sword she held, when in the struggle he lost his footing, and fell on his back. She at once jumped on him and cut off his head, driving the sword through and through. An incomparable joy suffused her heart.

RYUKA: Your highness. Are you all right? Is the boat still there?

NARRATOR: She staggered toward the boat.

RYUKA: It wouldn't do for me to join you in the boat in this condition. I will no longer be able to withstand the enemy if they come again; let yourself be carried wherever the tide takes you, and make your escape. Until your boat reaches the open sea I shall hold them on the land. Even if they come in thousands I will fight as long as I live, as long as I have any strength. Whether we two shall meet again can be determined only by fate and our lives. I pray with all my heart that you will be safe. I pray to the Buddhas of all the heavens, and in particular to the eight great dragon gods,[44] that they will protect the boat of the emperor's sister.

NARRATOR: Taking hold of the boat-beam, she pushed off the craft. Just then it was caught in the ebb-tide, and Sendan was at a loss to make her farewells.[45] In the salt-breeze she wept sad tears, as a wind from the offing granted by the dragon gods carried her boat far out to the open sea.

RYUKA: How relieved and happy I am! Now, even if I prolong my life, I shall be alone, and if I die, there will be no one to go with me, not even the companion-birds.[46] Though I may cross the sea of life and death, there will be waves of attachment to the mortal world, not knowing where my husband is, where my child, and where my sovereign. However difficult it may be to cross, the swift boat of my devotion will not break in the breaking waves of the sea, even if the oars of love and righteousness and the rudder of courage are broken. But are those war cries coming in this direction?

NARRATOR: Clutching her swords, she staggered about uncertainly. A storm blowing from the moutains down through the pines to the beach combed her dishevelled locks, and she stood there, glaring about her. Her story has been written down and preserved in the books of model women of Japan and China.

ACT TWO

Along the Beach

The oriole that calls in warbling notes alights on the corner of a hill. If a man does not rest in the place he should, he is inferior to the birds, is he not?[47]

Now, there lived a young man named Watōnai Sankan[48] in the town of Hirado, in the county of Matsura, in the province of Hizen in Japan, who made his living by casting his line and drawing his nets. His wife followed the same fisherman's work, and, like the creature *warekara*[49] that lives in the sea-weed, she had of herself, without go-between, joined her pillow to a man's. She was blessed with the name of Komutsu, " Little Friend",[50] and she lived on most friendly terms with the world. Now, the father of this Watōnai was originally not a Japanese. He had been a loyal minister of China called Grand Tutor Tei Shiryū, but had been unable to admonish the foolish emperor, and had of himself come to the Bay of Tsukushi[51] in the Land of the Rising Sun in order to escape the punishment of official exile.[52] In Japan he had changed his name to Rōikkan. He had married a woman who lived by the bay, and had begotten this son, to whom he had given the name of Watōnai Sankan, using the ideograph of *Wa* for the mother's land of Wa, Japan, and the sound of *Tō* because he had come from Tō, the Japanese name for China. The springs of twenty years and more had passed for the young man, and this autumn was going by, but October had the warmth of Indian summer.[53] As the evening calm settled, husband and wife went out together, their fishing baskets hung from their straight rakes, to earn their livelihood. As they looked about they could see the seagulls cutting their seals in the sand, and the bay-plovers had flocked together on the islands off the shore.[54] Raking the dry beach where the tide had been, they stepped on clams and gathered all kinds of shells. Komutsu's long dress was wet by the tide.[55] What were the shells that they gathered?[56]

Hermit-crabs, periwinkles, carpet clams... When the bamboo-blind shell is lifted by the tide, I see a princess-shell with whom I fall in love at first sight. I want to take my brush and send her a letter on a flat-shell. When her red-lips shell part, and she smiles-shell, my heart-goes-to-her shell. Ah, if-I-could-be-with-her shell! You draw me to you more-and-more shell, but my love is as one-sided as the abalone-shell. Oh, cruel one! I would like to give you a taste of my fist-shell in your monkey-face shell! Plum-blossom shells, cherry-blossom shells... Unable to sleep, I all alone spend-the-night shells. For whom do I wait-shell? I am sorry-I-saw-her shell, and wish I could forget-shell. But the two of us lying-in-bed shell, could sink-shell in one another's arms, and whisper words of joy-shells. We would celebrate-shell our happy departure, and we would then know bliss-shell. These were the shells that they gathered together.

Among them there was one big clam which had left its shells open in the sun. It did not know there was anyone there to seize it, and was blowing out clouds of foam. As Watōnai watched, thinking, "This must really be a case of a clam which can spit out vapour to form castles",[57] a shrike, which had been flying along the seaweed on the beach looking for something to eat, quickly discovered the clam, and came swooping down with a curious flapping of its wings, aiming to snap it up with one peck of its angry beak. Horrid master shrike! Didn't you who ponder the sutras[58] know this was a real violation of the commandment against taking life? And the clam, too, was committing a flagrant violation of Buddha's word in keeping its mouth open![59] The shrike flew at the clam and pecked at it quickly, but then the two shells clamped down on the bill and would not let it budge. The pleasure all at once drained from the shrike's face. It flapped its wings in an attempt to pull away. It shook its head and drew over to the base of the rocks, thinking, in its bird wisdom, to smash the clam against them. The clam tried to pull the shrike into a pool of sea-water, as it would with something it had caught on the beach, and sink down into the water tail-first. Stretching out its quills, the shrike flew up, rose about ten feet, hung in the air, and then fell. It rose again quickly, only to fall as suddenly. The shrike flapped its wings a hundred times, and struggled so hard its feathers stood on end. Watōnai watched this with absorption, then threw down his straight-handled rake.

WATONAI: This is most interesting. Now I see how it was that the sage became enlightened concerning his purpose in life when the bamboo was broken by the snow, cut off his arm, and founded in China the methods of Zen his teacher had brought from the West.[60] In keeping with my father's instructions, I had read the Chinese books of military science, and studied the reasons for victory or defeat in the battles of the famous Japanese generals of ancient and recent times. I had devoted my mind to military tactics, but it has only been by the battle between the shrike and the clam that I have just witnessed that I have all at once been illuminated about the secret of military strategy.[61]

The clam, relying on the hardness of its shell, did not know that a shrike would be coming along. The shrike, proud of the sharpness of its beak, did not realise that the clam would shut its shells. The shells will not let it go. The shrike, in its effort to get away, is straining all of its energies forward, and has no opportunity to look behind. Nothing could be easier now than for me to catch both of them at once. Then the hardness of the clam's shell will be to no avail, and the sharpness of the shrike's beak will have no effect. This is the secret of military strategy: to set two adversaries on one another, and then attack them both when they are off-guard. This was the strategy of the vertical and horizontal alliances by which Chin Shih-huang swallowed up the six kingdoms.[62] And in the *Taiheiki*[63] of Japan it tells how the Emperor Go-Daigo,[64] when ruling the country, did not control the government, but was like the clam with his shells opened wide. A shrike named Hōjō Takatoki was beating his wings in Kamakura;[65] the beak of his pride was sharp. He was defeated at Yoshino and Chihaya by Kusunoki Masashige and Nitta Yoshisada,[66] and his bill was caught by their two shells. It was the peerless General Takauji's supremacy in military strategy which enabled him to take advantage of Hōjō's unpreparedness as he struggled to free himself, and to capture him, the shells and the clam all at once. I have heard that in the land of my father's birth a shrike and clam battle is now at its height between China and Tartary. Now, if I were to cross over to China, and, applying what I have just learned to that situation, were to attack, I could swallow both China and Tartary at once!

NARRATOR: Not taking his eyes off the battle, he taxed his faculties. The product of the concentration of this warrior, who was first beginning to reason, was most impressive. It was reasonable, was it not, that this man should cross over to China, level China and Tartary, and make a name for himself abroad and in Japan. Coxinga, the Prince of Yen-p'ing, was this young man.

Komutsu, who was looking out in the distance cried out.

KOMUTSU: Look! The tide is already coming in. What are you staring at?

NARRATOR: She ran up to him.

KOMUTSU: Well! The shrike and the clam are kissing! This is the first I knew they were married. I can't stand watching them at it, just like dogs![67] I'll have to separate them somehow.

NARRATOR: Taking out a hair-pin she prized the shell apart. The shrike was delighted and headed for the reeds, while the clam thereupon buried itself in the sand as the tide flowed in.

The Chinese Boat

WATONAI: It looks as if it it's going to drizzle. Let's go back.

NARRATOR: As they looked out toward a little projection of land into the sea, they saw a rudderless boat of strange construction that came rocking toward them.

116

WATONAI: That's not a whaling-boat. Is it a Chinese tea-boat?

KOMUTSU: I don't know what it is.

NARRATOR: When they looked into the bottom of the boat, there was a high-born court lady of some sixteen years, who looked like a Chinese. Her face was like an hibiscus flower, and her brows like willow-leaves. Her sleeves were wet with the tears of the sea-wind that had washed the rouge and powder from her face, that was pale and drawn. She was touchingly beautiful like the first flowers of spring wilted by the rain. Komutsu lowered her voice.

KOMUTSU: She must be a Chinese empress like the kind I've seen in pictures, who has had some love affair and been exiled.

WATONAI: Yes, that's what she must be. You've made a good guess. I made the mistake of thinking that she might be the ghost of Yang Kuei-fei, and it frightened me. At any rate, she's a good-looking woman, isn't she?

KOMUTSU: You horrible man! Do Chinese women attract you? If your father had stayed in China where he used to be, you'd have been born there, and you'd be hugging a woman like that in bed. Instead, because you happened to have been born in Japan, you have a wife like me. What a shame for you!

WATONAI: That's silly. However pretty they may be, their clothing and the way they do their hair make Chinese women look like Benzaiten[68] to me. I could never get to sleep with one. I'd feel impious and my nerves would be on edge.

NARRATOR: He laughed as he said these words. Just then, the lady stepped on the shore and beckoned to them.

SENDAN: Japanese! Japanese! *Na mu kya ra chon nō to ra ya a a!*[69]

NARRATOR: Komutsu burst out laughing.

KOMUTSU: What sutra is *that?*

NARRATOR: She held her sides in merriment.

WATONAI: Don't laugh! She said, "Japanese, come here, I've something to request of you."

NARRATOR: Pushing her aside, he went up to the lady, who was blinded with tears.

SENDAN: Great Ming *chin shin nyō ro,* Lord *ken ku ru mei ta ka rin kan kyū, sai mō su ga sun hei su ru,* on the other hand, *kon ta ka rin ton na, a ri shi te ken san hai ro. To ra ya a a, to ra ya a a.*

NARRATOR: This was all she said, and then she melted in tears again. Komutsu plopped down on the beach, convulsed with laughter and unable to stand any more. Watōnai, who had never forgotten how his father's tongue was pronounced, struck his hands together and bowed his head.

WATONAI: *U su u su u sa su ha mō,sa ki ga chin bu ri ka ku san kin nai ro. Kin nyō, kin nyō.*

NARRATOR: He clapped his hands together, and then he and the lady took each other's hands in a most friendly manner. His tears of grief were sympathetic. Komutsu leapt up and seized him by the front of his robe.

KOMUTSU: See here, you. I don't want to hear any more of your Chinese talk. I always knew you'd been playing around, but how did you manage to get in touch with her in China? You've gone too far afield! And as for you, with your *to ra ya a ya*, how dare you go kinnyō-kinnyō-ing to my precious husband? You're not going to get a chance to taste what a Japanese man is like. Try a taste of this instead!

NARRATOR: She started to brandish her rake, but Watōnai snatched it away from her.

WATONAI: Open your eyes and stop being jealous. This is the Princess Sendan, the younger sister of the Emperor of China, my father's former sovereign, about whom he has always spoken. She is in a piteous state and we cannot abandon her. If I take her at once to our house, we will have to get permission from the village headman, there will be an investigation by the governor's office, and all kinds of trouble. In any case, I'll have to talk it over with my father. Go back home and bring him here at once! Hurry up, before people find out!

NARRATOR: Komutsu clapped her hands together.

KOMUTSU: Oh, the poor dear! I have heard how even in Japan ladies of royal and noble birth have come up against stormy winds. And to think that this pitiful figure is a descendant of the royal house of far-off China! It's because of the deep connection between sovereigns and their retainers that her boat put in here, of all the many places it might have gone. I'll go right away to fetch father. Oh, you poor thing, *to ra ya a ya. Kin nyō, kin nyō.*

NARRATOR: Her eyes filled with tears; she set off on the road back home. Ikkan and his wife, knowing nothing of this, were walking along the beach on their return from the shrine of Sumiyoshi at Matsura where they had gone to pay a visit after a strange dream that they had had.[70] Watōnai called out for them to come his way.

WATONAI: Princess Sendan has fled her disordered country, and her boat has put in here. She is a pitiful sight.

NARRATOR: As soon as they heard these words, Ikkan and his wife bowed their heads to the ground.

IKKAN: I believe your highness has heard of me. I was formerly known as Tei Shiryū. My present wife and my son are Japanese, but I should not be following the way of a loyal subject if I did not repay old obligations. I am

bent with years, but my son has a taste for matters of war and is, as you can
see, of a naturally powerful build. He is strong and bold. He will restore the
dynasty of the Ming and set at peace the mind of the late emperor in the other
world. Please rest easy on that score.

NARRATOR: The words that he addressed to the princess were most reassuring.
She, in tears, replied.

SENDAN: So you are the Tei Shiryū of whom I have heard! The traitor Ri
Tōten allied himself with Tartary, deserted my brother the emperor, and
usurped power in the country. I too was almost killed, but thanks to the
care of Go Sankei and his wife, nothing untoward has happened to me to
this moment. I entrust to you my wretched life, uncertain as the dew.

NARRATOR: With these words she again melted in tears. The words that passed
between them were those of oft-reiterated regret over the fate that had made
her dependent on this distant connection.[71] Stories of olden times are sadden-
ing. The mother too had difficulty in wringing out her tear-soaked sleeve.

MOTHER: This must be a sign that what we dreamt was really true. This
morning at dawn my husband and I had the same clear dream revelation,
that two thousand miles away[72] there would be a battle and victory in the
west. Watōnai, you must consider this dream and strive your loyal best for
the success of the imperial cause.

WATONAI: Just a little while ago I witnessed on this beach a strange encounter
between a shrike and a clam. From it I have gained a realisation of the
secret of military strategy. This is what is meant by "a victory in the west
a thousand miles away". China lies to the west of our country on the other
side of a thousand miles of waves. The ideograph for strategy 法 is written with the symbol for "water" 氵 and the symbol for "to leave" 去.
"To leave by water" is a divine message that I should entrust myself to the
water of this high tide and leave Japanese soil at once. My fortune is the
"hexagram of the general".[73] "The general" stands for an army. The hexagram is arranged with the trigram for earth above and that for water below.
When it says that with one *yang* you can command many *yin*, it means
that I shall be a general, myself commanding many thousands of troops. I
shall leave Japan at once on the rising tide to which the symbol for water
pointed, and push on to Nanking and Peking. I shall join my military
plans with those of Go Sankei, if he still survives in this mortal world, and
crush the traitorous followers of Ri Tōten. I shall raise an army and drive
the invaders back into Tartary. I'll twist off the shaven head of the chief of
the Tartars, and pursue and kill all the rest. Then I'll raise a song of victory for the long prosperity of the Ming Dynasty. Those are the plans that
fill my soul. "Opportunities of time sent by heaven are not equal to those

I

of situation afforded by earth, and advantages afforded by earth are not equal to the union arising from the accord of men." "Good or bad fortune depends on men and not on the sun."[74] I shall leave by boat without further preparations. I shall win over the barbarians of the islands I pass on the way, and then do battle as I plan. To the front!

NARRATOR: The ardour with which he spoke these words was such that it was as though they saw before them the fierce spirit of the Empress Jingū standing at the helm when she set off to conquer Korea.[75] The father was greatly impressed.

IKKAN: Most noble and reassuring words! The text is indeed true that says that a flower seed does not rot in the ground, but eventually grows into a plant with a thousand blossoms.[76] You are really a son of Ikkan! My wife and I should offer to accompany the princess in the same boat, but a crowd would attract attention, and there would be the danger that we might get in trouble with the shipping control posts at various places. My wife and I shall sail secretly from the harbour of Fujitsu. You board ship here and leave the princess at some easily accessible island on the way. Then change your course and catch up with us. A divine wind sent by the gods who dwell in the heads of loyal and honest fathers and sons will ensure that we have no difficulties while at sea. Let us wait for one another at the rendez-vous, the Bamboo Forest of Senri,[77] which is known throughout China. Hasten on your journey!

NARRATOR: The husband and wife took leave of the princess and set off on their distant journey. Watōnai took the princess by the hand and helped her aboard her own Chinese boat. He was about to push off when his wife ran up all out of breath, and seized the boat hawser.

KOMUTSU: When I got back home I found both your father and your mother were out. I thought there must be something up, and I see I was right. You and your father had this all planned long before. You sent for a wife from your father's country, and now the four of you are going off to China with all our property, leaving me, Komutsu, behind. This is too brutal and heartless! What kind of way is that to behave—abandoning me and taking off our possessions? We two who have exchanged vows to go together to India, to the ends of the clouds, much less to China or Korea, were joined by pledges and oaths contained in our hearts, and not by go-betweens or by formalities. However tired of me you may have become, for the sake of the love you once bore me, let me at least get on the boat with you. Then, though you throw me into the waves five or ten miles from the shore, and I there become the food of sharks, I will have died at the hands of my husband. Please, my lord Tōnai.

NARRATOR: She beat on the boat-beam, she wept, and she pleaded with him, showing no signs of letting go.

WATONAI: Your bawling face is a bad omen with which to start an important trip! Be off! Or I'll show you what I am capable of!

NARRATOR: He began to wave an oar at her.   The princess, in alarm, clung to him, but he pushed aside her restraining hand, and beat the side of the boat so hard he almost broke the oar. Komutsu took on her person the blows he struck in threat.

KOMUTSU: I want nothing more than to be beaten to death by you.[78]

NARRATOR: She fell down on the beach and rolled over, wailing at the top of her lungs.

KOMUTSU: And even with that I still can't die! Oh, I see it's all been because I've been so good-natured up to now. I'll throw myself down to the bottom of the sea, and my anger will become a great serpent of jealousy.[79] You, to whom I was pledged, are now my enemy! I'll show you!

NARRATOR: She picked up some stones and filled her sleeves with them. As she was climbing up the side of a cliff, Watōnai ran up to her and stopped her. He spoke in soothing tones.

WATONAI: Don't be foolish! Now that I have discovered what you are really like, I shall leave the princess in your care until China, now in the midst of war, is restored to peace. I had been thinking of leaving her here in Japan but I had to find out how you, a person of no birth, would react, and that's why I purposely seemed cruel. It is a proof of my unchanging manly devotion that I entrust to your care the princess, who is the equivalent of the four hundred and more districts of China. To serve the princess means a hundred times what is involved in filial piety to your father-in-law or duty to your husband. I make this vital request of you. When things are settled in China, you will accompany the princess there in the boat I shall send for you.

KOMUTSU: Don't worry about me. May all be well with you!

NARRATOR: She said these words, but her woman's heart was weak.

KOMUTSU: Not even one night to make your decision? This is a parting such as one sees in dreams.

NARRATOR: She clung to her husband's sleeve and began to weep and wail. She could not restrain her heart. Watōnai's heart was also full, and his eyes grew dim at the thought of the extreme step ahead. Together they stood in distraction, but then he thought, "At this rate I'll never end. I must be off!" and he took his last farewells. The Princess Sendan was also in tears.

SENDAN: I await the palanquin you soon will send for me. Then we shall return together. Be sure to send it quickly.

NARRATOR: Watōnai respectfully assented to her, and then, in tears, pushed off the boat. Komutsu again seized the boat hawser and stopped him.[80]

KOMUTSU: There is something I still have to tell you. Wait just a minute.

WATONAI: There is nothing for me to hear.

NARRATOR: He pulled the hawser away and rowed the boat out to the deep, where his body was soaked by the relentless waves of the sea. Komutsu lifted her hands and called out to the boat, but her words could not carry to the departed craft. She ran up the cliff and stood on her tip-toes. The object she was following with her eyes moved farther and farther away.

KOMUTSU: Now I shall take my example from the Watching Wife Mountain[81] in China and the Scarf-waving Mountain[82] in Japan. I won't move, won't leave this spot though I turn into stone, though I turn into a mountain.

NARRATOR: So she declared to him. They called to one another with all their tears and with their full voices, but salt-spray clouded and hid their figures from one another, and the waves of the sea drowned their voices. The sea-gulls and beach plovers that hovered off the shore called in sorrow and longing.

The Bamboo Forest of Senri

NARRATOR: Though when they left on their uncertain journey the coasts of Tsukushi where the sea-fire[83] burns were buried under the clouds, the boats of father and son met with the protection of a divine wind,[84] and cut through the myriads of waves, to arrive in the land of Cathay at one and the same time. Tei Shiryū Ikkan changed to his court costume of Chinese brocade,[85] as befitted his return to his country. He turned to his wife and son.

IKKAN: Though this may be said to be my own country, times have changed and the dynasty is not the same. The country is entirely in the grasp of Ri Tōten and has been enslaved by the Tartar barbarians. I have no way to call on any of my old friends or of my family. How can I raise a standard for loyal troops to follow when I do not even know whether President of the Council of War Go Sankei is dead or alive? There is no place in all the country where I can entrench myself.

However, when I departed this country in 1625 and crossed over to Japan, I left behind in the sleeve of her nurse a daughter just turned two years of age. The mother of this child died at once after having given her birth. I, her father, have been cut off from her by the boundless waves of the sea. She who has never known either father or mother has grown up as the plants and trees grow, by favour of the rains and the dew.[86] I have heard tell in the accounts of merchants that, thanks to the help of heaven and earth, who have been her parents, she has reached womanhood, and has now become the wife of the lord of a castle, a baron named Gojōgun

Kanki.[87] No other person can we trust. If my daughter's heart longs for her father, and she but consents, it will be easy for us to ask for aid from Kanki, my son-in-law. The distance from here is 180 miles. If we go together, people will become suspicious, and I shall therefore go by myself on a different route. Watōnai, you go with your mother. If you use your wits and tell people that you have been shipwrecked from a Japanese fishing boat, you can rest in their houses and catch up later. Ahead of us lies the celebrated Bamboo Forest of Senri, a great wood where tigers live. Beyond that is the Hsin-yang River, where orang-outangs dwell.[88] The towering mountain of beautiful scenery is the Red Cliff, which was the place of exile in olden times of Tung-p'o.[89] From there it is but a short distance to Kanki's castle, the Castle of the Lions.[90] Wait for me at the Red Cliff. There we will make our future arrangements.

NARRATOR: Unsure of the directions, they took the sun in the white clouds[91] as their guide, and separated to the east and to the west. Watōnai, following his father's instructions, steadfastly carried his mother on his back, looking for a house where they might hide. He jumped and leapt over dangerous rocks and boulders, over the roots of old trees, and over waterfalls and mountain streams, but though he speeded ahead like a bird in flight, China is a land of boundless distances, and he wandered into the vast Bamboo Forest of Senri, where no people dwell. Watōnai was at a loss what to do.[92]

WATONAI: Mother, my legs are beginning to feel the strain. We must already have come forty or fifty miles, but we have met neither man nor monkey. The farther we go, the deeper we get in the forest. Ah, I have it! It must be the work of Chinese foxes playing tricks on Japanese who don't know the way. Well, if they're going to bewitch us, let them. Since we are on a journey with no inn on the way, we'll be glad to share in a dish of rice and red beans.[93]

NARRATOR: Pushing and trampling through the low bamboo-grass and the high bamboos, he kept going ever deeper into the forest, when, strangely enough, they heard the sounds of thousands of voices, of hand-drums and bass drums sounding the attack and of loudly sounded bugles and trumpets.

WATONAI: Great heavens! Have we been discovered and surrounded by the enemy? Are those the sounds of his drums beating the attack? Or is it the doing of foxes?

NARRATOR: While he stood there, at a loss what to do, it suddenly grew cold, and a gale sprang up that scooped holes in the ground and curled up the leaves of the bamboo. The bamboos blown and broken by the gale were like swords, and everything was frightening beyond description. Watōnai was not the slightest afraid.

WATONAI: I have read all about this. It must be a Chinese tiger-hunt. Those horns and drums are the beaters. We are now in the Forest of Senri, about which we were told. I remember that when a tiger roars a wind springs up;[94] this is the doing of wild beasts. Yang Hsiang, one of the twenty-four examples cf filial piety,[95] was led naturally by the virtue of his filial actions to escape the danger of a ferocious tiger. Though I am inferior to him in filial piety, my courage is buoyed up by my loyalty. This will be the first test of my strength since coming to China. With the power of the gods, and, all the more, the power of Japan behind me, it would be unmanly to fight with a sword. I can crush with one blow an elephant or a devil, to say nothing of a tiger.

NARRATOR: He tucked up his skirts from behind and adjusted his clothing. As he stood there protecting his mother, it seemed as though even the Lion King of India would have been afraid of him.

Just as he had thought, on the heels of the wind came a raging tiger, who rubbed his muzzle on the base of a gall-nut tree, and sharpened its claws on a jutting rock, keeping his eyes on them all the while. Watōnai, paying no attention to the tiger's growls, struck it with his left hand, and fended it off with his right. He twisted it around, and when it sprang on him, he dodged. When it relented, he leapt lightly on its back. Now up, now down, they fought in a life and death struggle, a test of endurance. Watōnai gave great shouts to aid his strength, and the roars the tiger gave as his fur bristled seemed terrible as the noise of mountains crumbling. Watōnai's hair was in disorder, and half the fur of the tiger had been pulled out. The two of them were out of breath. When Watōnai stood up on a rock, the tiger hung its head among the the boulders, and the noise of its heavy panting was like that of a bellows working. The mother rushed up from the shelter of the woods.

MOTHER: Watōnai! don't harm the body, hair and skin you have received from the gods,[96] having been born in the land of the gods, in a contest with an animal. The land of Japan is far from here, but the gods are in your body. Why shouldn't this sacred charm from the Great Shrine by the Isuzu River[97] have an effect now?

NARRATOR: When she handed to him the charm she wore next to her person, Watōnai accepted it reverently, with the words "You are surely right". He pointed it at the tiger. Then, when he lifted it, what was the wonder of the secrets of the land of the gods! That force which had been fiercer than fierce suddenly drooped its tail, hung its ears, drew in its legs in fright, and then hid in a cave in the rocks, trembling with fright. Watōnai seized it by the base of the tail, hurled it backwards, pressed it down, and, when it flinched, jumped on it and pressed it firmly beneath his feet. For this he was indebted to the divine strength of the god Susanoo who flayed the piebald colt of heaven,[98] and to the benevolent virtue of Amaterasu-kami.

Just then the beaters came toward them in swarms, and one of them, who was recognisable as the chief, addressed them in a loud voice.

CHIEF: From what country have you drifted here, vagabond, that you should thus spoil my high name? This is a tiger we have been hunting so that my lord, the General of the Right Ri Tōten, whose name I mention with awe, might present it to the King of Tartary. Turn it over at once. If you have any objections, I shall slay you on the spot. Ho, officers!

NARRATOR: When he heard the name of Ri Tōten, Watōnai smiled with satisfaction.

WATONAI: Sometimes even a devil brings good tidings![99] You have babbled something I'm glad to hear. My land of birth is Great Japan, and in calling me a vagabond you said one word too many! If you want the tiger so badly, have the lord you depend on, Ri Tōten, or Tokoroten,[100] or whatever his name is, come here and beg for it. I have business with him and must see him personally. Otherwise, you won't get anything.

NARRATOR: He glared at him as he said these words.

CHIEF: Don't let him say another word! Kill him!

NARRATOR: They drew out their swords together. Watōnai cried, "I am ready!" and then, placing his charm on the head of the tiger, pulled it over beside his mother. There the tiger lay motionless as if tied to the spot.

WATONAI: Now I have nothing to worry about!

NARRATOR: Brandishing his broadsword, he slashed into the crowd. He sliced his way in every direction and rolled them back. The chief of the beaters, An Taijin, came back with his officers.

CHIEF: Kill him and the old woman both!

NARRATOR: With these words they fell on the pair, cutting with their swords held horizontally. As a further sign, then, of divine protection, the strength of the gods was added to the tiger's, and it sprang up with its body quivering. It faced the enemy, gnashed its teeth, and then leapt on them with a fierce roar. An Taijin and the beaters cried, "We are no match for him!" They flung at the tiger their hunting spears, their many lances, and anything else that came to hand, and struck him with the swords they wore. The tiger, possessed of divine strength, was infused with supernatural power. Snatching the swords high in the air with his jaws, he dashed them against the rocks and reduced them to fragments. The glint of the blades scattered in a hail of jewels, like splintered ice. The officers, deprived of their swords, gave way and fled in confusion. Then Watōnai appeared from behind with the cry, "You won't escape me!" He seized An Taijin by the head and lifted him in the air. He whirled him round and around, then flung him like a ripe persimmon against a rock. His entire body[101] was crushed and he perished. Such was the situation that when the officers withdrew, they were faced with the terrible jaws of the tiger, and when they went forward, with Watōnai, who stood there like one of the guardian kings.[102] They joined their hands in supplication, and crying, "Mercy! We crave your mercy!" bit into the ground and wept bitterly. Watōnai, stroking the tiger's back, replied.

WATONAI: You low creatures who despise the Japanese because we come from a small country! Have you seen how even a tiger is awed by Japanese prowess? I am the son of Tei Shiryū Ikkan, of whom you must have heard. Watōnai, who grew up at Hirado in Kyūshū, is none other than myself. I met the Princess Sendan, younger sister of the late emperor, and to repay the debt of three generations[103] have returned to my father's country where I am going to settle the disturbances. If you value your lives, join me. If you say "No", you will become food for the tiger. Yes or no?

OFFICERS: Why should we say no? We are reluctant to give up our lives by serving either the King of Tartary or Ri Tōten. Henceforth we shall be your followers. We crave your kind indulgence.

NARRATOR: They bowed, and their noses scraped the ground.

WATONAI: I've succeeded! However, if you are going to become my followers and serve me, you will have to have your coming of age ceremony performed[104] by shaving your heads in the Japanese style and changing your names.

NARRATOR: He had them take off their short swords.[105] Even these could serve as improvised razors. He and his mother took them in their hands. Then, using water from a pan on the lined-up brain-pans, they shaved brutally, without any thought of massaging or not massaging beforehand. Letting their razors cut as they pleased, they gave them *itobin* and *atsubin*[106] style haircuts, sometimes shaving only one side, sometimes hacking the whole. The shaving was done in an instant, and the Chinese were left with two and-a-half combs' worth of dishevelled hair.[107] Their heads were Japanese, their beards Tartar, and their bodies Chinese. They looked at one another. A wind that froze their heads blew, and naturally enough, they caught cold. They sneezed and sneezed, and their noses ran and eyes watered like the showers of summer. Watōnai and his mother burst out laughing.

WATONAI: All my followers are matched! Now change your names to Japanese ones, putting first the place you come from and adding -zaemon, or -bei, or tarō, jirō, all the way up to jūrō.[108] Then form in two ranks and clear the road ahead.

NARRATOR: "Yes, sir", they replied, and the first to lead the way were Chang-chowzaemon, Cambodiaemon, Luzonbei, Tonkinbei, Siamtarō, Champajirō, Chaulshirō, Honangorō, Unsunrokurō, Sunkichikyūrō, Moghulzaemon, Bataviabei, SanThomaschachirō and Englandbei. With his new followers in front, and their procession steeds and striped ponies behind, he helped his mother and gained a name for filial piety. He held the reins of his steed and conquered the country.[110] His fame spread in both directions, to China and Japan, like his legs in his saddle and stirrups, as he rode on the back of the tiger and showed his might to the world a thousand miles round.

ACT THREE

NARRATOR: Even the benevolent ruler cannot support worthless ministers; even the kind father cannot love a good-for-nothing child.[111]

Though they had parted on separate roads and travelled in different ways through Japan and China, the father, mother and son had not become lost, but had hurried along the right way, and had met at the foot of the Red Cliff. Then they had arrived at the Castle of the Lions, the residence of Kanki, about whom all they knew was that he was Ikkan's son-in-law. The fortress, of whose surpassing qualities they had heard, was built of stones piled up high. The tiles of the eaves sparkled in the frost of the still-cold spring night, and the dolphins[112] waved their fins in the sky. The water of the moat, straight as a taut rope, was like indigo, and flowed at its end into the Yellow River. The gate-tower was tightly bolted. Within the castle walls, the sound of a night-watchman's gong rang out noisily. In the loopholes were cross-bows closely packed together, and there were catapults installed at various places, to be fired in time of danger. This was a fortress more powerful than any that one is accustomed to see in Japan.

Ikkan was taken aback at the sight.

IKKAN: In view of the troubled times and the strict defences of the castle, it is unlikely ttha anyone will believe me and transmit my words if I knock on the gate in the middle of the night and say that I am Kanki's little-known father-in-law, come from Japan. Even if my daughter should hear me, I doubt if we could gain easy admittance to the castle, no matter how many proofs I might recite that I am the father separated from her when she was two years old, who crossed over to Japan. What shall I do?

NARRATOR: No sooner did Watōnai hear these whispered words than he cried out:

WATONAI: There is nothing to be surprised at now. It has been my expectation ever since leaving Japan that I would have no one on my side except

myself. Rather than suffer some humiliation after making friendly overtures of "Long lost father-in-law!", "Son-in-law!", we should make a direct
proposition to him, "Can we depend on you or can't we?" If he says "No", he
becomes our enemy on the spot. Since his wife is the daughter from whom you
were parted when she was two, that makes her my half-sister. If that hussy had
had any filial sentiments, she would have longed for word from Japan, and
there would have been letters from her, but as it is, we cannot rely on her.
If I can stage a close attack with the barbarians I subdued in the bamboo
forest tiger hunt, and whom I have made my initial military force, it won't
take any time for me to add another fifty or a hundred thousand men. Asking
favours from no one, I will kick down this gate and twist off the head of
my unfilial elder sister. Then I'll have a contest with your son-in-law Kanki.
NARRATOR: With these words he jumped up, but his mother clung to him
and stopped him.
MOTHER: I don't know what is in the girl's heart, but it is the custom for
women to follow their husbands, and not to do what they themselves wish.
With her father she had the relationship of parent and child, and she is of
the same seed as you. I am the only outsider, and though we have been
separated by a thousand miles of ocean and mountains, I can't escape the
name of a step-mother.[113] It's not possible that the girl does not long in her
heart for her father and her brother. If you cut your way in there, it will
be said that it was because the girl's step-mother was jealous, and that will
be a disgrace not only to me but to Japan. Since you plan the noble project
of crushing the powerful Tartar enemy and restoring the Ming dynasty by
yourself, you should avoid the disgrace to me, put up with your own
annoyance, and gain their friendship. I have heard that the basis of military
strategy is to win over to your side even one of the common soldiers of the
enemy. How much more true this is of my son-in-law Kanki, who is the lord
of a castle and an independent general! Do you think we can get such a man
on our side by any ordinary means? Control your feelings and ask him!
NARRATOR: Watōnai stood outside the gate and shouted:
WATONAI: Gojōgun Kanki! There is something I want to discuss with you
personally. Open the gate!
NARRATOR: He beat on the gate, but there was only an echo within the walls.
Then the soldiers on duty shouted all at the same time:
SOLDIERS: Our general, Lord Kanki, left yesterday by command of the Great
King. We haven't any idea when he'll be back. What crass impudence of
you, no matter who you are, to ask for an interview with him when he's
away, and in the middle of the night! If you have anything to say, speak
up! We'll tell him about it when he comes back.

NARRATOR: Ikkan replied in a low voice.

IKKAN: What I have to say cannot be relayed by anyone. If Lord Kanki is away, I must meet his wife and speak with her. If you tell her that someone has come from Japan, she is certain to understand.

NARRATOR: Barely had he finished his words than there was an uproar within the castle.

SOLDIERS: How audacious to seek to meet the lady whom even we have never seen! And especially when you're a Japanese! Watch out!

NARRATOR: They waved their lanterns and beat their gongs and cymbals. Many of the soldiers on top of the wall pointed their musket barrels at them, and made a great clamour.

SOLDIERS: Release the catapults! Crush them! Fuses! Shells!

NARRATOR: Kanki's wife, who must have heard them in her apartment, rushed up to the gate-tower.

KINSHOJO: Stop your racket! Don't fire your guns or do anything rash until I myself approve and tell you to.

You outside the gates! I am Kinshōjo, the wife of Gojōgun Kanki. The whole country bows before the Great King of Tartary, and my husband, too, conforms with the times, and belongs to his staff. He has been entrusted with this castle. I do not understand why you wish to meet me when my husband is away, especially now when strict defence measures are in effect. However, since you have something to do with Japan, I long to listen to your words. Tell me who you are. I wish to hear.

NARRATOR: While she was thus speaking, she was wondering, "Can it be my father? Why should he have come?" And, though she felt both apprehension and danger, her longing was foremost in her heart.

KINSHOJO: Soldiers! Don't do anything rash! Don't fire your muskets recklessly!

NARRATOR: Her fears were understandable. When Ikkan first looked on his daughter's face, it was to him like the misty moon in the sky,[114] and he raised a voice that was clouded with tears.

IKKAN: It is presumptuous of me to speak of it, but your father was Tei Shiryū of the Ming, and your mother died in giving you birth. Your father incurred the imperial wrath and fled to Japan. At the time you were but two years old and unaware of the sorrow of parting of parent and child, but you must have heard about it in the gossip of your nurse or in stories. I am your father, Tei Shiryū. I have passed years at the Bay of Hirado in Hizen, and my present name is Rōikkan. This man is your younger brother, born in Japan, and this is your new mother. As there is something I would like to discuss and request of you in private, I have come here, not concealing the shame of my reduced station. Would you please have the gate opened?

NARRATOR: These words of earnest persuasion struck Kinshōjo's heart. She wondered, "Is it indeed my father?" and she wanted to rush down, cling to him, and gaze into his face. Her heart was agitated, but she remained true to her part of wife to Kanki, the lord of a castle. She held back her tears lest the soldiers might see.

KINSHOJO: You have remembered every particular, but your argument is useless without proofs. If you have any proof that you are my father, I would like to hear it.

NARRATOR: When she had said these words, the soldiers all shouted, "Proof! Proof! Furnish proof!" "He has no proof other than to say that he's her father!" "He's a liar!" They all pointed the barrels of their muskets at him. Watōnai ran in between them and his father.

WATONAI: If you even make a gesture of firing your worthless rifles, I'll cut off your heads!

SOLDIERS: Don't let that rogue escape either!

NARRATOR: They raised the caps of their matchlocks and, covering the party from all sides, began to threaten them, demanding, "Proof! Proof!" When the situation seemed dangerous, Ikkan raised both his hands.

IKKAN: Here you are! The proof must be in your possession. When you were one year old and I was about to leave China, I had a portrait of myself painted, thinking that it would serve as a memento for you when you were grown. I left that picture with your nurse. My appearance has changed with age, but compare my features with those preserved in the portrait and clear up your doubts.

KINSHOJO: Those words are already proof!

NARRATOR: On the parapet she opened out the portrait of her father that never left her person, and drew forth a mirror with a handle. Reflecting in the surface of her mirror her father's face, on which the moonlight fell, she matched and compared it with the portrait. When she examined them carefully, she saw caught in the picture the face as it was of old, with its sleekness and glossy side-locks. In the mirror was the present old-age and gauntness. The head had turned to snow, but left unchanged, as they had been, were the eyes and the mouth, that closely resembled her own features. The beauty-mark on her forehead that she had inherited from her father was a positive sign that they were father and daughter.

KINSHOJO: Ah, are you really my father? How I have longed for you! How dear you are to me! They told me only that my mother lay under the sod in the other world, and that I had a father in Japan. I sought word of you, but I had no one to help me. Since I had heard that Japan lay at the eastern end of the world, at dawn I worshipped the rising sun as my father. At dusk I would spread out a map of the world, and would say to myself, "Here is China, and here Japan. This is where father lives." On a map they seem so close, but Japan is thousands of miles away. I had given up all hope of meeting you in this world, and I waited for the world to come, thinking I might meet you there. I passed my days in sighs and my nights in tears. The nights and days of twenty years have been difficult for me to bear. How grateful I am that you are alive and that I can behold my father!

NARRATOR: She wept with joy, not caring who could see or hear her. Ikkan, choking with tears, clung to the gate-tower. When he looked up, she looked down, their hearts too full for words; their ceaseless tears moved all who saw them. Watōnai, who was so filled with martial spirit, knelt down with his mother, and even the heartless soldiers dampened the rope-fuses of their guns with their overflowing tears. After a while, Ikkan spoke.

IKKAN: We have come here to make an important request of Kanki in private. But first I would like to relate it to you. Please have the gate opened and let us in the castle.

KINSHOJO: Although I should ask you to come in even without your request, the country is still in the midst of war, and by order of the King of Tartary it is strictly prohibited to admit any foreigner within the walls, be he a relative by blood or marriage. But this is a special case. Say there, soldiers, what should be done?

NARRATOR: The unfeeling Chinese cried, "No, no! This is unheard of! We can't allow it! Go back! Go back! *Bin kan ta satsu, bu on, bu on*"[115] and they levelled their muskets at them again. This they had not expected, and it made them despair, but then the mother came forward.

MOTHER: That is only right. Since there is an order from the Great King, you cannot help it. However, you don't have to take any precautions against an old woman like me. All I would like is a word with the lady. Please let me in, just by myself. That would truly be the kindness of a lifetime.

NARRATOR: She joined her hands together in pleading, but the soldiers would not listen to her.

SOLDIERS: No! There was nothing exempting women from the order... However, we will be reasonable. While in the castle you must be bound with ropes. If we let you in tied up like a criminal, our general will have some excuse and we will be cleared even if the King of Tartary should hear of it. Hurry up and put on the ropes. If you don't like it, go back! *Bin ka ta satsu, bu on, bu on!*

NARRATOR: Watōnai's eyes flashed fire.

WATONAI: Dirty Chinese! Do you have ears? Can you hear me? This lady has the honour of being the wife of Tei Shiryū Ikkan. She is my mother, and also the mother of your lady. I, a Japanese, have never heard of such stupidity as to think that my mother is going to get through your gates tied up with a rope like a dog or a cat on a leash![116] It doesn't make a great deal of difference even if we don't get into your miserable castle. Let's be on our way!

NARRATOR: He started to lead his mother off, but she shook loose.

MOTHER: Have you forgotten what I just said? When you have something important to ask of a person, you are bound to have all kinds of unpleasant experiences and even humiliation at times. If by being put in stocks at my hands and feet, much less by being tied with a rope, our request were to be granted, it would be like getting gold for broken tiles.[117] Though Japan is a small country, neither her men nor her women will abandon the cause of righteousness. Please tie me up, my lord Ikkan.

NARRATOR: Though he was humiliated, there was nothing he could do about it. He took out a light rope tied about the waist as a precaution against escape, and then bound her at the elbows and wrists.[118] The mother and son looked at one another. That they could then force a smile shows how gallantly Japanese are brought up. Kinshōjo found it difficult to bear, but hid her look of grief.

KINSHOJO: In these times there is nothing that can withstand the laws of the country. Do not have any fears about your mother while she is in my care. I do not know what her request may be, but I shall listen to it through, and then tell it to my husband, and beg him to grant it.

Now, the water in the moat dug around this castle comes from a conduit in the garden by my dressing-room, and flows eventually into the waters of the Yellow River. If my husband Kanki hears me, and grants your request, I shall dissolve some powder and send it flowing through the conduit. If the river water flows white, you will know it to be a sign of good fortune. Enter then the castle in high spirits. If he does not grant your request, I shall dissolve some rouge and let that flow. If the river water flows red, you will know it has not been granted. Go then to the gate to call for your mother. Look and tell by the whiteness or the crimson of the water whether good or ill fortune has been your lot. Farewell!

NARRATOR: Then, in the moonlight, she opened the gate. The mother, who was with her, stood on the border between life and death, but instead of the Gate of Enlightenment, she was faced with the Gate of Delusion.[119] The sound of the bolt being drawn was like that of a weapon going off. Kinshōjo's eyes grew dim; weakness is the way of the women of China. Neither Watōnai nor Ikkan wept; that is the way of a Japanese warrior. The opening and closing of the great gate resounded like a fired catapult; that is the way of Tartary. Just to hear this catapult-like noise resound carried them all off to distant thoughts.

It was only on coming to China, a land she had not visited before even in her dreams, that the mother first knew what it was to have a daughter. They were bound together by ties of kindness and love, and there was no need for the criminal bonds with which the mother was tied.[120] Such an example of affection was rare, even in China, as rare as plum flowers that blossom in the snow, and the sound of their voices was the same, like the song of the oriole, so that they needed no interpreter. Kinshōjo, with deep filial piety, led her mother to a chamber in her apartment, and presented her with double-thickness mattresses and triple-thickness blankets, with delicacies from the mountains and the sea, and with famous wines. The splendour with which she treated her mother was like that afforded in heaven, but it would have been heart-breaking to see those bonds at the elbows and wrists even on a criminal guilty of ten sins and the five great crimes.[121] Kinshōjo performed various tasks for her mother, and was as loving toward her as if she were her real mother. Her heart was indeed most excellent.

All her maid-servants gathered round.

FIRST SERVANT: Have you ever seen a Japanese woman before? Her eyes and nose are like ours, but what a funny way she has of doing her hair, and her clothes are so peculiarly sewn![122] I suppose even the young women must dress the way she does. Her lower and upper skirts billow out, so that if a sudden wind came along, you could see right up to her thighs! Wouldn't she be embarrassed if that happened?

SECOND SERVANT: No, no. If I'm going to be born again as a woman, I want to be a Japanese. This is why. Japan is called the Land of Great Gentleness.[123] Wouldn't a country where everyone is gentle be fine for a woman? Oh, it's just the country for me.

NARRATOR: She narrowed her eyes with envy, and nodded her head. Kinshōjo came toward them.

KINSHOJO: Now, now, what are you talking about in so amusing a way?

Since that lady is not the mother who bore me, I pay her greater respect, both because of filial piety and because of duty, than I would a real mother, but I am helpless against the laws of the country. How pitiful it is to see her bound and tied! If word of this should leak out to the King of Tartary, my husband might be blamed for it, and it would be difficult for him to secure pardon. I am alone in my troubles. I want you all to help me. I understand that the food she eats is unlike ours. Inquire what things suit her taste and offer them to her.

SERVANT: If it please you, my lady, we prepared most carefully a meal for her, rice cooked with longans,[124] soup made with duck and fried beancurd, pork stew, barbecued mutton and beef-paste cakes. But though we offered these to her in various ways, her ladyship said, "How disagreeable! I don't like such things at all. I can't manage them with my hands when I'm tied up. Just make me some *musubi.*" I didn't understand what kind of food *musubi* might be. I gathered everyone together and asked about it, and someone said that in Japan they call a wrestler a *musubi.*[125] I thereupon searched everywhere for one, but just now the season is poor, and they were all out of wrestlers such as might suit her ladyship's taste.

NARRATOR: A carriage rumbled outside, and the shout was raised, "His excellency has returned!" Gojōgun Kanki was borne forward in his palanquin, a splendid silken parasol above him, in a manner worthy of his dignity. Kinshōjo went out to meet him.

KINSHOJO: How quickly you have returned! What happened at court?

KANKI: The Great King of Tartary was highly pleased, and granted me a generous promotion. I have been appointed banner leader of one hundred thousand horsemen, with the rank of General of Cavalry.[126] He bestowed on me the headgear of a prince and court robes, and entrusted me with an important position. No higher honour could come to our house.

KINSHOJO: I congratulate you on your accomplishments. One fortunate thing after another has happened to our family. My father, about whom I have spoken to you so often, and for whom I have always longed, came to our gate with my Japanese mother and brother, and said he had something to request. I told him you were not here, and the men, respecting the strict laws of our country, both went away. Only my mother have I kept here. As I feared, however, that the government might hear of it, she was brought in tied with ropes. I have offered her entertainment in the women's pavilion, but it is sad that the mother from whose womb I did not come[127] should have to be tied up in that way.

KANKI: You were wise to have her bound. Now I have an excuse if the government happens to hear of it. Treat her most kindly. But first I should like to meet her. Please show me the way.

NARRATOR: The sound of his voice must have carried, for from within the double doors

MOTHER: Kinshōjo, has Lord Kanki returned? He does me too great an honour in coming. It is for me to go to him.

134

NARRATOR: Her figure, as she struggled to rise, was like that of an old pine-tree twisted and bound with wisteria and vines. At the sight of her painfully standing there, Kanki's eyes expressed his pity.

KANKI: Truly has it been said that one will cross ten thousand miles of mountains and rivers if one has a child somewhere in the world. Those cruel bonds are necessitated by the inflexible laws of our time. Wife, see whether her arms are hurt. So rare and important a guest[128] must not be disrespectfully treated in any way. Whatever you may have to request, I, Kanki, shall grant it, so long as it is in keeping with my dignity. Do not hesitate to tell me.

NARRATOR: He treated her in so friendly a manner that the old mother relaxed her expression.

MOTHER: Why should I hesitate since you have spoken to me in so reassuring and kind a way? I would like to tell you in secret the important thing I have to request. Please come closer.

NARRATOR: She dropped her voice to a whisper.

MOTHER: It was not only because we longed to see our daughter that we have crossed over to China on this occasion. In the early winter of last year, the Princess Sendan, sister to the Ming emperor, was blown ashore in her little boat at a place called the Beach of Matsura in the province of Hizen. She told us how China had been seized by the Tartars. As soon as they heard this, your father, who was formerly a vassal of the Mings, and my son Watōnai, who though he follows a humble fisherman's calling has studied the military texts of China and Japan, decided that they would crush the Great King of Tartary, restore the former dynasty, and place the princess on the throne. We left her for the time being in Japan, and the three of us came here to China. But, alas, how distressing it has been to find that everything, down to the plants and trees, sways before the Tartars, and there is not a single person who desires to join the adherents of the Ming. Watōnai would like to ask that you, Lord Kanki, be his chief lieutenant, and that you please add your strength to the cause. I have come to beg this of you most earnestly. Behold my heart that bows before you.

NARRATOR: She forced her forehead down to her knees, and seemed possessed of but a single purpose and determination. Kanki was greatly surprised.

KANKI: So this Watōnai about whom I have been hearing is the brother of Kinshōjo and the son of Tei Shiryū Ikkan! His bravery is famous even in China. His plan is promising, and will very likely succeed. My ancestors were also vassals of the Ming, but after the emperor was overthrown, I had no sovereign to rely on, and I accepted the rewards conferred on me by Tartary. Your request is what I have most desired at a time when I had been wasting my days. I should like to declare myself an ally at once, but since it is a matter

135

K

that requires a little consideration, I cannot make any answer just yet. I shall think it over carefully and then give my reply.

NARRATOR: Before he could finish

MOTHER: Your cowardly words are wrong. Once so important a matter as this is mentioned, it becomes common knowledge. If, while you are thinking it over, word should leak out, and we suffer defeat as a result, no amount of regret will mend matters. I do not think Watōnai will bear you any hatred no matter how you answer. Whether willing or not, make your reply immediately.

KANKI: If you want to hear an answer at once, it is very simple. Kanki will most assuredly be Watōnai's ally.

NARRATOR: Even before he had finished speaking, he seized Kinshōjo by the front of her robe and pulled her toward him. Drawing out a knife, he pressed it against her throat. The old mother rushed over in agitation and pushed between the two of them. She kicked away Kanki's hand that held her daughter, and then pushed Kinshōjo down with her back, and lay in protection over her. She cried out in a loud voice.

MOTHER: You monster! What does this mean? Is it the custom in China to stab your wife to death when somebody asks you a favour? Or have you become infuriated because the person who made a disagreeable request of you is a relative of your wife's? Or is it madness? You lawless creature! I can imagine how you behave toward her on ordinary days, if you attempt to kill her before my eyes on the rare occasion of my first visit. If you don't want to join us, don't! My precious daughter has a mother now.

There is nothing to be afraid of. Hold tight to your mother.

NARRATOR: In an act of self-sacrifice she became an intervening wall between Kanki and her daughter. As she lay there protecting her daughter and weeping, Kinshōjo, who could not understand her husband's intentions, felt grateful for the affection her mother showed.

KINSHOJO: Don't hurt yourself!

NARRATOR: This was all she could say, and the two of them choked with tears. Kanki jumped back.

KANKI: It is natural that you should fail to understand. I am not in the slightest lawless or mad. Yesterday I was summoned by the King of Tartary, who said, "A low fellow named Watōnai has recently crossed over to this country from Japan with the intention of overthrowing me and restoring the country to the Ming. Base and vulgar though he is, his cleverness and military skill are impressive. Who will be his adversary?" Then, of all the thousands of feudal lords, he picked me out, and appointed me to the post of General of Cavalry, and gave me a command of one hundred thousand men. I had never dreamt that Watōnai was my wife's brother until I heard it just now, and I therefore answered boldly in accepting the command, "I've heard it said that in that rogue's country, Japan, Kusunoki, or some such, once showed his bravery, and that Asahina and Benkei were renowned for their strength, but I shall penetrate the strategems of K'ung-ming, and borrow the secrets of Fan K'uai and Hsiang Yü.[129] I shall defeat him in one battle and track him down, and come back with Watōnai's shaven head borne aloft." If I, who boasted thus, should ally myself with him nonchalantly, without having crossed swords or shot a single arrow, I am sure that the Tartars would all say that since Gojōgun Kanki is not a man to be frightened by what he hears of Japanese military prowess, it must be because he is tied to his wife's apron-strings and influenced by his in-laws that he is fearful and has forgotten the heroism of his bow and arrows. If they talk in that way, my descendants will be unable to escape shame. If I harm my wife, for whom I feel love and sympathy, it is because I want to ally myself cleanly with Watōnai, not influenced by his relationship with my wife, and holding in reverence still the words "righteousness" and "fidelity". Kinshōjo, a heart of compassion was contained in the words of your mother who stopped me. Loyalty was contained in the point of the knife of your husband who tried to kill you. For the sake of your mother's love and your husband's loyalty, give up your life!

NARRATOR: These were the words of a brave warrior who did not ornament the rights and wrongs of the matter.

KINSHOJO: I am willing. I am equal to that test of loyalty, and do not think it will be regrettable if, for the sake of filial piety, I sacrifice the body I have received from my parents.

NARRATOR: Pushing aside her mother, she approached her husband, opened the front of her robe, and drew to her the icy blade so terrible to behold. Her mother cried, "Alas!" and ran in between them. She tried to push them apart, but to no avail, and she was unable to take away the knife. When she took her daughter's sleeve in her mouth and pulled her back, the husband came closer. When she pulled the husband's sleeve with her mouth, the daughter approached again, determined to die. She was like a mother-cat changing her nest and taking one kitten after another in her mouth. Then her eyes grew dim and her body lost its strength. She fell with a cry, and seemed insensible to her surroundings. Kinshōjo clung to her.

KINSHOJO: All my life I never knew my mother. At last when I met her, I showed no filial piety. How shall I return my obligation to her? Oh, let me die, mother.

NARRATOR: She pleaded and lamented, and then burst into tears.

MOTHER: What sad things you say! You have three parents, here and in the world of the dead. You owe to your two real parents the great obligation of having been born. I, your other mother, have never shown you kindness or compassion. Alas! however hard I try to escape the reputation of a step-mother, I cannot escape it. If I let you die now, people will say that your Japanese step-mother hated her step-child in China three thousand miles away, and had her killed before her eyes. This would not only be a disgrace for me, but since everyone would then say that Japanese are cruel-hearted, and give the country that reputation, it would also be a disgrace to Japan. The sun that shines on China and the sun that shines on Japan do not differ in their light, but the "rising sun" is where the sun comes from, and there humanity and justice, the five constant virtues and kindness may be found. Could this mother, who was born in the land of the all-merciful gods, look on while her daughter was killed and still go on living? I make a request of you: these ropes that bind me are a manifestation of the sacred ropes[130] of the Japanese gods. Strangle me with them now. Then, though my corpse be exposed in a foreign country, the ropes will lead my soul to Japan.

NARRATOR: She wept, and there was reason and love in her touching pleadings. Kinshōjo clung to her and the mother's sleeve was wet by the tears they both shed. Kanki was also extremely moved by the truth of her words, and, without realising it, melted in tears. After a little while, however, Kanki struck his chair with impatience.

KANKI: It's unavoidable, then. I am powerless to change things. Since your mother will not consent to your death, Watōnai and I are enemies from this day hence. If we keep your old mother here, people will think that she is a hostage, which is contrary to my intention. Have a palanquin prepared therefore, find out where she wishes to go, and send her back!

KINSHOJO: No, there is no need to send her anywhere. I promised that if I had good news, to let white powder flow from this conduit down into the Yellow River, or if I had unfavourable tidings, to let rouge flow. In that case they were to come for her. Now I shall dissolve some rouge and let it flow.

NARRATOR: She went into her room. The mother was immersed in thought, wondering what to tell her husband and her son when she returned, now that everything had gone contrary to their expectations. There was no way for her to console them, and her tears were redder than rouge.[131] Kinshōjo was at this time dissolving rouge in a lapis bowl.

KINSHOJO: Thus is the brocade bridge broken before the father and daughter could cross.[132] Now is the time of parting.

NARRATOR: The rouge slipped through the moonlit waters of the spring as crimson leaves rush through fords, waterfalls and the shallows of autumn in this passing world, and fell together with the red-tinged bubbles through the conduit down to the Yellow River. There Watōnai was sitting on a boulder, his straw rain-coat thrown about him, watching to see whether it would flow red or white.

WATONAI: Great Heavens! The water's flowing red! He's refused my request! I can't trust my mother to the care of that rogue Kanki who won't join me!

NARRATOR: He rushed forward so fast that his feet stopped the flow of the swift river, and then he leapt over the moat that lay in his path. He climbed over the wall, trampled down wattled fences and palisades, and reached the spring in the garden of the women's apartments of Kanki's castle.

WATONAI: Thank heavens mother is safe!

NARRATOR: He rushed up to her and cut the ropes that bound his mother, then planted himself in front of Kanki.

WATONAI: So you're that dirty Chinese of a Gojōgun Kanki! I tied up my mother, the only one I have in heaven or on earth, because I honoured you for what I thought you were, and because I wanted to ask you to become my ally. But you have abused the high respect I paid you. Is it because you find me inadequate as a general that you won't join me? I expected you to follow me if only because I am your wife's relative. Now, make your answer to my request directly to me, Watōnai, who am without peer in Japan.

NARRATOR: He laid his hand on his sword-hilt and drew himself up before Kanki.

KANKI: If you mention your relationship to my wife, you will be all the less successful. You may be without peer in Japan, but I am Kanki, unique among the men of China. I am not a warrior to make an alliance because I am tied to my wife. I have no grounds for divorcing my wife, and I can't idle my time away waiting for her to die a natural death. Take advantage of the favourable breeze and go back at once. Or would you like to leave your head behind as a souvenir?

WATONAI: No! I'll take your head as a souvenir for Japan!

NARRATOR: Both of them were about to draw their swords when Kinshōjo cried out.

KINSHOJO: See! See! You won't have to wait for me to die. Behold the source of the rouge I just set flowing!

NARRATOR: When she opened the front of her robe, they saw that she had stabbed herself with her dagger, slashing sideways from under her breasts to her liver. When the mother saw the wound bathed in crimson, she cried out and swooned on the ground. Watōnai was astonished, and even her husband, who had been prepared for her death, could not help but be amazed. Kinshōjo painfully spoke to them.

KINSHOJO: My mother did not let me be killed because she was thinking of the disgrace it would be to Japan. It would be a disgrace to China if I now held my life so dear that I would not offer it up for my parents and my brother. Now, Kanki, there will surely be no one to slander you and say that your mind was influenced by a woman, so join my father and my brother, and add your strength to theirs. Please tell this also to my father, but please do not tell him anything else. Oh, I am in pain!

NARRATOR: These were all the words she uttered, and then fell into a coma. Kanki hid his tears.

KANKI: You have succeeded. I won't disregard your suicide.

NARRATOR: He bowed his head before Watōnai:

KANKI: My ancestors were vassals of the Ming, and I should gladly have joined you had I not feared I would be criticised for having been led astray by your relationship to my wife. Now that my wife has encouraged me in the ways of righteousness by her death, I can become your ally with a pure heart. I honour you as commanding general, as a king among feudal princes. I now change your name, and give you the title of Tei Seikō, Coxinga, Prince of Yen-p'ing,[133] and I offer you a ceremonial robe.

NARRATOR: From a Chinese chest laden with the fortunes of war, he took forth a scarlet court robe of double-thickness brocade with sleeves of silken gauze, a ceremonial hat, shoes with woven crests, a belt set with coral and amber, and a sword of polished gold like Mo Yeh.[134] Then, when a silken parasol was held over him, and the hundred thousand troops lined up, armoured sleeve against sleeve, bearing imperial flags with pendant streamers, conical pennants, raised spears, bows and muskets, it was as if the King of Yüeh had come a second time to Kuei-chi Mountain.[135] The mother cried out in immense joy.

MOTHER: How happy I am! This is what I hoped for! See, Kinshōjo! The great desire of my husband and my son has been realised because you have sacrificed your life! And, though it might be thought just the desire of my husband and son, it is actually the great desire of the whole world. This knife is but nine and a half inches long, but by your suicide it has altered the destiny of the country. If I should protract my life now, my first words will prove to have been empty ones, and I will again bring shame on Japan.

NARRATOR: Seizing her daughter's knife she plunged it into her throat. When everyone exclaimed in horror, she cried, "Don't come any closer", and looked at them fiercely.

MOTHER: Kanki, Coxinga. You must under no circumstances bewail or regret the death of your mother or her daughter. If you regard the King of Tartary as the enemy of both of us, you will be strong enough to defeat him. This is the kindness of a mother who will not permit your spirits to slacken. Do not forget these last words. Since your father is alive, Watōnai, you still have one parent left. Your mother in dying exhorts you. If your father lives on and instructs you, you will become a general without defect. My thoughts of this fleeting world go no further.

MOTHER: Kinshōjo, do you feel no longing for this world you are leaving?

KINSHOJO: Why should I feel any longing?

NARRATOR: Though she spoke thus, there was the longing for her husband left behind. Mother and daughter took each other's hands and drew close. Looking up and down Coxinga's new attire happily, they expired at the same moment, leaving behind smiles on their faces as mementoes to this world.

Coxinga, who could cheat devils, and Gojōgun, who was as brave as any dragon or tiger, melted in tears, but the one was determined not to disobey his mother's last words, and the other not to act contrary to his wife's intentions, and so Coxinga was ashamed to show his feelings before Kanki, and Kanki before Coxinga, and they hid their downcast faces. Along the road over which the sad remains were borne to the grave their armies started out; thus the quick and the dead trod the same road.[136] For Coxinga, the last words of his mother were like a sutra to Buddha, and his father's teachings would be an iron bar in the hands of a devil.[137] When he struck, he would win; when he attacked, he would conquer. Here was a warrior of wisdom and benevolence for all ages to marvel at.

The banks of a pool where there are pearls cannot be broken. The pond where the dragon lives cannot dry up.[138]

That he was the most wonderful of men from Japan, where such heroes are born, where the land is as land should be, and the sovereign is a true sovereign, he showed by illuminating a foreign country with the brilliance of his martial talents.

ACT FOUR

NARRATOR: The days and nights at Komutsu's house on the Beach of Matsura were spent in waiting for news from China. The Chinese princess living with her had become the subject of the neighbours' gossip, and it was suspected that she was a countryless wanderer from the land where the waves of China and Japan meet.[139] Komutsu's heart had filled with courage when she learnt that her husband's name had been changed to Coxinga, Lord of the Imperial Surname, and that he was now the commanding general of many tens of thousands of troops. She changed her appearance to that of a young actor. In the thick braids of her combed-out side-locks, and in her flowing back-hair of glossy black, she suggested the son of a Shinto official or an unguent vendor,[140] and did not look like a woman at all. She wore light blue[141] breeches and coat, and carried a wooden sword in a red lacquered scabbard with a scarlet sword-knot. Her rouged lips were like a flower, and her face was white with powder like snow. Her sedge-hat pulled deep over her face, she lifted her legs high as she walked along the beach with the light steps of a beach plover, on her daily visit to the Matsura shrine of Sumiyoshi. She vowed that she would fulfil her desires. For a while she paused, her hands joined in prayer, but then she leapt up in a flash with her sword drawn, and stood facing the opponent she had chosen, a sacred pine-tree. Holding her wooden sword over her head, she sprang up at it, shouting bravely. Swift as summer lightning and furious as a lion in the leap were her movements as she wielded her broadsword now high, now low. She charged in with nimble steps, skilfully feinting and dodging,[142] and felled with a stroke of her wooden sword a branch from the old pine-tree. Such skill earned her the right to be called a modern Ushiwaka.[143]

Before she knew it, the Princess Sendan had run up to her from the shadows of the forest.

SENDAN: Lady Komutsu! Every day at the same hour you have indulged in these strange practices. To-day I have followed you and discovered you at them. Who has taught you military tactics? How skilful you are!

KOMUTSU: I haven't had any teacher. It has been more a matter of becoming accustomed to my husband's practice-sword than of learning. The news from China has made me anxious, and since no boat has come for you, I have been praying I might escort you there myself. I have asked the god of this shrine for a sign, and look! I believe that the fact that I could cut through this pine-tree as if I had a real sword is a proof that the god has granted my prayers. There is a merchant ship sailing for our destination. Let us take advantage of it.

SENDAN: Your words delight and reassure me. Send me back without a moment's delay!

NARRATOR: Her joy was deep indeed.

KOMUTSU: Set your mind at ease. The god of this shrine, Sumiyoshi, is the god who watches over the sea-lanes. When the Empress Jingū set out to conquer Korea, he protected her ship with his ebb-pearl and flow-pearl,[144] and he is also known as the God of Ships. Long ago a man from China named Haku Rakuten[145] crossed over to the Islands of the Dragon Fly[146] to test the wisdom of Japan. As soon as he saw its scenery before his eyes, he wrote a poem.

> Green moss donned like a cloak
> Lies on the shoulders of the rocks.
> White clouds, like a belt
> Encircle the mountain's waist.

The great god appeared in the guise of a humble old fisherman, and recite a poem in reply.

> Rocks that wear a cloak of moss
> Have no need of belts,
> But the Cloakless Mountain
> Wears a belt of clouds.

Rakuten, at a loss to match this poem, returned to his own country. I shall take the cloak of moss the god who protects our country mentioned in his poem, and it will be my travelling robe. Let us be on our way!

NARRATOR: The two of them set off together. The journey by water ahead seemed to stretch far away.

Michiyuki of Princess Sendan

NARRATOR: For the Chinese style of hairdress they use Satsuma combs; for the Shimada style of hair-dress they use Chinese combs. Thus are Yamato and Cathay united.[147]

How poorly they were prepared for the journey that lay before them! On their travels over sea and land they would need bamboo hats, and pillows on which to pile up the dreams of many nights. They had resolved to voyage a thousand miles, for even the strong bow of a woman's heart may be drawn because of a man. Komutsu thought, "I am on a journey that will take me from my home; you are returning to yours". Different though her thoughts[148] might be, Sendan had been led by Komutsu's courage to contemplate the trip to China, and her heart was far away. What did she who had parents and a husband have to grieve about? Though the moon at dawn would be the same in China, it was difficult to leave the chamber where they had seen it together. As they passed the Bay of Ōmura, the beach wind brought a shower, a shower that cleared as her tears did not, tears that she hid within her sleeve, and wiped away with her trailing under-sleeve. They left their images in the Mirror Temple. They did not weep lest people should see at Seaweed Bay.[149] When they looked out over the water, the sun and sky of their destination seemed far away. "When shall I return? Oh, geese[150] of heaven, lead me, lead me to my husband, whose years are twenty-five, for we are joined together as lute strings are. Come, let us play our lutes, and when we hear the music among the pines of Hakozaki, we shall think of those who are pining for us, and hurry ahead." As they followed along the beach, the children of the fisherfolk who rake the seaweed were gathered there, playing at jacks, marbles, odd or even, counting three, four, five; these were children's games of innocence.[151] Even the water that flowed through the Pool of Seven Rapids hid itself in games of hide-and-seek, and sang while the "devil" was away,[152] but their sleeves were wet with tears that did not dry. They waited for the boat for Cathay at the Matsura River, as the harbour was swept by wind from Nearby Bay.[153] When they looked out that way, they saw in the Kuguri River, where the nets were drawn up on shore,[154] a boy with his hair parted and tied, who was fast asleep in a fishing boat that was rocked by the waves, with no nets lowered and only a string dangling from his fishing pole.[155]

SENDAN: Say there, my lad! We are travellers bound for China. Please take us aboard and guide us to the place we seek.

BOY: Nothing could be simpler! I see that one of you is from China, and the other from Tsukushi. For ladies such as you to be travelling to China, there must be someone there you love. Though this is not the night of the full moon, of which the poet wrote,[156] you must long for old friends two thousand miles away. Come at once aboard my moonlit boat.

NARRATOR: He stretched toward them his water-wise fishing-pole.

BOTH WOMEN: What strange chance is this!

NARRATOR: They went aboard his boat. The white waves that led to their longed-for destination[157] calmed, and they sailed over the smooth surface of the sea.

SENDAN: Would you inform a stranger what groups of islands we see, so that she may tell those at home when she returns?

NARRATOR: The boy stepped up to the prow, and pointed far out over the fields of the sea.

BOY: Listen well to me, voyager. Stretching out there are the twelve islands of Kikai, in groups of five and seven.[158] That one, where the white birds gather in flocks is Whitestone Island, and there, where the smoke is rising, is the Island of Sulphur. To the south, where the mist hangs high, is Chido Island. There is the island where in ancient times the god Sumiyoshi played his flute and danced for the goddess Amaterasu, and the island is called Two Gods because it was there that the two gods played. There you are, my Chinese lady.

NARRATOR: Even as he spoke to her, they had left behind Shikishima,[159] the Land of the Dragon Fly, and the islands that lay ahead of them or what seemed islands, were peaks of clouds, and what seemed mountains were the sky and the sea. Though there was no wind, their fisherman's boat raced ahead as once the bird boat and the rock boat of the gods had travelled through the sky,[160] and to the west where there had been no mountains, mountains appeared. Travelling with the sun, ahead of the moon, they reached the harbour of Sung-chiang, where men were fishing for carp[161] in the same autumn wind that had left the Land of the Rising Sun with them. They went ashore from the boat.

SENDAN: You have really been most kind, my lad. What manner of person are you, you who have sent our boat in a moment's time crossing through heavy seas while seated so tranquilly?

BOY: I have no name such as mortals bear. Since I have lived in the Land of the Rising Sun from ancient times, I am called the Boy of the Great Sea from Sumiyoshi.[162] Now this boy must take his leave of you, and return to Sumiyoshi. I shall await your return to Japan.

NARRATOR: Rowing back his little fishing-boat that had been at the water's edge in the evening waves, he rode upon a favouring breeze and went out to the open sea, far out to the open sea.

The Mountain of the Nine Immortals

NARRATOR: The story is told how T'ao Chu-kung accompanied Kou Chien to Kuai-chi Mountain, where he remained in meditation. He conceived various schemes, and finally overthrew the King of Wu, thus realising Kou Chien's desires, or so it is told.[163]

The present fate of Go Sankei, an example of similar devotion in times distantly removed from those of old, was to wander from one cloud-covered mountain to another with the crown prince he was raising. With the reversal of their fortunes, they had learned to sleep on mats of moss, and the willows in front of the temples and flowers in front of the shrines they once had known gave way to withered trees on mountain peaks.[164] When the mists gathered in the evening, Go Sankei would make of his body a mattress for the infant prince. He even fashioned an imperial palanquin and side-carriage, and wove brocade of ivy. When the dew lay thick in the morning, the prince would ride on the shoulders of the valley monkeys. Two years soon passed, as quickly as yesterday turning into to-day. At dusk of day they were in the mountains, and dawn still found them there. Go Sankei had hidden from the world both his own name and the prince's identity. The rainbow bridge that led to the court had been broken by the clouds.[165] In the cries of the crows and the night-birds deep in the mountains, or even in those of the parrots that came to the tips of the branches to screech, there was nothing to recall the past.

Far from the water, deep in the mountains, Go Sankei had been trampling through fields of bamboo-grass, of black pine and of cypress, and was now wearied by a mountain path that led up to a towering summit. He was climbing the Mountain of the Nine Immortals in Chiang-hua-fu, known to him only by name. As he paused for a while in the breeze that came from the pines, he saw two old men with shaggy eyebrows and white hair, who seemed in perfect harmony, as friends who have long lived together. They had put a *go*-board on a rock, and were profoundly absorbed in a game, placing their black and white stones in scattered triangular pockets or in linked lines like flights of geese, on the 361 intersections of the board. Their minds moved freely, like a spider's thread in the air, and their bodies had become like dried cocoons on a withered branch. This was the art of the game of *go*, far removed from the usages of the world.

GO SANKEI: Is this the lofty world[166] where desire is no more and there are only pure acts?

NARRATOR: He moved the prince to a ledge of rock, and himself leaned his chin on a withered stump. As he gazed on in fascination, it seemed as though he too were purified of the dust of worldly ideas. Go Sankei was driven by inspiration.

GO SANKEI: I should like to speak to you, old men! The game of *go*, removed as it is from mundane desires, is most interesting, but can there be any real pleasure in playing your matches without the Three Friends—music, poetry and wine?[167]

NARRATOR: One old man, without seeming to answer him, said

OLD MAN: If you see a *go*-board, then it is a *go*-board. For the eye that sees *go*-stones, they are *go*-stones. But there is a text that likens the world to a *go*-board.[168] For those who see with their minds, it is the centre of the universe.[169] If we look from here at the mountains, rivers, grasses and trees of all China, what will cloud our view? In each quarter of the board are ninety intersections, for the ninety days of each of the four seasons. Together they come to 360 intersections. How foolish of you not to realise that we spend one day on each intersection!

GO SANKEI: Most interesting! And why should two men choose to oppose one another as their sole pleasure in heaven or on earth?

OLD MAN: If there were not a *yin* and a *yang*, there would be no order in the things of creation.

GO SANKEI: And the winning and the losing?

OLD MAN: Is not the good or bad luck of man dependent on the fortune of the moment?

GO SANKEI: And the black and the white?

OLD MAN: The night and the day.

GO SANKEI: What of the playing of the game?

OLD MAN: The methods of war.

GO SANKEI: Breaking up combinations, checking, opening offensives,

BOTH OLD MEN: War is a game of *go* in which the stones are scattered. The black and the white may be likened to crows that fly back and forth or to snowy herons that gather in flocks, or to the regular procession of the night and the day. No wonder that in olden times a king was so absorbed in watching a game of *go* that he failed to notice the passage of nights and days, and his axe-handle rotted before he knew it.[170]

NARRATOR: The first old man spoke again.

OLD MAN: An heroic general named Coxinga has crossed over from Japan and become an adherent of the Ming. He is now in the midst of fighting. Though the battle is far from here, you may see it clearly, through the power of sight that comes from concentration on the game of *go*.

NARRATOR: His voice and the mountain wind both echoed in the sound of the *go*-stones. The thought suddenly came to Go Sankei.

GO SANKEI: Indeed, this must be the Mountain of the Nine Immortals!

NARRATOR: The Mountain of the Nine Immortals commanded a view of the four hundred and more districts of China. When Go Sankei looked he saw a peak, so faint and hazy that he thought it might be a cloud, but the mist dropped to the foot of the mountain, where it was blown away by the will of the spring breeze. The time was the middle of March. He could see a castle swathed in brocade woven of the green of young willows and the pink of cherry-blossoms.[171] Of what nation is he who is there entrenched? The gates are tall and the moats are deep. Shielding walls are built about the fortifications, and the towers are girded round with imposing bastions. The soaring larks and the returning wild-geese, thinking the many-coloured pennants are flowers, rest their wings on them. The light of the rising sun calmly shining was superimposed on the light of the moon, and showed the beauty of the name of the Land of the Rising Sun. This is Shakutō Castle,[172] captured by Coxinga, Prince of Yen-p'ing.

What need to tell of the white sandalwood bows, the muskets, the Korean spears, the lances and the halberds, of the flags large and small that are inclined to one another, or of the conical pennants, shrine flags and commander's banners that flap in the wind? They dye the sky in every hue, and it is as if the colours of the wisteria, azaleas and primroses were all reflected there. The days of spring pile up like *go*-stones on a board.

BOTH OLD MEN: The young leaves have grown to their full deep green, and through a rift in the clearing clouds we see the Yun-men Pass to Nanking through which the cuckoo flies. Around the tents are tall hedges of verbena. It is the middle of the summer of the year.

GO SANKEI: For thirty miles around abattis have been laid. The generals of of the pass, Saryūko and Uryūko,[173] are there with over three thousand troops.

OLD MAN: The stars on their helmets shine.

GO SANKEI: They beat their drums in disorder.

OLD MAN: Even if one could i-

GO SANKEI: -mi-

BOTH OLD MEN: -tate the crowing of the cock, there would be no way to penetrate so strong a place.[174] Swords disturb the pampas grass in the summer fields, and rope-matches for match-locks glow like fireflies over a marsh, but not even a bird could pass through the gates of this imposing pass.

GO SANKEI: For Coxinga who was raised in Japan, it would be easier to break through this pass, even if it were strengthened with iron and stone, than for a boy to break through a thickness of paper pane, but drawing to mind the catalpa bow of Musashibō Benkei who, long ago, in the Bunji era of Japan,[175] deceived the gate-keeper of Ataka, for one of the most brilliant of military feats, he winks to his soldiers as a signal, and cries

    COXINGA: Hear ye! Hear ye! This is the foot of Mount Li, where lies the grave of Yang Kuei-fei. We are travelling priests gathering funds wherewith to build again the T'ai-chen Palace. Listen to our Book of Gifts, and pray subscribe, oh gate-keeper.

Taking out a scroll of lists of troop arrivals, he prays for the prosperity of his allies and the defeat of his enemies, and reads in a loud voice,

    COXINGA: The autumn moon of enlightenment lies hidden by pitiless clouds from the Tartar rebels, and none can rouse them from the long uncertain dream of life and death. Here once in days gone by, there lived an emperor, who bore the name Hsüan Tsung. When parted from the princess he so dearly loved, he could not master his longing, and tears flowed in strings of jewels from his eyes. Then, turning his thoughts to the Good Way, he built the T'ai-chen Palace. I, a descendant of the magician from Lin-ch'iung,[176] grieving that so holy a place should fall in ruin, am gathering funds throughout the land. Those who fight for the enemy in the coming battle will have their heads transfixed by our spears; those that fight for us will raise cries of triumph after our victory. I bow my head in devotion and respect.

Thus he read aloud to make the heavens resound.

OLD MAN: Saryūko and Uryūko, the generals of the pass, cry

TWO GENERALS: Look! Coxinga has flown into the flames like a summer insect!

GO SANKEI: And is like a cicada that attacks a branch by singing!

OLD MAN: They smiled with pleasure.

COXINGA: There was nothing remarkable in Fan K'uai's style of warfare. See how Asahina of Japan used to break down gates!

NARRATOR: With these words he broke through the bolts of the gate and through the abattis. He felled those who opposed him, and, seizing those who fled before him, tossed them about like pebbles. He slew Saryūko and Uryūko, and went without difficulty through the pass, as time was passing on the *go*-board.

BOTH OLD MEN: An autumn wind that blows across the pass clears away the mist at the mountain castle where the Tartar general Prince Kairi is entrenched. In front of the castle is a cliff, and behind it, the sea. Coxinga, observing the carelessness that comes from confidence that the fortress is unassailable, stages a night attack. As his troops rode on their ponies, the bit-crickets[177] and the pine-moon crickets can clearly be heard, so stealthily do they advance to the moat. Then, when suddenly they lift together their thousands of paper lanterns on poles, it is just like seeing the thousand suns and moons of a thousand worlds at the same instant, and the soldiers of the castle, dumb-founded, stand in utter bewilderment. They put their helmets where their leggings should be, don their armour upside down, and carry their horses on their backs. With great cries of confusion they push open the front gate. When they come out waving their swords, the attacking forces sound horns and bells, and shout war cries. The general, taking up his round signalling fan,[178] flashes it to his troops.

GO SANKEI: In the Japanese style of battle commands, to attack and crush was Yoshitsune's method; to put the enemy off-guard and then strike was Kusunoki's style.

BOTH OLD MEN: As in the pursuit of Kurikara, the downhill charge at Ichi-notani, and the battle on the beach of Yashima, the attacking force was here most powerful.[179] They pound the enemy who, cut to pieces, with-draws within the castle walls. "Now is the time!" cries Coxinga, and in the evening darkness they let fly grenades,[180] the secret Japanese weapon. The roar of their explosion is like that of the central mountain of the universe crumbling. To what should the destroyed shields and towers be compared —to the smoke from the salt that the fishermen burn, or to charcoal kilns? The flames were like the massed red leaves of autumn, or the Hsien-yang Palace when reduced to ashes by the torch of the man from Ch'u.[181]

Coxinga, raising shouts of victory, pulls on the reins of his pony, and rides around, around, and around, and as the days and months go around, it becomes a world without deceit.[182] In the tenth moon after the late autumn rains have fallen, a high-gated citadel on a hill is seized by Coxinga, Chōraku Castle in Hokushū.[183] The tiles of the eaves glittered with the coloured jewels of the first frost. Later there came the night storms mixed with hail, and then, as winter deepens, how wonderful it is to see the snow blowing in, piling up, and burying the walls and the towers!

NARRATOR: Besides this castle, he captured thirty-eight places, including the capitals of Min and Ken Provinces.[184] In anticipation of the future visit of the crown prince, he strengthened the castles at various places with outworks, laid in military stores, and fortified these places with troops. His power showed itself in the very atmosphere.

All this could be seen as clearly as though it were something one held in one's hands. Go Sankei was in an excess of joy. Completely forgetting himself and the others, he clasped the crown prince in his arms, and started to run off toward the mountain with the castle on it. The two old men stopped him.

FIRST OLD MAN: How foolish of you! Everything you saw was many miles from here, though it seemed to happen right before your eyes. You think it has been but a moment since you came to this mountain, but you have spent the springs and autumns of five years here. You do not realise that the battles you witnessed took place in the four seasons of four years. Even while we are thus talking, time is speeding by. Observe how the prince has grown, and look well at your own face reflected in the water-mirror.[185] Since the water is pure, the image will be clear. I, who am reflected in the mirror of your loyal and honest heart, am the first sovereign of the Ming.

SECOND OLD MAN: And I am Liu Po-wen of Ch'ing-t'ien.[186]

BOTH OLD MEN: Our home is on the moon, where the leaves of the katsura-tree are blown by the wind.[187]

LIU: To the eyes of the enlightened, the waxing moon

EMPEROR: seems the same as the waning moon, but

LIU: the ordinary man is confused of mind, and takes it for a go-stone.

EMPEROR: And the fish swimming in the water

LIU: mistakes it for a fishing hook.

EMPEROR: The bird that flies above the clouds

LIU: is frightened, thinking it a bow.

EMPEROR: The moon does not come down

LIU: nor do the waters rise.[188]

BOTH MEN: Behold the moon which waxes only to wane, and wanes only to wax.[189] Hidden for a while by clouds, it is at last clear, and shines in the heavens.[190] Through the divine strength of Japan, the Land of the Rising Sun, a day will soon come for the crowning of the prince.

NARRATOR: Their voices mingled with the wind that blew through the pines. Their bodies disappeared, and only their faces were left behind;[191] then, they too were blown away by the wind from the peak of the mountains on which stood the pines.

Go Sankei thought it must have been a dream, but did not feel drowsy. And, as a sign that five years had really passed, a beard had sprouted on his face. The prince's appearance had changed in an instant; he had grown and already had the bearing of a seven-year-old. His voice that cried, "Go Sankei, Go Sankei" was gentle, and made him think he heard the first cries of orioles deep in snow-covered mountains. Go Sankei bowed his head in reverence, then worshipped heaven and earth. His joy was so great that his legs trembled and he felt for a second time that he was dreaming. He clasped his hands before the prince.

GO SANKEI: I have learned that Coxinga, the son of Tei Shiryū of old, has crossed from Japan, and raised loyal armies for our cause. His military achievements during the past five years have been glorious. Since he has already retaken half of China, I should like to communicate with him and inform him that your majesty is here.

NARRATOR: Hardly had he spoken than, from far up the valley opposite, he was called.

IKKAN: You over there! Are you not Go Sankei, President of the Council of War? Go Sankei!

NARRATOR: He looked carefully in that direction.

GO SANKEI: Are you not Tei Shiryū of old?

IKKAN: Go Sankei! How wonderful it is that you are still alive! My son's wife, from his native village, has escorted the Princess Sendan here.

NARRATOR: He beckoned to them.

SENDAN: Dear Go Sankei! Thanks to the self-sacrificing loyalty of your wife, Lady Ryūka, I was carried to Japan in a boat that drifted over the sad shoals of the world. Now, by the kindness of Ikkan and his children, I have met you again to my great surprise. Where is Lady Ryūka? What has happened to your baby? I should like to see them. Please take me there.

NARRATOR: Her longings were understandable.

GO SANKEI: Alas, my wife perished from the severe wounds she received at that time. The empress also lost her life to enemy guns, and I cut open her womb to deliver her child. Then I killed my own son, and deceived the

151

L

enemy into thinking he was the empress's. I have brought the prince up safely in the mountains. He has already passed his first seven years here.

NARRATOR: When he had related these things, the princess uttered a cry of dismay and fell to the ground. Heedless of the eyes of other people, she lamented, and it was touching to see her expressions of sympathy. Ikkan, looking back to the foot of the mountain, cried.

IKKAN: That rogue Prince Bairoku has discovered the princess and is coming after us with thousands of troops. Though I put forth the strength left in these old bones, stand my ground, and defend her to the death, her life will still be in grave danger. I should like to take her over there to safety somehow, but I am unfamiliar with these mountains. Is there no way to cross the gorge?

GO SANKEI: No, it is sixty miles around the mountain, and the gorge is so profound that its bottom cannot be told. Our place of safety cannot be brought over here, and we cannot cross over there. What shall we do?

NARRATOR: He worshipped the empty air.

GO SANKEI: First Emperor of the Ming and Liu Po-wen of Ch'ing-t'ien, who just now appeared to me in a vision! Lend your heavenly, miraculous strength and save us from this extraordinary peril!

NARRATOR: The crown prince joined with him in devout prayer. The princess and Komutsu brought their hands together in worship.

SENDAN AND KOMUTSU: Hail to the great god Sumiyoshi of Japan, gatherer of happiness boundless as the sea!

NARRATOR: They earnestly prayed with undivided hearts. Heaven was affected and earth heard their prayers, for there trailed a stream of cloud from the mouth of a cave, to form a bridge like the cloud-bridge of heaven built by the magpies,[192] or, though it was not night-time, like the stone bridge of Kume, built by the god of Katsuragi.[193] They crossed as over a road in dreams, and having no feeling of motion, found themselves climbing up the peak on the other side of the gorge, their legs shaking with fright.

Soon afterwards the rebel soldiers came rushing up in swarms.

SOLDIERS: What a piece of luck to have found the Crown Prince and Go Sankei too! We've been casting for sardines and caught a whale! Aim your bows and guns on them! Kill them! Shoot them down!

NARRATOR: Thus they clamoured. Prince Bairoku gave orders.

BAIROKU: Wait! They have plenty of space behind them to make an escape. Your bows and guns will be of no use. Look at the cloud bridge! That is something I have never seen before! It must be a Japanese-style abacus or folding bridge built by that rogue Coxinga! He has made a blunder in military strategy by helping his enemy! Follow me, men! Over the bridge!

NARRATOR: His fivehundred and more troops, letting out great cries, pushed and crowded to be first across the bridge over the gorge.[194] When they were about half-way across, a wind from the mountains and a wind from the gorge sprang up, and blew the cloud bridge to bits. The general and all his troops plummeted down and fell on top of one another. Their foreheads were split open and their skulls crushed. Their cries and howls rose higher and higher, and they filled the gorge with their bodies. Go Sankei and Tei Shiryū cried, "Success! Hurrah!" and they threw at the Tartars whatever rocks and logs they could lay their hands on, until there was not a single man of them alive, and all had been turned into mincemeat. Only Prince Bairoku, the commander, had been able to climb hand over hand up the vines along the base of the rocks. Then Go Sankei, lifting up the *go*-board of the mountain immortals, cried.

GO SANKEI: This *go*-board is strengthened with vine, and is harder than a rock. It's bitter and doesn't taste good, but won't you have a taste? It's your turn to play, but you're not much of an opponent! Now see what a strong game is like!

NARRATOR: When Bairoku showed his head, Go Sankei struck it squarely, and when he showed his face, he struck it with a bang, over and over, until Bairoku's brains and skull had been smashed, and he perished.[195]

IKKAN: Just as I wished it! There's an example of something like this in Japan, Tadanobu of the *go*-board from Yoshino.[196] His board was made of torreya-wood, while this one is of vine from the Mountain of the Nine Immortals.

We have taken the lead in our battle! Breaking up their strong points, surrounding them, splitting them in attacks from front and behind, bursting through their traps, we will defeat them, and then, picking up the enemy pieces, we will wager our country and our dynasty on one final effort, and go on to triumph.[197] Thus is the way of loyalty, thus is the way.

NARRATOR: Hand in hand they entered the castle of Foochow.

ACT FIVE

NARRATOR: No man can take Mount T'ai under his arm and jump over the North Sea, but for a king to act in a kingly manner is not an impossibility, or so it is told.[198]

Coxinga, Prince of Yen-p'ing used military forces effortlessly, as though he were turning them in the palm of his hand. He slaughtered over fifty cities, and his military power grew with every day. His wife had escorted the Princess Sendan from his native village, and Go Sankei had accompanied the Crown Prince from the Mountain of the Nine Immortals. The imperial sash and seal had been offered to the prince, and he was given the reign name of Emperor Eiryaku.[199]

In the fields of the Dragon-Horse a siege-engine[200] half-a-mile square had been constructed. The curtains that hung round his camp and the curtains at the doors were of brocade. Over the camp flew pennants of the Great Shrine of Ise, and the sacred staff with cut-paper was displayed. The Crown Prince was installed in a palace of his own.

Coxinga was seated on a stool in the centre of the camp. President of the Council of War Go Sankei and General of Cavalry Kanki both sat on camp stools to his left and right. There were military discussions of all sorts about the decisive struggle between the Tartars and the Mings. Go Sankei picked up his military fan.

GO SANKEI: Nothing is better than to have plans that arrive at great results from small beginnings.

NARRATOR: He took out a bamboo tube.

GO SANKEI: This tube contains honey and a great many hornets. We should make thousands of such tubes, and have our front line troops carry them. Then if they throw away the tubes and retreat hastily on contact with the enemy, the Tartar forces, with their usual gluttony, will certainly think that they contain food, and will pick them up. Then, as soon as they have removed the stoppers, tens of thousands of hornets will swarm out and sting the rebels severely. They will flee in confusion, and we can kill them by firing on them from all sides. Look!

NARRATOR: When he removed the stopper, a great many hornets came buzzing out.

GO SANKEI: If, on the other hand, the rebel soldiers make fun of the tubes, saying, "What a silly childish scheme to frighten us! Let's burn them and make them ashamed of themselves!" pile them up, and set them on fire, at the instant that the powder contained in the bottom of the tubes catches fire, it will explode with a roar, and there won't be a single soldier left alive for half a mile around.

NARRATOR: As soon as he applied a rope-match to the tube, it shot off flames that made it clear that it would really work as he said.

Gojōgun Kanki then brought out a basket filled with fruit.

KANKI: Go Sankei's unusual scheme is feasible, but I have another plan. We should make two or three thousand baskets like this, and fill them with all kinds of poisoned sweetmeats, rice-balls and appetisers. Then we should stack them up within the camp. We'll draw the enemy on, until they're close to the camp, and then retreat about ten miles, under guise of having been defeated. The Tartars, flushed with victory, will enter the camp after one of their usual long marches. When their eyes fall on the food, they will certainly think they have come to a treasure mountain, and the officers and men will struggle to see who will be first in seizing the food and gobbling it down. As soon as the food touches their lips, they will vomit up poisoned blood one after another, and we will thus have massacred them without staining our swords.[201]

NARRATOR: Each of them had taxed his brain in military planning, and offered very different suggestions. Coxinga nodded and said:

COXINGA: You have each put forth a plan with some merits, and I have no criticisms to offer. However, my mother's last words have penetrated my soul and I cannot forget them. "Bear in mind that the King of Tartary is the enemy of us both, and realise your great plan! We have killed ourselves so that your spirits would not slacken." Her words have soaked into my bones and permeate my entire being. I have never forgotten them for a single instant. What is the use of such complicated plans? I shall be guilty of unfiliality to my mother, even if I accomplish a million military exploits, even if I am loyal to my sovereign and kind and just to the people, unless I attack boldly, seize both the King of Tartary and Ri Tōten with all my strength, and cut them to shreds.

NARRATOR: Tears flowed copiously from his mirror-clear eyes, and the whole camp, high and low alike, from Go Sankei and Kanki down, wetted their sleeves with their tears.

COXINGA: Even though she were a woman, she did not forget her old home, and paid reverence to the land that gave her birth. Until her last breath she thought of the honour of Japan. I, too, was born in Japan, and I shall not deny the country of my birth. Behold! I bow in devotion before the great goddess Amaterasu. It has entirely been due to the divine strength of Japan that I have risen from the common people, captured many cities, become chief of the lords of the empire, and am entrusted with every service to his majesty.

I shall place in the front ranks the barbarians I subdued in the bamboo forest, whose hair has been cut in the Japanese manner. Then, when it is announced that we have received reinforcements from Japan, the Tartar barbarians will be frightened, for they have heard that Japan has always excelled in the use of the bow and arrow, and is famous for her training in the military arts. While they are hesitating what to do, we shall draw close and seize the city. This is the plan that my wife and I have devised. Minamoto no Ushiwaka![202] Lead your soldiers here!

NARRATOR: When he lifted his military fan in command, Komutsu replied, "Yes, sir!" and came forward. Her hair was tied with a cord,[203] while her

155

troops had their heads shaven in the Japanese manner. She presented a most resplendent appearance in her Chinese brocade of Japanese pale blue.

Princess Sendan came rushing forth from within the curtains of the temporary palace.

SENDAN: Coxinga, this flag is your father's ensign, and here is a note in your father's writing, most grievous tidings.

NARRATOR: Coxinga sank on his knees and read it aloud.

LETTER: I returned to this land thinking rashly I might repay my debt to the late Ming emperor, but I have achieved nothing, and merit no praise. What pleasure may I anticipate from the years of old age left me? To-night I shall seek death in battle by the walls of Nanking, to leave behind a fair name in Japan and China. I am now in my seventy-third year. Tei Shiryū Ikkan.

NARRATOR: Before he had finished reading it, Coxinga sprang to his feet.

COXINGA: Now is my hatred of the enemy complete. The enemy of my mother is now also the enemy of my father. I need no artifices. What good will military science do? Everything assuredly devolves on one person alone, Coxinga. I shall ride into the city of Nanking and twist off the heads of the King of Tartary and Ri Tōten. If I do not avenge my father's death on the spot, I shall die in battle and accompany my parents on the journey to the other world. I take leave of you for this life.

NARRATOR: He was about to rush off when his two generals seized him by the sleeves.

KANKI: You have no feeling for other people! They are the enemies of my wife and also of my father-in-law.

GO SANKEI: And the enemies of my wife and my baby too.

COXINGA: We are none of us inferior to the enemy. Together we three are a match for the world. Come on!

NARRATOR: They galloped off. No demon, however cunning, would have dared face the sword-points of these three men.

Tei Shiryū Rōikkan had cleverly attired himself in his black-braided armour as he set out in the dark of the evening mists. He rapped on the great wooden door of the outer wall of Nanking.

IKKAN: I am Coxinga's father, Ikkan. I am an old man. My knees are weak, and I am not equal to the demands of an ordinary battle. And yet I cannot listen idly when the young people talk of battle. I have come to the gates of the city and wish to die quickly in battle, thus to end my life as I have always hoped. Come out, Ri Tōten, and take if you please this white-haired head. No other kindness will I ask of you while I live.

NARRATOR: A strapping fellow six feet tall called out from within the castle.

MAN: That's easy, Ikkan. I'll take you on as an opponent.

NARRATOR: He opened the gate and came out swinging his sword. "I'm ready," cried Ikkan. It seemed as though Ikkan would be finished off in two or three strokes of the sword, but suddenly he closed in and cut off his opponent's head. He cried out in a great voice filled with displeasure.

IKKAN: I may be old, but my head is not to be yielded to common soldiers like that one. Come out and fight me, Ri Tōten! Anyone else who comes out will be dealt with in the same way.

NARRATOR: He stood there glaring at the city. The Great King of Tartary appeared on the tower of the Shou-yang Gate.

KING: That rogue is Rōikkan, Coxinga's father. I have many little things to ask him. Don't kill him, but capture him and bring him to me.

NARRATOR: Forty or fifty men brandishing clubs went out and surrounded Ikkan. They beat him furiously, not allowing him an opportunity to defend himself, then twisted him down, tied him up, and dragged him off into the castle. Ikkan was chagrined beyond all words.

Shortly afterwards, Kanki and Go Sankei, with Coxinga leading them, rode up to the front gate. Following them, sixty thousand troops, with Komutsu as general of the rear guard, pressed forward, resolved to make this the day of decisive battle. Coxinga gave orders.

COXINGA: We still cannot tell if my father is alive or dead. There are twelve main gates and six small ones around the city of Nanking. If even a single avenue of escape is left open, the enemy will certainly take it. Keep a sharp lookout on all sides and then attack.

NARRATOR: In response to his words, they took their stations, struck their quivers, and uttered war cries so fierce it seemed as if heaven would be overturned. Komutsu advanced to the fore wielding with skill her short sword of the Ushiwaka style.

KOMUTSU: This young warrior chooses no opponent, chooses no time, nor even any location, but will take on as an opponent anyone wishing to die!

NARRATOR: She proclaimed these words boldly, cut into the enemy ranks, and fought furiously.

Although many of the rebel soldiers were killed, there was no way of capturing the city of Nanking, in which seven hundred thousand troops were entrenched. Coxinga rode about everywhere, hoping to learn in some way whether his father were dead of alive, but it was in vain. Then he proclaimed at the front ranks:

COXINGA: During the five years since I've come to China, I have fought a number of battles, but never one without swords. Today, strangely enough we shall not lay our hands on our sword-hilts. You Tartars who are such masters of horsemanship, and who pride yourselves so on your skill with your swords, come out and fight!

TARTARS: Let's kill that disgusting braggart!

NARRATOR: They came at him shouting, each anxious to take him on. When they approached, Coxinga's men twisted away their swords, beat them, crushed them, hit them, squashed them, and wrested away, twisted away, pushed away and broke away their lances, spears and halberds. If the on-rushing enemy soldiers came in contact with their feet, they trampled them to death. If the enemy touched their hands, they twisted off their heads or strangled them to death. Thus they tossed the enemy like pebbles before them. The mounted warriors they seized together with their horses, and hurled them into the air. Picking up the horses by the four legs, they tossed them before them, then the riders, then more horses, and finally some rocks for good measure. It did not seem like the work of human beings. The Tartars, mighty though they were, were being forced back. Then, just when it seemed as though the city would fall, Ri Tōten came out, the King of Tartary ahead of him, with Ikkan, who was tied to the front of a shield.

RI TŌTEN: Coxinga, you crawled out of your little country of Japan and have trampled all over China. You have captured a number of cities, and now have even approached the seat of the Great King. Because of your countless outrages and your effrontery to-day, we have tied up your father in this way. Shall we cut his belly in the Japanese manner? Or, if you and your father will return to Japan immediately, we are willing to spare his life. If you won't agree, we shall perform hara-kiri on him while you watch. Give us your answer at once.

NARRATOR: Coxinga, who had been in high spirits until that moment, suddenly felt his eyes grow dizzy; his strength ebbed and he was utterly dejected. The troops also fell in low spirits, and the camp became perfectly still. Ikkan gnashed his teeth.

IKKAN: Coxinga! What are you hesitating about? Why are you delaying? What use would there be for me, already over seventy, to have my days prolonged? Have you forgotten that I too have been informed how gallantly your mother died? It will be a disgrace in the eyes of all ages to come, and a source of ill fame for your country if it is said that out of anxiety for this wrinkled old man's life you allowed your judgment to stray, and thus ruined the great cause which otherwise would have been won by now. Would it not be a disgrace to Japan if in other countries Japanese are given the bad name of people who surrender themselves to love and know nothing of duty? Have you forgotten that, although she was a woman, your mother respected the place she was born, and gave up her life for the honour of

Japan? When matters have reached so decisive a point, you should attack them without wavering in your attention, even if I am torn to pieces before your eyes, and go on to succeed. Where have you lost your resolution to restore the Mings? Ah, you are weak-willed, you are ignoble!

NARRATOR: Stamping on the ground, he admonished his son. Coxinga, stung by his father's words, plucked up his courage and rushed at the Great King. Then Ri Tōten pressed his sword against Coxinga's father. Coxinga cried out, his senses failed him, and he stood stockstill. His uncertain legs could not go ahead. Had the central mountain of the universe then begun to crumble over his head, Coxinga would not have been startled, so bewildered did he seem. Kanki and Go Sankei exchanged glances, suddenly rushed forward, and bowed their heads before the King of Tartary.

BOTH MEN: We have been successful up to now, oh King of Tartary, but your fortunes have been more powerful. Coxinga's luck came to an end when you captured Ikkan. His future is empty of hopes. If you will be so merciful as to spare our lives, we shall take Coxinga's head and offer it to you. May we have your answer affirmed with an oath?

NARRATOR: No sooner had they spoken than the King of Tartary cried out,

KING: Wonderful! Wonderful!

NARRATOR: Just then they sprang at him and kicked him down in a fury. They were holding him by the throat when Coxinga, an instant later, rushed up to cut away his father's bonds. He seized Ri Tōten and tied him to the face of the shield to which Ikkan had been bound, in the same severe manner at the elbows and wrists. The three men looked at one another and let out a great shout of joy, so powerful that it resounded throughout the country. The troops regained their high spirits. When the Crown Prince and the princess arrived, Coxinga declared,

COXINGA: I shall put to punishment these rogues in your presence without delay. Since this man is the King of Tartary, barbarian country though that is, we shall send him back to his country after we have horse-whipped him.

NARRATOR: He divided those about him into two groups with five hundred whips, and they beat the king until he was half-dead, and then let him make his escape.

COXINGA: And now we come to Ri Tōten, the man guilty of the eight great crimes, the five inhuman acts, and the ten sins, the man who is the cause of all that has happened. To avoid partiality, I, Coxinga, will myself cut off his head. You two hold his arms!

NARRATOR: Standing on three sides of Ri Tōten, they all at once raised a great cry, and the head was slashed off. Then all wished the Emperor

Eiryaku a reign of ten thousand years, and expressed their hopes for the long peace and tranquillity of the country, and they prayed that by the blessing of prosperity for the nation and the people, prosperity filled without end by the divine virtue, military virtue and illustrious virtue of the sovereign of Great Japan, the five grains would continue to yield in abundance for ever and ever and ever.

VII

NOTES FOR CHAPTERS I-VI

Chapter I

1. "Coxinga." The name here used for the leading character of Chikamatsu's play is the one by which he was best known to Europeans. In the play he is called by two names, Watōnai 和藤內 and Kokusenya 國性爺. The latter name is curious in that the second character is Chikamatsu's mistake for 姓. The pronunciation is also unusual because normal Japanese usage would require a reading of "Kokuseiya". The pronunciation of "sen" was probably an attempt to approximate the current southern Chinese "seng", but Mizutani Yumihiko (*Chikamatsu Kessaku Zenshū*, Volume III, page 515) suggested that Chikamatsu was influenced by a fashion of the Kyōto dialect of his time to pronounce "sei" as "sen" in certain words. *Kokusenya Kassen* is written 國性爺合戰.

2. Takano (in *Edo Bungaku-shi*, Volume II, p. 451) calculated that some 240,000 persons saw the play during its first run in Osaka. He estimated the population of the city at that time to have been about 300,000. The next most popular *jōruri* play ran about fourteen months, (*cf.* Kitani Hōgin: *Dai-Chikamatsu Zenshū*, Volume III, p. 81) but Chikamatsu's plays usually ran from one to three months. When one play had run a hundred days it was considered so significant that the words "hundred days" were added to its title. *Love Suicides at Sonezaki* (曾根崎心中), Chikamatsu's next most popular work, ran for only seven months. (*Cf.* Sonoda: *Jōruri Sakusha no Kenkyū*, pp. 86-93 for dates of plays.)

3. Kitani: *op. cit.*, Volume III, p. 102.

4. A good account of the career of Masatayū 政太夫 is found in Kitani: *Dai-Chikamatsu to Takemoto Masatayū*, pp. 21-5.

5. At the Takemoto Theatre (竹本座) alone it was revived in 1720, 1731 and 1750. *Cf.* Shuzui Kenji: (article in) *Nihon Bungaku Daijiten*, Vol. II, p. 102.

6. Mizutani: *op. cit.*, p. 515.

7. Watōnai (where *wa* 和 stands for Japan, and *tō* 藤 for 唐 , China) is the name by which Coxinga, the hero of the play, is known before the imperial surname is conferred on him. The name may have been derived from that of Odera Tōnai 小寺藤內 (the historical 小野寺十內), a minor figure in Chikamatsu's play *Goban Taiheiki*. The two personages bear no resemblance, however. The name may also be a kind of joke, where the characters 和唐內 are read *wakaranai*, meaning "I don't know". Ikkan (一官) is Watōnai's father.

8. *Amboyna* in *The Works of John Dryden*, ed. Sir Walter Scott, Volume V, p. 81. The play was acted and printed in 1673. Scott said of it, "This play is beneath criticism, and I can hardly hesitate to term it the worst production Dryden ever wrote" (p.3).

9. *Ibid.*, p. 80.

10. *Ibid.*, p. 87.

11. Of course there have been Japanese zealots of all times who have believed that Japan was the all-important country, particularly those of the Shintō school like Kitabatake Chikafusa, who wrote the *Jinnō Shōtōki* 神皇正統記, a work setting out to prove the divine descent of the emperor. But such men were few in number in comparison to the many important figures who wrote their serious works in Chinese, painted in the Chinese manner, and used allusions to Chinese history and literature as often as they were able.

12. The marriage of Japan and China is literally the subject of *Taishokkan*, 大職冠, a play Chikamatsu wrote five years before *Kokusenya Kassen*, 國性爺合戰. It concludes with a Japanese princess leaving for China where she is to marry the Chinese sovereign (in *Chikamatsu Jōruri-shū*, ed. Tadami Keizō, Volume III, pp. 1-53).

13. Particularly important was the painter Shen Nan-p'in 沈南蘋 who visited Nagasaki about 1735.

14. The play and its connections with Chikamatsu's is discussed in Yamaguchi: *Kokusenya Kassen no Beni-nagashi*, pp. 236-8. Yamaguchi presents a fairly strong case for his belief that Chikamatsu read and was influenced by *Kokusenya Tegara Nikki* 國仙野手柄日記, but there is no positive proof that this was true. Nishiki Bunryū 錦文流 enjoyed considerable fame in his time. Takano: *op. cit.*, Volume II, p. 445, put forward the suggestion that Chikamatsu might have met Coxinga's younger brother, Shichizaemon, if the latter visited Ise in 1706. Takano believed that since Shichizaemon was sixty years old, and it was customary to make a pilgrimage at that age, he may have been one of the large number of pilgrims from Nagasaki recorded for that year. Takano offered an alternative suggestion, that Chikamatsu saw the Ryūkyū Islands native who visited Osaka in 1714 and may have been inspired by his exotic costume to write a play on a non-Japanese subject. These suggestions are interesting but of doubtful validity.

15. *Kokusenya Gonichi Kassen* 國性爺後日合戰 and *Tōsen-banashi Ima Kokusenya*. 唐船噺今國性爺. The former is a real sequel to *Kokusenya Kassen*. The latter deals with the Chu I-kuei 朱一貴 rebellion on Formosa in 1721.

16. Kitani: *Dai-Chikamatsu Zenshū*, Volume XIV, p. 207.

17. Nishizawa Ippū (1665-1731): *Konjaku Ayatsuri Nendai-ki*, p. 518.

18. This set of definitions was supplied by Professor Serge Elisséeff.

19. In his *Shinjū Ten no Amijima* 心中天の網島 (1720).

20. In *Naniwa Miyage*, p. 47, Hozumi Ikan (穗積以貫) compared the headdresses with the story in Chuang Tzŭ of two kingdoms which exist on the antennae of a small insect.

21. *Cf.* such puns as "currants-currents" in Eliot's *The Waste Land*. Elizabethan poets sometimes sought the same effect.
    Their reasons straining through their bodies still
    Waterish and troubled, as thro' clouds and mists;
    And wrastler-like, rush'd ever on their lists
    Too straight and choked with press to comprehend
    The struggling contemplation of their end.
    (quoted in C. Day Lewis: *The Poetic Image*, p. 42). There is a play on the word "straining" (meaning both as the light of sun or moon is strained through the clouds, and the active sense of strain which leads to the wrestler simile).

22. Ihara Toshirō in Tsubouchi: *Chikamatsu no Kenkyū*, p. 293.

23. The game of *go* 碁 is of Chinese origin. It is played on a board with 324 squares. One player has white stones and the other black, and they take turns in placing their stones on the intersections formed by the squares. The object of the game is to surround the pieces of one's opponent. It is traditionally a game that teaches the secrets of military strategy. It figures importantly in the fourth act of the play and is further discussed in appropriate footnotes.

24. It may be interesting to compare this summary with one by Mr. B. Kure in his *The Historical Development of Marionette Theatre in Japan* (p. 45). "The well-known play *Kokusenya Gassen* was his work. In the plot is cleverly woven the two features—bravery and lovableness. The plot is of two faithful lovers who could not be united in this world but they consoled themselves in their belief that they would be united in the world to come."

Chapter II

1. Katō: *Chikamatsu Kenkyū*, p. 34. The play coupled with *Kokusenya Kassen* is *Keisei Hangonkō* (傾城反魂香). Katō goes on to say of *Kokusenya Kassen* that it is a work abounding in "strength and feeling" and that it "lifts to the highest degree the power of the *jōruri*". He further states, "It is an unprecedented work which has never since been excelled." (p.35).

2. The word *jōruri* is used to describe the entertainment which combines puppets and music to the narration of a text. The name itself is derived from that of the Princess Jōruri about whom various ballads were sung in medieval Japan. These ballads were the first play-books used in the later puppet *jōruri* theatre.

3. *Genji Monogatari* (源氏物語) by Murasaki Shikibu (紫式部).

4. *Cf.* Grube: *Chinesische Schattenspiele*, p. xv. Grube traces the word *kugutsu* 傀儡 from the older Chinese word 窟礧子. "In the Fukien dialect the word still has a k-ending, kuk-le, and this word is none other than the Middle Greek *koûkla* 'puppet'. The word evidently reached the Chinese through the Turks or the Iranians of Central Asia or perhaps from Kucha. The Osmans obtained the word from the Byzantines (Osman *kukla* 'puppet', *kuklaci* 'marionette operators'). The word is the same in the Slavic languages (Russian and Bulgarian *kukla*). . . Not only the word but the thing itself was taken over by the Chinese in the T'ang Dynasty."
   Against this view there is the one of certain Japanese scholars that the word is the same as the ancient Japanese *kugutsu* meaning "basket". They contend that the puppets were produced from a basket carried by the operators. But this seems an unlikely derivation as the operators used a box and not a basket, and even if they had used a basket, the extremely rare word *kugutsu* would almost certainly not have been used to describe it.

5. Ōe: *Kairaishi-ki* 傀儡師記. In *Gunsho Ruijū, kan* 135.

6. Kuroki: *Jōruri-shi*, p. 37.

7. *Ibid.*, p. 40.

8. A good introduction to the Nō is Waley's *The Nō Plays of Japan*.

9. *Jōruri Monogatari* 淨瑠璃物語. The work is also frequently known as *Jōruri Jūnidan Zōshi* 淨瑠璃十二段草紙. Wakatsuki, in *Kinsei (Shoki) Kokugeki no Kenkyū*, p. 593, states that he has seen close to forty versions of the story.

10. Wakatsuki: *(Ningyō) Jōruri-shi Kenkyū*, p. 17. (The work is henceforth referred to as *JK*.)

11. *Cf.* account in Kuroki: *op. cit.*, pp. 29-35.

12. Sonoda in *Jōruri Sakusha no Kenkyū*, pp. 6-9, gives this and other accounts including one which claims that the samisen was derived from the Portuguese rabeca. He states that all sources are agreed that the instrument was introduced to Japan from the Ryūkyū Islands. The characters used are *jabisen* 蛇皮綿 and *shamisen* 三味綿.

13. Terashima: *Wakan Sanzai Zue* (1715) *kan* 16, p. 7a, b.

14. The terms "stiff" (硬い) and "flexible" (軟い) used of the styles of Sawazumi 澤澄 and Takino 瀧野, refer to the nature of the music to which the texts were chanted. Presumably the "stiff" style was a harsher, more powerful type of music than the gentler, more melodious "flexible" style.

15. Quoted in Wakatsuki: *JK*, p. 68. From *Tōkaidō Meisho-ki* 東海道名所記 (*c.* 1658) by Asai Ryōi 淺井了意.

16. Quoted *ibid., loc. cit.* From *Yōshūfu-shi* 雍州府志 (1684) by Kurokawa Genichi 黑川玄逸.

17. Wakatsuki: *JK*, p. 70.

18. Kuroki: *op. cit.*, p. 48. The names of the pieces in Japanese are *Jōruri Monogatari*, *Amida Munewari* 阿彌陀胸割 and *Go-ō no Hime* 牛王の姫.

19. Wakatsuki: *JK*, p. 69.

20. *Ibid.*, p. 72. This is interesting in the light of the statement in the preface to Hozumi: *Naniwa Miyage*, p. 2, that a woman first combined puppets to the existing type of *jōruri*, but the woman chanter mentioned there, Rokuji Namuemon 六字南無右衛門 flourished much later.

21. Wakatsuki: *JK*, p. 87.

22. Amida or Amitābha (in Sanskrit) is the manifestation of Buddha worshipped by some sects which believe that it is only necessary to repeat the prayer *Namu Amida Butsu* to gain salvation.

23. Wakatsuki: *Chikamatsu Ningyō Jōruri no Kenkyū*, pp. 79, 133, 359.

24. Wakatsuki: *JK*, p. 70.

25. *Ibid.*, p. 94 ff. Sugiyama Shichirozaemon 杉山七郎左衛門 was known later as Tango-no-jō 丹後掾. In the sections following I have given only one or two names for each chanter although any of them may have been known by many different names in his lifetime.

26. *Ibid.*, p. 104 ff. Satsuma Jōun 薩摩淨雲, also called Koheita 小平太.

27. *Ibid.*, p. 164.

28. *Ibid.*, pp. 109-10.

29. Kuroki: *op. cit.*, p. 42.

30. Wakatsuki: *JK*, p. 625.

31. Kuroki: *op. cit.*, p. 65.

32. Wakatsuki: *JK*, p. 595.

33. *Ibid.*, p. 154.

34. *Ibid.*, p. 163.

35. Kuroki: *op. cit.*, p. 116 ff. Izumi-dayū is written 和泉太夫. Kimpira 金平 is the name of the bold hero of the highly adventurous stories that bear his name.

36. Wakatsuki: *JK*, pp. 187-8.

37. *Ibid.*, pp. 188-90.

38. Kuroki: *op. cit.*, pp. 118-9 and Wakatsuki: *JK*, p. 190 give a few details concerning Oka Seibei 岡清兵衛.

39. Wakatsuki: *JK*, p. 196.

40. Kuroki: *op. cit.*, pp. 82-3. Wakasa-no-kami is written 若狹守.

41. *Ibid.*: p. 135. Toraya Kidayū 虎屋喜太夫.

42. Wakatsuki: *JK*, p. 232. Toraya Gendayū 虎屋源太夫. Shijōgawara 四條河原. Inoue Harima-no-jō 井上播摩掾.

43. 愛護若.

44. Kuroki: *Chikamatsu Igo*, pp. 213-4.

45 Kuroki: *Chikamatsu Monzaemon*, pp. 121-4. Kuroki believed that this play, *Kazan-in Kisaki Arasoi* (花山院后諍) was a juvenile work by Chikamatsu, but his opinion has not been shared by all critics.

46. Wakatsuki: *JK*, p. 437.

47. Wakatsuki: *JK*, p. 431.

48. *Ibid.*, p. 441.

49. *Ibid.*, p. 630.

50. *Ibid.*, p. 611.

51. *Ibid.*, pp. 626-30.

52. The career of Uji Kaga-no-jō 宇治加賀掾 is described in Wakatsuki: *JK*, pp. 463-92.

53. *Ibid.*, p. 566. The text of the diary (*Matsudaira Yamato-no-kami Nikki* 松平大和守日記) is found in Wakatsuki: *Kinsei (Shoki) Kokugeki no Kenkyū*, pp. 13-180. The diary contains entries between 1658 and 1695 and offers much valuable information on the *jōruri* works presented during those years.

54. *E.g.* Takahashi: *Chikamatsu no Gikyoku Taiyō*. *Yotsugi Soga* 世繼曽我 was presented in 1685.

55. Wakatsuki: *JK*, pp. 495-551 has an account of Yamamoto Tosa-no-jō 山本土佐掾 (also often called Kakudayū 角太夫).

56. *Ibid.*, p. 542.

57. 竹本義太夫, known also as Shimizu Ridayū 清水理太夫 and as Chikugo-no-jō 筑後掾.

58. Sonoda: *Jōruri Sakusha no Kenkyū*, p. 33ff. contains a biography of Gidayū.

59. 清水理兵衛.

60. Wakatsuki (in *Chikamatsu Ningyō Jōruri no Kenkyū*, pp. 656-7) states that the successive chanters sometimes had assistants who either took parts in a scene or chanted in rough unison with the regular chanter. This would explain how the broken lines and words of the fourth act of *The Battles of Coxinga* could be recognised as having been spoken by several people.

61. Many books give 1685, but Wakatsuki (*JK*, p. 658) and Kuroki (*Jōruri-shi*, p. 224) argue convincingly for 1684.

62. *Yotsugi Soga*, *Aisome-gawa* 藍染川 and *Iroha Monogatari* 以呂波物語.

63. *Koyomi* 暦.

64. *Kenjo no Tenarai narabi ni Shingoyomi* 賢女手習並新暦.

65. Wakatsuki: *JK*, p. 660.

66. *Shusse Kagekiyo* 出世景清.

67. *Sonezaki Shinjū* 曽根崎心中.

68. Kuroki: *Jōruri-shi*, p. 226.

69. Wakatsuki: *JK*, p. 627. See also Plate II.

70. The art of puppeteering continued to develop after Chikamatsu's death. In 1727 puppets could open and shut their mouths and eyes, and could grasp things with their hands. In 1733 puppets could move their fingertips. The most important development came in 1734 with the adoption of the three-man puppet, still in use to-day. A final refinement of 1736 was enabling puppets to move their eyebrows. (Miyake: *Bunraku no Kenkyū*, p. 346.)

71. Descriptions of the appearance of the stage in Chikamatsu's time are rare. The puppet theatre apparently seated about 400 persons. The stage was some forty or fifty feet across. Only in the time of Takeda Izumo 竹田出雲 was more scenery used than a simple drop curtain. His innovations included golden sliding-doors and hangings of silk and satin. (*cf.* Takano: *Chikamatsu no Kushō*, p. 33). Competition between the Takemoto 竹本 and Toyotake 豊竹 Theatres was probably responsible for the increasing splendour of the costumes and sets. *Cf.* Ichiraku: *Chikuhō Koji*, p. 536.

72. 豊竹若太夫.

73. 紀海音.

74. Kuroki: *Jōruri-shi*, p. 388 ff.

75. Ichiraku: *Chikuhō Koji*, p. 543.

76. The names of Chikamatsu Monzaemon 近松門左衞門 include Nobumori 登盛, (名); Heiandō 平安堂, Sōrinshi 巢林子, Fuisannin 不移山人 (號); and Heiba 平馬 (通稱). Tōshirō 登四郎 is not commonly given as one of his names.

77. Futagion Shujin: *Gikyoku Shōsetsu Tsūshi*, pp. 245–9.

78. The pioneer article by Tanabe, *Chikamatsu Monzaemon no Shoshutsu ni tsuite*, was published in the periodical *Kokugo to Kokubungaku*, August 1925. Tanabe discovered a genealogy of the Sugimori family which established Chikamatsu's place of birth and family background. Mori Shū, in *Chikamatsu Monzaemon* (pp. 12–15), presents a reinterpretation of the genealogy.

79. The characters 近松 may be pronounced Chikamatsu, Kinshō and Gonshō.

80. Even the author of *Higashi-matsura-gun-shi*, the history of the subprefecture in which the Chikamatsu (or, more properly, Kinshō) Temple mentioned in Futagion's account is located, is unable to show any connection between the dramatist and the temple, although he strives desperately to do so. The suggestion about the actor's name is given in Katō: *Chikamatsu Kenkyū*, p. 38.

81. Satō: *Chikamatsu no Kokugoteki Kenkyū*, p. 4.

82. Tokutomi: *Sesōhen*, p. 392.

83. Higuchi: *Chikamatsu Monzaemon no Gakushiki*, p. 121.

84. Kitani: *Watakushi no Chikamatsu Kenkyū*, p. 100.

85. Kuroki: *Chikamatsu Monzaemon*, p. 11. Chikamatsu's poem appeared in a collection entitled *Takaragura* 寶藏, edited by Yamaoka Genrin 山岡元隣. His poem and those of his family are in the appendix to the volume. Sonoda mistakenly dates the book 1667 (*op. cit.*, p. 74).

86. Sonoda: *op. cit.*, p. 76. See also footnote 46 of this chapter.

87. Wakatsuki: *JK*, p. 704. The term *zenkō* means the "father of a Kwampaku (prime minister), who shaved his head and entered a Buddhist's life" (Brinkley: *Japanese-English Dictionary*, p. 1676). Ekan 惠觀 was the ninth son of the Emperor Go-Yōzei (whose interest in puppet plays will be remembered). His personal name was Akiyoshi 直昭. He became head of the Ichijō 一條 branch of the imperial family and was made *kwampaku* in 1629. He took Buddhist orders in 1651 and died in 1672 in his sixty-eighth year. (Kuroki: *Chikamatsu Monzaemon*, p. 11.)

88. Kinshō is an alternative reading of the characters of Chikamatsu.

89. Quoted in Kuroki: *Jōruri-shi*, pp. 240-1. The original work is entitled *Nora Tachi-yaku Butai ōkagami* 野直立役舞臺大鏡. Its author is unknown.

90. All of Chikamatsu's famous works, both *jidaimono* and *sewamono* were written as *jōruri*. Many were afterwards performed on the *kabuki* stage, however.

91. Sonoda: *op. cit.*, pp. 84-96.

92. *Ibid.*, pp. 121-2.

93. Kuroki: *Chikamatsu Monzaemon*, pp. 22-8. Tanaka Shinji (in *Chikamatsu to Jidai*, p. 35) makes a similar division, except that his second period extends to 1702.

94. Elisséev and Iacovleff: *Le Théâtre Japonais*, pp. 64-6.

95. *Nihon Furisode Hajime* 日本振袖始.

96. *Sagami Nyūdō Hyappiki Inu* 相模入道百匹犬; *Keisei Shimabara Kaeru Kassen* 傾城島原蛙合戰; *Goban Taiheiki* 碁盤太平記.

97. Van Doren: *The Poetry of John Dryden*, p. 108.

98. *Ibid.*, p. 110.

99. The play was entitled *Karigane Bunshichi Aki no Shimo* 雁金文七秋の霜. *Cf.* Wakatsuki: *JK*, p. 766.

100. Lamartine; *Graziella*, p. 86. Chikamatsu's interest in what made for pathos is discussed in Chapter V, p. 95.

101. Kuroki: *Chikamatsu Monzaemon*, p. 99.

102. Kondō: *Kamigata Edo Jidai*, p. 50.

103. *Cf.* Katō: *Chikamatsu Kenkyū*, p. 52. Elisséev: *Le Théâtre Japonais*, p. 10, gives a list of the eight stock roles in a *kabuki* play. The *jōruri* was probably influenced by the *kabuki* in this feature.

104. It would be pointless to attempt to quote all the critics who have praised the play. Apart from Katō's comment mentioned in footnote 1, I may cite Yamaguchi (in *Kokusenya Kassen*, etc., p. 262), "This piece is the greatest masterpiece of Chikamatsu's *jidaimono*, and the crowning achievement of all *jōruri* works". Tadami (in his introduction to *Chikamatsu's Jōruri-shū*, Volume III, p. 1) calls it one of Chikamatsu's three masterpieces. Early critics (like Hamamatsu in *Nansui Manyū Shūi*, p. 554) considered it the great work of Chikamatsu's career.

    Meiji critics were the least favourable. Men like Takayama Chogyū (in *Chogyū Zenshū*, Volume II, p. 43) had a poor opinion of the historical plays in general.

105. Tadami: *op. cit.*, Volume III, p. 138.

106. Unless Komutsu considered she had been pledged to Coxinga since his birth, a possible interpretation. The lute was often used to symbolise conjugal harmony.

M

Chapter III

1. The account of the bestowing of the imperial surname of Chu 朱 by Lung Wu 隆武 is found in many accounts, although not always accurately. For example, Giles (in *A Personal Memory of Formosa*, p. 1) stated that it was "a dignity conferred upon him by the Manchus in order to secure his loyalty".
Chiang Jih-sheng in *T'ai-wan Wai-chi, chüan* 55, gives the story of Coxinga's cousin.

2. *Dagh-Register gehouden int Casteel Batavia*, Anno 1653, ed. Van der Chijs, p. 15.

3. *Tweede en Derde Gesandschap na het Keyserryck van Taysing of China*, p. 55.

4. Montanus: *Atlas Chinensis*, tr. Ogilby, p. 73.

5. The list of variants here given is by no means exhaustive. Cogseng, Con-seng, Kuesim, Cogsin, Coseng, Kue-sing, Maroto and Pompoan occur chiefly in Spanish accounts. Quoesing is in a Dutch account. Coxiny occurs in the narrative of a German mercenary serving with the Dutch. Quesim is from the Italian. Cocxima and Quesin are French. Quesingus, of course, occurs in Latin accounts.
An almanac preserved in the library of St. John's College, Cambridge, bears a handwritten inscription, "Anno Domini 1676. This Almanack was given to Mr. John Dacres merchant in the East Indys by Pun Poin, then King of Tyon." This "Pun Poin " must be the same as the Spanish "Pompoan" or "Pumpuan". From the place that the name occurs in Spanish translations of Coxinga's letters, it is clear that the Chinese original of the word was 本藩, which would have been pronounced something like Pun-puan in the Amoy dialect. This word is commonly used as an appelation of Coxinga in Yang Ying: *Ts'ung-cheng Shih-lu*. It came to mean "our leader". The origin of the name Maroto was probably the Portuguese word *maroto*, related to the English word "marauder".

6. This date is found in the text of an inscription prepared for a monument to Coxinga. The author, Asakawa Zen'an, does not give his source, but the date otherwise agrees with what we know of Coxinga's life. (*Cf. Zen'an Zuihitsu*, p. 311.) Cheng Chü-chung, in *Cheng Ch'eng-kung Chuan*, an early (date unknown, but probably seventeenth century) biography of Coxinga, says only, "The night that Coxinga was born, the Japanese islands were lit by ten thousand fires, and it was bright as day" (p. 1a).

7. Ponsonby-Fane (in *Koxinga, Chronicles of the Tei Family*) made the gallant attempt to prove Coxinga's mother was a lady. Certain Japanese writers were less kind. Maki Bokusen (1736-1824) (in *Isshōwa*, p. 705) stated that she was a courtesan. But Yang Shu-fang (in *Fu-chien Wen-hua*, Volume III, No 17, p. 28) declared that Coxinga's mother was of royal descent. He further quoted an account of the courtship of the lady, as found in the *Kuang-yang Tsa-chi* (*chüan* 2) by Liu Hsien-t'ing (1648-95). "When Cheng Chih-lung (鄭芝龍) was young he fled to Japan. There he did sewing for people in order to earn a living. He had sewn his savings of three coppers into the collar of his clothes, but they fell out. He wandered along a road looking for them. When he could not find his money he burst into tears. There was a Japanese woman, newly widowed, who was standing inside her gate. She saw him searching and asked what the matter was. Chih-lung told her. The woman said, 'With your talents it should be as easy for you to earn three million coppers as it would be to pick up a blade of grass. How could you come to such a state for three coppers?' She gave herself to Chih-lung and spent the night with him. When Chih-lung achieved success he married her."

8. Boxer: *The Rise and Fall of Nicholas Iquan*, p. 418.

9. Inō: *Taiwan Bunka-shi*, Volume I, p. 91. Fukumatsu 福松 is not found in Chinese works where Cheng Sen 鄭森 is given as his boyhood name.

10. Arai Hakuseki: *Shinsho*, p. 685, and elsewhere. Tagawa Shichizaemon never again saw his brother, but they continued to correspond in later years, and Coxinga sent him a generous allowance. Some letters of their correspondence may be found in Ōta: *Ichiwa Ichigen*, Volume II, pp. 732-6.

11. Huang Tsung-hsi: *Ssu-hsing Shih-mo*, p. 1. The words translated "Imperial Collegiate School" are literally "Nanking University". The school was actually one intended to prepare young men for the civil service examinations. The translation adopted, if not strictly accurate, is closer to the meaning than Nanking University. Ch'ien Ch'ien-i is written 錢謙益. Ta-mu is written 大木.

12. 董氏 (Miss Tung); 經 (Ching).

13. *Cf.* Hummel *et al.*: *Eminent Chinese of the Ch'ing Period*, Vol. I, p. 192.

14. Boxer: *op. cit.*, p. 435.

15. Coxinga seldom actually used the "national surname" of Chu 朱, but he frequently used Ch'eng-kung 成功.

16. Chu Hsi-tsu, in his essay *Cheng Yen-p'ing-wang Shou Ming Kuan-chüeh K'ao*, has determined the dates on which various titles and court ranks were bestowed on Coxinga by the Ming court. As they are not usually of interest in a narrative of his life, they will all be mentioned here instead of in the main body of the text.
    1646: Marshall of Punitive Expeditions (招討將軍).
    3rd moon 1646: Count of Loyalty and Filial Piety (忠孝伯).
    10th moon 1646: Marquis of Wei-yüan (威遠侯).
    7th moon 1647: Duke of Chang-kuo (漳國公).
    7th moon 1652: Prince of Yen-p'ing (延平王). Title declined.
    4th moon 1653: Prince of Yen-p'ing. Title accepted.
    11th moon 1655: Prince of Ch'ao (潮王).

17. Takano: *Edo Bungaku-shi*, Volume II, p. 443.

18. Cheng: *op. cit.*, p. 1 b.

19. Boxer: *op. cit.*, p. 436.

20. Huang: *op. cit.*, "In the eighth moon [of 1652] the Vice-President of the Board of Punishments arrived from Five Fingers Mountain (五指山), and said that the Emperor Ssu-wen (思文) had become a monk at that place. Shortly afterwards a messenger arrived in Amoy with an edict. At that time all the old ministers could not decide if the message were genuine... In the second moon of 1653 another envoy came from Five Fingers Mountain to enquire about the health of the various ministers. The envoy said that the Emperor Ssu-wen had now left the mountain and had moved to P'ing-yüan (平原), and was going to raise a military force. The old ministers joined in presenting a memorial requesting permission to look into his claims, but it was never granted." Ssu-wen was the posthumous designation of Lung Wu.

21. Thus in the *Ming Shih*, Volume CXVIII, but other authorities state that Lung Wu was strangled at Ting-chou, the scene of his defeat.

22. *Cf.* Chu: *op. cit.*, p. 93.

23. Boxer: *op. cit.*, p. 437.

24. Nishikawa: *Nagasaki Yawa-sō*, p. 261.

25. Huang: *op. cit.*, p. 1b. The "facts" as recorded by various Chinese historians were interpreted in a Japanese way by Saitō Setsudō in *Kaigai Iden* (p. 9a): the mother committed suicide because she had been violated, and Coxinga cut open her abdomen in order to cleanse the defilement from her entrails. Brinkley: *History of the Japanese People*, p. 586, states the mother committed suicide after Coxinga had fallen fighting at Macao!

26. My source of information about the Chinese story-tellers has been Dr. William Hung who heard such tales as a boy in Fukien. I have not found any written version of them.

27. Yang: *Cheng Ch'eng-kung Shih-chi K'ao*, p. 29.

28. The work, *Ts'ung-cheng Shih-lu,* is a record of Coxinga's campaigns by Yang Ying, one of his officials. It was discovered in manuscript in 1922 and published in 1931.

29. Ishihara: *Nihon Kisshi no Kenkyū,* p. 67. There may have been a fifth mission, but its date is uncertain.

30. An account of the debate among the Shogun's advisers in 1658 on the question of sending aid to Coxinga may be found in Hayashi Nobuatsu: *Kan'ei Shōsetsu* (p. 36) and elsewhere.

31. Yang Ying: *Ts'ung-cheng Shih-lu,* p. 15 b.

32. *Ibid.,* p. 22a. Some Chinese of the time thought that the only reason Coxinga did not surrender was that the Manchu offers were not big enough. Chu Hsi-tsu, in his preface to Yang Ying's account (*loc. cit.*) shows, however, that this was not the case.

33. "Islanders" because Coxinga's chief base was the island of Amoy.

34. Huang: *Ssu-hsing Shih-mo,* pp. 5b-6b.

35. Greslon: *Histoire de la Chine sous la Domination des Tartares,* p. 8.

36. Rougemont: *Historia Tartaro-Sinica nova,* pp. 49-55.

37. Ferrando: *Historia de los PP Dominicos,* Volume III, p. 49. Saitō: *op. cit.,* p. 10 b, stated that 200,000 picked troops were sent by the Manchus to relieve Nanking, and they easily overcame Coxinga's battle-weary soldiers.

38. Yang Ying: *op. cit.,* p. 121a. Kan Hui is written 甘輝.

39. Ferrando: *op. cit.,* p. 47. Other writers put the figure as low as 2,300 ships. Li Chieh, a pro-Manchu Chinese who was an eye witness, wrote that there were "not) less than two or three thousand ships". (In *T'ien-hsiang-ko Sui-pi,* chüan 2, p. 3a.'

40. Hummel *et al.: op. cit.,* Volume I, p. 109.

41. Blair and Robertson: *The Philippine Islands,* Volume XXXVI, p. 251.

42. Ferrando: *op. cit.,* pp. 64-5.

43. *Ibid.,* pp. 65-6.

44. Vojeu de Brunem: *Histoire de la Conquête de la Chine,* Volume II, p. 120.

45. Ferrando: *op. cit.,* p. 67.

46. Pelliot: *Michel Boym,* p. 97.

47. *Ibid.,* p. 99.

48. The best article on the subject of the would-be Christian emperor is a review by Pelliot entitled *Michel Boym* in *T'oung Pao,* Second Series, Volume XXXI. See also Parker: *Letters from a Chinese Empress.*

49. *Cf.* Inō: *op. cit.,* p. 96. Chang Huang-yen 張煌言 continued to resist the Manchus on the mainland after Coxinga had left for Formosa. Another general, Wu Hao 吳豪, opposed the Formosan expedition on the grounds that his personal observations on the island had convinced him it would be extremely difficult to take, and that a campaign would therefore only succeed in wasting the strength of Coxinga's forces. Wu may have been one of the numerous soldiers in Coxinga's army who took refuge in Formosa after the débâcle at Nanking. (*Cf.* Shidehara: *Kokusenya no Taiwan Kōryaku,* pp. 275-83.)

50. Boxer: *op. cit.*, p. 412.

51. Huang: *op. cit.*, p. 7. But Boxer: *op. cit.*, p. 414, gives a letter written by the son of Li Han, a famous pirate, claiming that it was Li who encouraged the emigration of Chinese settlers from the mainland to Formosa.

52. Chiang Jih-sheng: *T'ai-wan Wai-chi, chuan* 11, has the Chinese view. For the Dutch account of Ho T'ing-pin 何廷斌, see Campbell: *Formosa Under the Dutch*, p. 390.

53. Campbell: *op. cit.*, p. 401. The merchant, Juko, is probably the same man mentioned in Coxinga's letter on page 57.

54. *Ibid.*, p. 459. The Dutch apparently thought that "I-quan" was in the service of the Manchus at this time!

55. *Ibid.*, p. 386.

56. Yang Ying: *op. cit.*, p. 12 a.

57. Campbell: *op. cit.*, p. 390. This and the following citations from Campbell's work are translations by him from *'t Verwaerloosde Formosa* by C. E. S. (Jan Claesz ten Hoorn) written in 1675.

58. Imbault-Huart: *L'Ile Formose*, p. 59, and elsewhere.

59. Campbell: *op. cit.*, pp. 391-2.

60. *Ibid.*, p. 405.

61. *Ibid.*, p. 407.

62. Hobson: *Fort Zelandia, and the Dutch Occupation of Formosa*, p. 37. Luh-urh-men is properly Lu-erh-men (鹿耳門), and Chi-khan is Ch'ih-k'an (赤嵌). Ch'ih k'an was known to the Dutch as Saccam and also as Fort Provintia.

63. Ishihara (in *Taiwan Teishi Shōyu Ruson Shimatsu*, p. 94) lists the years during which Coxinga considered attacking Formosa: 1646, 1652, 1654, 1655, 1657 and, more seriously, in 1658-9. But the campaign against Nanking must have occupied first place in his attentions until 1660.

64. Yang Ying: *op. cit.*, p. 23 b.

65. *Cf.* Shidehara: *op. cit.*, p. 277.

66. Yang Ying: *op. cit.*, p. 149a, b.

67. Herport: *Reise nach Java*, etc., p. 51.

68. *Archief voor de Geschiedenis der Oude Hollandsche Zending*, Vol. III, p. 218.

69. Campbell: *op. cit.*, p. 416.

70. *Ibid.*, p. 422.

71. *Ibid.*, p. 427.

72. Probably the same man mentioned before as the friend of Ho T'ing-pin.

73. The characters are 大明招討大將軍國姓. The letter is quoted from *Archief*, etc., Volume III, p. 219 ff.

74. Indick must be an approximation of Yung Li (永曆).

75. Campbell: *op. cit.*, p. 439.

76. *Ibid.*, pp. 441-2.

77. Yang Ying: *op. cit.*, p. 5a. The author gives a graphic account of the hardships suffered by the Chinese forces on account of lack of food. By the eighth moon of 1661 they were reduced to eating berries and nuts. The forced evacuation of the coastal area is described in Hsieh: *Removal of Coastal Population.* (See below, note 92.)

78. Campbell: *op. cit.*, pp. 445, 448.

79. Huang: *op. cit.*, p. 7.

80. *Cf.* van der Aa: *China en Zijne Bewoners*, p. 222. Oddly enough, the same man is mentioned in a different connection in the Batavia *Dagh-Register* for 1661. In the entry for 24th June of that year we find, " . . . At the same time the yacht *Maria* also came, quite unexpectedly, both because it is now against the monsoon, and because the ship was supposed to remain in Formosa according to latest advice received from the sloop *Urk.* The captain, named Cornelis Claez Bennis, and a certain corporal named Hans Juriaen Rader(*sic!*), who had spent about seven years in Formosa, and who in March last had boarded the said yacht with several soldiers, were sent for, and had, on coming ashore, brought very unpleasant and grievous tidings." The news in question was of the arrival of Coxinga's forces. Clenk, Coyett's appointed successor, had left for Formosa two days before this news arrived. Caeuw's fleet, presumably with Radis aboard, sailed on 5th July to the aid of Formosa.

81. Tavernier: *Recueil de plusieurs Relations et Traitez*, pp. 250-1. A Dutch reply to Tavernier's charges is Quellenburgh's *Vindiciae Batavicae.*

82. Tavernier: *op. cit.* p. 251.

83. There is some confusion about the date. Herport, for example, who was an eyewitness, stated that the surrender took place on 10 February (*op. cit.*, p. 80), but the difference may perhaps be explained by the confusion arising from the fact that in 1662 some states of the Netherlands used the Julian calendar while others had adopted the Gregorian calendar. At the time there was a difference of ten days between the two.

84. Campbell: *op. cit.*, p. 455.

85. A rijksdaalder equals 2½ guilders.

86. Campbell: *op. cit.*, p. 455 ff.

87. Vixseboxe: *Een Hollandsch Gezantschap naar China*, p. 18.

88. Helmers: *Nagelaten Gedichten*, p. 191.

89. Nomsz: *Anthonius Hambroek of de Belegering van Formoza*, p. 81.

90. Baldaeus: *Naauwkeurige Beschrijvinge*, p. 119. This figure is possibly too high. Murillo (quoted in Navas del Valle: *Catalogo de los Documentos, etc.* p. clvi) estimated that the Dutch had lost 1,400 soldiers. When the number of civilian lives lost is added, the two figures are approximately the same. Others, such as the author of *'t Verwaerloosde Formosa*, fail to give any estimates of the deaths.

91. Campbell: *op. cit.*, p. 458.

92. Yang Shu-fang: *op. cit.*, p. 31. The plans of Huang Wu 黃梧 (1618-74), though submitted as early as 1657, were not put into effect until late in 1660, and only affected Coxinga to a limited extent. The evacuation of the coast of Fukien did not end until after 1680.

93. Maas: *Cartas de China*, p. 120. The date of the letter should probably be 12 January 1661, a mistake in dating natural early in the year, or possibly resulting from confusion over the calendar, as the New Year did not begin until Lady Day under the old calendar.

94. *Tweede en Derde Gesandschap*, p. 53. The Dutch account is confirmed by a Japanese one (in Asakawa: *op. cit.*, pp. 314-5). The latter account runs, "A minister declared that since his (*i.e.* Iquan's) prison was close to the water and since Coxinga's pirate ships could travel anywhere, Iquan should be fastened with three iron chains and should have fetters placed on his hands and feet . . . This was done."

95. Alcobendas: *Las Misiones Franciscanas en China*, Volume V, p. 3.

96. Palafox: *History of the Conquest of China by the Tartars*, p. 147.

97. *Ibid.*, pp. 300-1. *Cf.* G. P. (George Phillips): *Life of Koxinga*, p. 68.

98. Boxer: *op. cit.*, p. 438.

99. Rougemont: *op. cit.*, pp. 64-5. The Four Regents mentioned were Soni, Suksaha, Ebilun and Oboi, who ruled for the boy emperor of the K'ang Hsi era.

100. Wei Yüan: *Sheng-wu-chi, chüan* 8, p. 12. Another account credited the interception to Iquan's barber, and said that Iquan thereupon bit off his tongue and the fingers of his right hand to keep himself from giving the Manchus further information! (Hill: *Notes on Piracy*, p. 73.)

101. Hummel *et al.*: *op. cit.*, Volume I, p. 111, states that there is no indication that Iquan was ever sent to Manchuria.

102. Navarrete: *Tratados Historicos, Politicos, etc.*, p. 416.

103. Diaz: *Conquistas de las Islas Filipinas*, p. 553, and elsewhere.

104. Nieuhof: *Het Gezantschap der Neerlandtsche Oost-Indische Compagnie*, p. 234.

105. Orléans: *Histoire des Deux Conquérans*, pp. 98-9.

106. Haguenauer: *Mélanges Critiques*, p. 42.

107. Maas: *op. cit.*, p. 119. For the date, see note 93.

108. *Ibid.*

109. Imbault-Huart: *op. cit.*, p. 77.

110. The word "Sangley", used in the Philippines of the Chinese, is of uncertain origin. A manuscript of about 1590, written in Spanish with illustrations, probably by a Chinese artist, contains a picture of a Fukienese couple above which appears the word Sangley together with the characters 常來. Professor C. R. Boxer, the discoverer of the manuscript, interprets the characters as meaning traders who were "constantly coming" to Luzon, but whether this was the original meaning of the term is not clear. Other Chinese characters have been suggested by various people, but the word may also be of Filipino origin.

111. Blair and Robertson: *op. cit.*, Volume XXXVI, p. 232.

112. *Ibid.*, p. 222.

113. *Ibid.*, p. 229.

114. *Ibid.*, p. 241.

115. *Ibid.*, p. 242. The text incorrectly gives 10 June, but the correct date, 10 July, may be found in Navarrete: *Tratados Historicos*, p. 418 and elsewhere.

116. Pastells: *Historia General de Filipinas*, p. clviii.

117. Coxinga's death is sometimes given as 23 June (usually in Chinese sources) and sometimes as 2 July 1662 (usually in European works). See Ishihara: *Taiwan Teishi*, p. 95. In either case, he was already dead when Ricci received the governor's message.

118. Diaz: *op. cit.*, p. 636.

119. Ferrando: *op. cit.*, p. 98.

120. Rougemont: *op. cit.*, pp. 108-10.

121. Careri: *Voyage Round the World*, p. 390.

122. Orléans: *op. cit.*, p. 105.

123. Ides: *Three Years Travels from Moscow Over-Land to China*, p. 150.

124. Davidson: *The Island of Formosa*, p. 52. Davidson's source was Cheng Chü-chung's *Cheng Ch'eng-kung Chuan*. The date of Coxinga's death here given is by the Chinese calendar. The Western equivalent is 23 June.

125. Ross: *The Manchus or the Reigning Dynasty of China*, p. 405.

126. Vizetelly (ed.): *New Standard Encyclopedia*, Volume XVII, p. 140. See also Brinkley: *History*, p. 586.

127. Saitō: *op. cit.*, p. 12 b.

128. Ishihara: *Taiwan Teishi*, p. 95.

129. Blair and Robertson: *op. cit.*, pp. 218-60, contains a translation entitled *Events in Manila*, 1662-3. This work is neither dated nor signed, but if it were written in 1663, as appears to be the case from the text, it was possibly the first account of Coxinga's death. The details (p. 248) are extremely close to those given by Rougemont, suggesting that this work was either Rougemont's source, or the two accounts have a common origin.

    The account of the madness and death of Coxinga is further substantiated by a poem in the collection *Borts Voyagie* by Matthijs Cramer. The poem, apparently written about November 1663, describes Coxinga's vision of attacking enemy soldiers, then continues with the memorable lines:

> Sijn gruwelijcke mondt doet desperate beeten,
> Soo dat hy niet ontsiet sijn eigen vleesch te eeten,
> Soo wapent sich Godts recht in Goddelijcke straf,
> Die and're handen kapt, eet eygen handen af:
> Soo kryght d'onnos'le hulp, en soo wort overrompelt
> Der Christen dwingelant, en in de aert gedompelt. (p. 62)

> His mouth most horrible now bites in desperation,
> So that to eat his flesh he shows no hesitation,
> Thus arms itself in God-like punishment God's might
> As he who chopped off others' hands his own does bite.
> Thus th'innocent are helped, and thus the Christians' foe
> Is taken by surprise and to the earth brought low.

    One further authoritative source of the death of Coxinga is disappointing. Shichizaemon, Coxinga's Japanese brother, wrote in a letter of 1676 that Coxinga had "died of illness", but this is too vague an expression to furnish proof as to the manner of his death. (See Ōta: *Ichiwa Ichigen*, p. 735.)

130. Cheng: *op. cit.*, p. 12. Also quoted in Akizato: *Shūi Miyako Meisho Zue*, p. 105.

131. *Cf.* Wang Chih-hsin: *Ts'ung Kuo-nan*, etc., p. 4.

132. Yang Ying: *op. cit.*, p. 16 b.

133. The view here expressed may be found more fully developed in Huizinga: *Herfsttij der Middeleeuwen* (Haarlem, 1947), p. 76.

134. Even careful scholars such as Sansom (in *Japan*, p. 484) refer to Coxinga as "a pirate chief", but surely it must be obvious from the material in this chapter that Coxinga was no Captain Kidd of the East. It was natural, however, that the Manchus sought to stigmatise him as a pirate in order to discredit his efforts at re-establishing the Ming Dynasty, and that the Dutch and Spaniards, for reasons of their own, gave him the same uncomplimentary name. There is evidence that Coxinga insisted that skippers who wished to trade from his ports pay dearly for the privilege—a letter to his brother Shichizaemon (in Ōta: *Ichiwa Ichigen*, p. 733) states that ships engaged in trade with Japan must be furnished with certificates by Shichizaemon at the rate of one or two thousand taels of silver for big ships and five hundred taels for small ships. If they failed to have such certificates their cargoes would be confiscated by the Nagasaki officials. But this is still a far cry from the images usually conjured up by the name of pirate.

Iquan can be defended less easily from the charge. It was probably his own well-founded reputation as a freebooter that led people to call his son, who was the last best hope of the Mings, "a pirate chief".

135. *Peking Gazette*, 15-16 February 1875, p. 24.

136. For example, Coxinga's biography is to be found in the *Isetsu Nihonshi*, Volume VI, a work not otherwise devoted to foreigners. In such uncritical works as Nishikawa's *Nagasaki Yawa-sō* it is claimed that Coxinga used to celebrate the New Year in the Japanese manner because of his "deep longing" for his native land (p. 260).

Chapter IV

1. The play is critically described in Brewster: *Aaron Hill*, p. 95. It was presented in February, 1716, or about two months after *The Battles of Coxinga*.

2. *Dramatic Works of Aaron Hill*, Volume I, p. 151.

3. See above, Chapter I, p. 6.

4. *Cf.* Takahashi: *Chikamatsu no Gikyoku Taiyō*, p. 92.

5. It should be noted that the possibility exists that some book may yet be found that will prove to be a much closer source of Chikamatsu's play than any yet uncovered. The comparative lack of interest by Japanese scholars in Tokugawa literature has meant that much valuable source material of the period still lies neglected in the great Japanese libraries.

6. For a list of Chinese works on Coxinga written before Chikamatsu's play, see Hsieh Kuo-chen: *Wan-ming Shih-chi K'ao*, chuan 13, pp. 1-6.

7. The importance of the *Minshin Tōki* (明清闘記) is described in Noma: *Kokusenya Gozen Gundan to Kokusenya Kassen, etc.*, p. 625 ff.

8. Chinese sources all agree on this point. *Cf.* Huang: *Ssu-hsing Shih-mo*, p. 1a.

9. Nishikawa: *Ka'i Tsūshō-kō* (written 1695) p. 300. Arai: *Shinsho*, p. 685, states that Coxinga was in his eighth year rather than his seventh.

10. A biography of Li Tzu-ch'eng (李自成) may be found in Hummel *et al.*: *Eminent Chinese of the Ch'ing Period*, Volume I, p. 491.

11. See Chapter VI, note 14.

12. Ross: *The Manchus or the Reigning Dynasty of China*, p. 151.

13. Coxinga was actually married to a Chinese woman of the Tung family. See Chapter III, p. 46.

14. See Chapter I, p. 6.

15. *Cf.* Hummel *et al.: op. cit.*, Volume II, pp. 877-8, for life of Wu San-kuei (吳三桂).

16. This work was actually written four years after *The Battles of Coxinga*, but appears to reflect an independent tradition about the loyalty of Wu San-kuei. The author seems to have gathered his information from Chinese living in Nagasaki. Chikamatsu may have read an earlier work of similar content.

17. Nishikawa: *Nagasaki Yawa-sō*, pp. 258-62.

18. It is interesting that in Vondel's drama *Zungchin* (1667) Wu San-kuei (Uzangueius) also figures as a model of loyalty.

19. Noma: *op. cit.*, p. 629.

20. *Ibid.*, p. 635. The original story of the shrike and the clam is in *Chan Kuo Ts'e* (戰國策) (Szu Pu Pei Yao edition), Chapter 30, p. 10a.

21. Noma: *op. cit.*, pp. 635-7.

22. Yamaguchi: *Kokusenya Kassen no Beni-nagashi ni tsuite*, pp. 237-8.

23. Noma: *op. cit.*, p. 638.

24. Shuzui: Article in *Nihon Bungaku Daijiten*, Volume I, pp. 917-8, describes the play 傾城國性爺.

25. *Ibid., loc. cit.*

26. Tsubouchi et al: *Chikamatsu no Kenkyū*, p. 304. *Kokusenya Takenuki Gorō* is written 國性爺竹拔五郎; Oshimodoshi is 押戻.

27. Kitani: Introduction to *Kokusenya Kassen* in *Dai-Chikamatsu Zenshū*, Volume III, p. 106.

28. Other plays on the theme include *Hiragana Imagawa-ō* 平假名今川狀 (1732) (described in Tsubouchi: *op. cit.*, p. 305); *Tōjin-mage Ima Kokusenya* 唐人髷今國性爺 (1825) (described *ibid.*, p. 343); *Wakoku-bashi* 和國橋 (1863) (in Kawatake: *Kawatake Mokuami*, p. 152); and *Kokusenya Rihatsu no Sugatami* 國性爺理髪の婆視 (1887) (in Iizuka: *Kabuki Saiken*, p. 242).

29. Ihara: *Meiji Engeki-shi*, p. 189-90. The play is called in the original *Kokusenya Sugata no Utsushie* 國性爺婆の冩眞鏡.

30. Takeda: *Chūshingura*, tr. Inouye, pp. 156-7.

31. Koizumi: Article in *Nihon Bungaku Daijiten*, Volume II, p. 103, describes the work, *Kokusenya Gozen Gundan* 國性爺御前軍談.

32. *Keiseiya Gundan* 傾城野群談 may be found in *Kokusho Kankōkai: Kinsei Bungei Sōsho*, volume 5. The title is untranslatable, being a combined play on the names of Ki no Kaion's work and of the novel *Kokusenya Gozen Gundan*.

33. In *Teikoku Bunko, Kiseki Jishō Kessaku-shū*, Volume I. The title is written 國性爺明朝太平記.

34. *Ibid.*, pp. 173-178.

35. *Ibid.*, p. 202.

36. Kanagaki: *Kokusenya Ichidai-ki*, p. 3b.

37. Ponsonby-Fane: *Koxinga*, p. 72. It was probably not coincidence that in the same year, 1898, the tale *Watōnai* was added to Iwaya Sazanami's great collection of children's stories.

38. *Cf.* Akizato; *Shūi Miyako Meisho Zue* (written 1787), p. 105.

Chapter V

1. Lee: *Studies of the Eighteenth Century in Italy*, pp. 171-2.
Burckhardt (in *Civilization of the Renaissance*, p. 192) related how ballets and pantomimes served as interludes when classical plays were presented in the Renaissance courts. "...That while the play was going on everybody was longing for the interludes is quite intelligible, when we think of the picturesque brilliancy with which they were put on the stage. There were to be seen combats of Roman warriors, who brandished their weapons to the sound of music, torch dances executed by Moors, a dance of savages with horns of plenty, out of which streamed waves of fire—all as the ballet of a pantomime in which a maiden was delivered from a dragon." Wakatsuki (in (*Ningyō*) *Jōruri-shi Kenkyū*, p. 591) described the less elaborate Japanese counterparts of the Italian interlude entertainment.
It is interesting to note what J. Middleton Murry (*Shakespeare*, pp. 189-90) wrote about *The Merchant of Venice*. "We may say that it is, as nearly as possible, a pure melodrama or tragi-comedy, an almost perfect example of the art-form which being prior to art itself, most evidently and completely satisfies the primitive men in us all...*The Merchant of Venice* is the type of entertainment the theatre should supply—villain discomfited, virtue rescued, happy marriages, clowning, thrills, and a modest satisfaction of the general appetite for naughtiness." This description might almost as well apply to *The Battles of Coxinga*. The difference in the nature of the two plays is that Chikamatsu's is at times deeply pathetic, at times even horrifying, and at times low comedy, while, as Murry points out, *The Merchant of Venice* is essentially a fairy-tale throughout, and has a uniform tone which *The Battles of Coxinga* lacks.
I have chosen not to call *The Battles of Coxinga* a melodrama because the word generally has a pejorative sense, although if used as in the quotation above from Murry's work it comes fairly close to describing Chikamatsu's play.

2. Wakatsuki: *JK*, p. 618, quotes an account which reads, "Up to and including the work *Jitō Tennō Uta Gumpō* [presented three months before *The Battles of Coxinga*] there were puppet comic pieces in between the acts because the *jōruri* plays were short. This practice stopped with *The Battles of Coxinga*." Another reason why the practice may have stopped was that it may have been felt that the comic interludes were already incorporated in the text itself.

3. *Cf.* Sonoda: *Jōruri Sakusha no Kenkyū*, p. 101.

4. *Ibid.*, p. 102.

5. It was the tradition of the old *jōruri* to begin acts with certain set expressions and to end them with the praise of some great figure, such as the first Tokugawa shōgun, Ieyasu (*cf.* Wakatsuki: *JK*, pp. 150, 217). This fact in itself gave a degree of independence to the form of each act.

6. An example of a truncated version of the play may be found in Atsumi: *Zoku-zoku Gidayū Kyōgen-shū*, pp. 494-522. This is an acting version dating from about 1835. After a short introductory scene on the beach of Hirado, where Watōnai witnesses the battle between the shrike and the clam, an abbreviated version of the third act is given. The play ended with the death of Kinshōjo and of Watōnai's mother.

7. See glossary.

8. *Cf.* Tsubouchi *et al.*: *Chikamatsu no Kenkyū*, p. 299.

9. Hozumi in *Naniwa Miyage*, p. 3, made this statement.

10. In this connection, the writings of Takayama Chogyū might in particular be cited. In *Chikamatsu Sōrinshi*, p. 11, he wrote, "A time has now at last come for our Chikamatsu, who has been likened to England's Shakespeare and Germany's Goethe, to be appreciated". Although Chikamatsu's plays were popular on the stage and were widely read, they were not considered worthy of consideration by serious literary critics until it was discovered that Chikamatsu's Western "equivalent", Shakespeare, was so highly regarded.

11. Wakatsuki: *JK*, p. 735.

12. Tōgi Tetteki: *Ongaku-jō yori mitaru Kokusenya Kassen*, p. 318. Extracts from the music are reprinted in this article.

13. *Ibid.*, p. 319.

14. An excellent example of how a musical accompaniment consisting of a stringed instrument playing melodies which have no direct relation to the scenes they accompany may serve to heighten the emotional intensity of a film is found in *The Third Man*. Presumably the effect of the *samisen* at a *jōruri* performance would have been much the same.

15. In Miyajima: *Contribution à l'Etude du Théâtre des Poupées*, pp. xii-xiv.

16. Particularly those about "la frontière indécise". The attribution of the *Naniwa Miyage* to Hozumi Ikan is almost universal, but the *Kokusho Kaidai*, p. 1524, credits the work to Konoshita Kisei 木下希聖.

17. A *waka* has come in modern times to mean the same as a *tanka*. The latter is a poem written in 31 syllables arranged in lines of 5, 7, 5, 7 and 7 syllables. *Haikai* are poems of 17 syllables arranged in lines of 5, 7 and 5 syllables.

18. *Saimon* 祭文, here probably short for *saimon-yomi*, the name given to persons who made a living by chanting ballads about the miracles of the gods. These were chanted to the tunes of popular songs. By the time of Chikamatsu, however, the only thing to distinguish the *saimon-yomi* from others who sang or told stories in the streets to gain a few coppers was the style of chanting.

19. For additional information about Kaga-no-jō and Chikugo-no-jō (Takemoto Gidayū) see Chapter II, p. 29.

20. *Bunyabushi* was the name given to the style of *jōruri* practised by Okamoto Bunya 岡本文彌. It was noted for its sentimentality.

21. The word I have here translated as "restraint" is *giri* 義理. The word normally means "propriety" or "duty", but in the context, "restraint" seems to be the meaning indicated, although it is not a recognised meaning of the word. The meanings of "propriety" and "restraint" are actually not so far removed, however. If one acts in accordance with the principles of propriety one will not gush over into uncontrolled emotion but will be restrained. I think that is what Chikamatsu meant.

22. The word Chikamatsu used, *rikugi*, refers to the six types of poetry recognised in the prefaces to the *Kokinshū* (*cf.* Ueda: *Chikamatsu Go-i*, p. 371). The word is here used to indicate all parts of the art of *jōruri* including music, words, etc.

23. Yang Kuei-fei (d. 756) was the most famous of Chinese beauties.

24. Hozumi: *Naniwa Miyage*, pp. 5-11.

25. This device was imitated in *Chūshingura*, see Chapter IV, p. 82.

26. *Cf.* Aeba Kōson (in Tsubouchi *et al.*: *Chikamatsu no Kenkyū*), p. 292.

Chapter VI

I have attempted in these notes firstly to explain parts of the translation which might not be clear because of allusions or unfamiliar terminology. Secondly, I have given all but the most obvious of the plays on words, so that students using my translation as a "pony" might be able to follow some of the added intricacies of the text. Thirdly, I have given the sources of most of the quotations in the play. In this last respect I have been helped enormously by the work of Ueda and Higuchi, *Chikamatsu Go-i*, which lists virtually every quotation in the entire body of the works of Chikamatsu.

1. Derived from a poem in the collection *Poems in Three Forms* (*San-t'i-shih*) compiled by Chou Pi in 1250 A. D. The poem is entitled *The Palace of Yeh* and is by Lu Kuei-meng (d. about 881 A. D.) The poem in the original runs, "Flowers scatter, butterflies take fright, but it does not worry man. In the Water Pavilion and Cloud Gallery spring is specially established. [The Emperor sees] early in the morning a thousand painted and powdered equestriennes, Under the white cherry and peach blossoms wearing purple kerchiefs." (Quoted in Ueda: *op. cit.*, p. 528). Lu's poem was one criticising the extravagance of the Chinese court, and is thus aptly used to raise the curtain on an act showing the evil consequences of the similar misrule of the Ming emperor.

2. The rare incense named was *ranja*, and was obtained from the musk deer (*ja*). It was given the name of "orchid" (*ran*) because its fragrance resembled that of the flower.

3. The usual name for the sovereign, Chuang-lieh Ti, is here prefixed with the word *ssu* 思, as was customary before the name of a martyred emperor. Chikamatsu probably saw the name in some pro-Ming writing and did not know that it could be used only after the sovereign's death. Chuang-lieh-ti ruled from 1628 to 1644. He committed suicide on April 25th, 1644 by hanging himself with his sash, leaving behind a note written in his blood. *Cf.* Hummel *et al.*: *Eminent Chinese of the Ch'ing Period*, Volume I, p. 172. The father of this emperor was Kuang Tsung, who reigned from 1620 to 1621.

4. This list is derived from the *Chou Li. Cf.* Biot: *Tcheou-Li*, Book 7, fol. 28, 30.

5. The image is derived from another poem in *Poems in Three Forms*, by the T'ang poet Wang Chien. The poem is entitled *The Palace of Hua-ch'ing*, and refers to the Emperor Hsüan Tsung (685-762), another emperor who brought ruin upon himself by his personal indulgence. (*Cf.* Ueda: *op. cit.*, p. 528.)

6. From Po Chü-i's poem *Chang-hen-ko*, translated by Jenyns in *A Further Selection from the Three Hundred Poems of the T'ang Dynasty* as *The Song of neverending Grief*. The lines in question run, "In the palace there are three thousand beauties, But the favour that should have been extended to three thousand, Is concentrated on the person of one". (Jenyns: *op. cit.*, p. 10.)

7. Go Sankei is the Wu San-kuei (1612-78) of Chinese history. For Chikamatsu's use of the character, see Chapter IV, p. 78. His wife, the Lady Ryūka, is fictitious.

8. The year 1644.

9. Junji or Shun Chih (1638-61) became Emperor of China later in 1644. In that year he would scarcely have been of an age to conceive a passion for Lady Kasei.

10. This was supposed to be cloth woven from the hair of mice that lived in a volcano off the south coast of China. (*Cf.* Ueda: *op. cit.*, p. 117.) It is similar in properties and in legendary association to the Western asbestos.
    Many commentators prefer to take the Shishi-koku of the original as the name of a country at the eastern end of Mongolia, from the name of the famous Khan Chih-chih (Shishi in Japanese). I prefer the interpretation in Ueda (*op. cit.*, p. 605) of Ceylon, because it adds to the effect of exoticism. The Heibonsha *Daijiten*, Volume XII, p. 606, also gives Ceylon and quotes this passage as well as one in the *Taiheiki*. The horse-liver stone is described in the *Tung-ming-chi*, a collection of fantastic tales attributed to Kuo Hsien (*c.* 26 B.C.-*c.* 55 A.D.), quoted in Ueda: *op. cit.*, p. 278, "In the fifth year of Yüan Ting (112 B.C.) the country of Chih-chih presented a horse-liver stone as tribute. If, in the spring, one crushed it, mixed it with Nine Change Pills, and swallowed it, one would know neither hunger nor thirst for a whole year. If one stroked one's hair with it, all the white hairs would turn black."

11. Chikamatsu uses the word *bairoku* as if it were a proper name. Actually, *pei-le* designated a secondary rank of Manchu prince.

12. The seven precious things were: gold, silver, lapis lazuli, crystal, coral, agate and pearls, by one classification. "The ten thousand treasures" has no specific meaning; it indicates simply great wealth.

13. Parent and child. I have adopted this possible meaning of the Japanese word *shinshi*, for purposes of translation, but am inclined to prefer the one of "lips and teeth" (唇齒). This would be a reference to the *Tso Chuan* (in Legge: *Chinese Classics*, Volume 5, Part I, p. 145) " 'When the lips perish, the teeth become cold' illustrates the relation between Kwoh and Yü". Here, Tartary would be the "lips" protecting China, the "teeth", from the cold. Chikamatsu's almost invariable use of chiasmus makes this reading more likely, but I have found it easier to use the more natural image of "parent and child" adopted by Tadami (in the text of his edition of *Kokusenya Kassen*, p. 92).

14. Ri Tōten. No person named Li Tao-t'ien 李踏天 is to be found among the chief officers of the Ming court. The character is probably modelled on that of Li Tzuch'eng (1605?-1645), the famous bandit chief who captured Peking in 1644. The name may have been derived from the Chinese expression *tao-t'ien* (滔天) ("to dash to the skies") often used as an intensifer before words denoting disaster.

15. Three emperors: Fu Hsi, Shen Nung and Huang Ti. Five rulers: Shao Hao, Chuan Hsü, Ti K'u, Yao and Shun. At least two other lists of five rulers exist.

16. Five constant virtues: benevolence, righteousness, propriety, knowledge and sincerity. (Definitions from Mathews: *Chinese-English Dictionary*, p. 1071.) Five human relationships: between prince and minister, father and son, husband and wife, elder and younger brothers, and friends.

17. A quotation from Mencius (in Legge: *Chinese Classics*, Volume I, *Works of Mencius*, p. 251). "But men possess a moral nature; and if they are well fed, warmly clad, and comfortably lodged, without being taught at the same time, they become almost like the beasts."

18. Kuan Chung was the famous counsellor of Duke Huan of Ch'i (d. 643 B.C.). The account of his summoning of the feudal lords may be found in a great variety of texts, including *Han Fei-tzu* (tr. Liao, p. 89), "In by-gone days, Duke Huan of Ch'i called the feudal lords to meet nine times, brought All-under-Heaven under one rule, and became the first of the Five Hegemon Rulers. And Kuan Chung assisted him. . ."

19. Wu Tzu-hsü was a counsellor of the King of Wu. When the King of Wu defeated the King of Yüeh at Kuai-chi Mountain, and then made peace with him, Wu Tzu-hsü criticised him, declaring that he should instead crush Yüeh. Wu Tzu-hsü was slandered and his plan rejected by the King of Wu, who presented him with a sword with which to commit suicide. Wu, in despair over the king's stupidity, decided to cut out his eyes and place them on the eastern gate. Then they would see the troops of Yüeh advancing on Wu. Later, he committed suicide by cutting off his own head. When the attack by the troops of Yüeh actually occurred, Wu's eyes are said to have shown their pleasure. (*Cf.* Chavannes: *Mémoires Historiques de Se-ma Ts'ien*, Volume IV, p. 428.)

    Fan Li was the counsellor of King Kou Chien of Yüeh at the time of the happenings described in the above paragraph. It was his wisdom that was responsible for the final victory of Yüeh. (*Cf.* Chavannes: *op. cit.*, Volume IV, pp. 428ff.)

20. Sendan was a fictitious character derived from the Princess Sendara in Nishiki Bunryū's *jōruri*, *Kokusenya Tegara Nikki*.

21. A reference to Kaguya-hime in the *Taketori Monogatari*. *Tsuki* is used as a pivot-word, going both with *izayoi* "moon of the sixteenth night" and with *miyako* "capital of the moon".

22. A reference to the preface to the *Kokin-waka-shū*, written by Ki no Tsurayuki (883-946). In the preface it says, "It is the *uta* that makes sweet the ties between men and women and brings solace to the hearts of brave warriors as well". The *uta* is the classic Japanese verse form.

23. Plum-blossoms, because they come out very early in the spring, are associated with coldness and chastity.

24. This refers to an incident said to have occurred during the reign of Hsüan Tsung. "One day, when the emperor was drunk, he had the princess (Yang Kuei-fei) lead over a hundred court ladies, while the emperor led over one hundred court ladies. They were disposed in two files to form a *feng-liu-chen* (風流陣). They attacked and ran against one another. The side that lost was penalised by having to drink great pots of wine." (In *T'ien-pao I-shih*, quoted Ueda: *op. cit.*, p. 308.)

25. The meaning of the line is, "Watch out for ambushes!" The passage is derived from the Nō play *Yorimasa*. "Tadatsuna gave these orders to his subordinates, 'You can tell that there must be rocks in the stream where it swirls around. . .' " (Ueda: *op. cit.*, p. 427.)

26. From the Nō *Futari Shizuka*, "They trod on the flowers and together regretted their youth". This is in turn derived from the poem *Spring Night* by Po Chü-i (both quoted in Ueda: *op. cit.*, p. 549). "We turned our backs on the candlelight and one and other regarded the late night moon; we trod on the flowers and together regretted the springs of our youth."

27. From a poem by Tachibana Zairetsu in the *Wakan Rōei-shū* (quoted in Ueda: *op. cit.*, p. 550). "Breaking a branch of plum-flowers, I hold it over my head; the snows of February fall on my clothes."

28. The kalavinka was a bird that dwelt in paradise; here used to indicate the sweetness of the women's voices.

29. From the *Great Learning* (tr. Legge, p. 376). "From the loving example of one family, a whole state becomes loving, and from its courtesies the whole state becomes courteous."

30. Cheng Chih-lung (1604-61), the father of Coxinga. See Chapter III, p. 45.

31. The ideograph *ming*, meaning "bright" is written with the "sun" and the "moon" 日 , 月 to form 明.

32. All of nature is divided into *yin*, the female, negative, dark principle; and *yang*, the male, positive and light principle.

33. Branding, cutting off the nose, cutting off the feet, castration, and death.

34. The first poem in the *haiku* book *Ayanishiki*, was one by Tokugen 德元 (1559-1647). "However you may regard it, there is nothing so black as snow", "Nan to mite mo, yuki hodo kuroki mono wa nashi." (Quoted in Sekine: *Kokusenya Kassen*, in *Chikamatsu no Kenkyū*, p. 328). The idea goes back to the Chinese sophists and their remarks on hardness and whiteness.

35. The third stroke ㇏ in *ta* 大.

36. Kaidō may have been the town of Hai-teng in Fukien, but this is so far away it hardly seems likely. The name was not written in Chinese characters in the original, and may have been no more than a Chinese-sounding name invented by Chikamatsu.

37. The words Chikamatsu used, *toki* and *hiji*, are Buddhist. *Toki* was the usual noontime meal of Buddhist monks, while *hiji* was a kind of light collation taken in the afternoon, when fasts were generally observed. Here, Go Sankei refers to Ri Tōten as the more important meal, and to Ri Kaihō as the lesser. There is also a pun imbedded in the text, *toki ni hazureru*, "to come at the wrong time" or "to miss an opportunity"

38. The seal was proof of the legitimacy of the emperor, and the sash was tied about it. *Cf.* Ueda: *op. cit.*, p. 38.

39. Literally "the fruit left on the tree after the rest have been gathered".

40. Taisufu is probably T'ai-chou-fu, the modern Lin-hai-hsien, Chekiang.

41. Emperor. The word *jūzen*, "ten virtues", means one who is not guilty of any of the ten sins (killing living beings, theft, adultery, lying, obscene language, cursing, being double-tongued, covetousness, anger, and foolishness). It was an adjective used for the emperor.

42. A proverb for something when one needs it; also, a familiar subject of paintings.

43. "Seagulls" is used to describe the clumsy behaviour of the Tartar soldiers, as clumsy as seagulls on shore.

44. These gods had control of the oceans.

45. The pun is here made between *nani wo sen*—"What shall (I) do?" and the name *Sen*dan, *sen* being used as a pivot.

46. Here, as often in the play, the desire for a play on words leads the author into an irrelevant phrase. *Tare wo tomo* "taking whom as friend" links with *tomo-chidori*, a kind of plover.

47. From the *Great Learning* (tr. Legge: *Chinese Classics*, Vol. I, p. 362). " 'The twittering yellow bird rests on the corner of the mound.' The Master said, 'When it rests, it knows where to rest. Is it possible that a man should not be equal to this bird?' "The quotation is from the *Shih Ching*. Modern research has shown the adjective *mienman* to mean "delicate" rather than "twittering", but Chikamatsu was most probably guided by Chu Hsi's interpretation which was "twittering".

48. Watōnai Sankan was a name of Chikamatsu's invention.

49. *Warekara* is the word of a pun. It is at once the name of a sea-creature, *Caprella*, and means "by oneself".

50. There is a play on words between the name Ko*mutsu* and the word *mutsu*majiku, meaning "friendlily" or "harmoniously".

51. Tsukushi was an old name for Kyūshū.

52. This refers to the exile of Chia I 賈誼 who was sent to Ch'ang-sha.

53. Literally, "a little June".

54. "Cutting their seals" means that the birds were leaving their tracks on the sand. The phrase is found in the *Heike Monogatari*, volume 3. A Chinese poem by Ōe Tomotsuna in the *Wakan Rōei-shū* goes, "The seagulls wander on the sand cutting their seals; the wild geese pass their time tracing letters on the bottom of the sea". (Quoted Ueda: p. 469.)

55. There is a pun between *kaidori*, a long outer-garment worn by ladies, and *kaidori*, "shell-gathering".

56. The following passage is known as the *kai-zukushi*, or "catalogue of shells". Most of the shell-names are used as puns. These are sometimes difficult to reconstruct. The shell-names are linked by short phrases, and tell a story, which is roughly the following:
    When the bamboo-blinds (*sudare*) are lifted by the tide, (I see) a princess (*hime*) with whom I at once fall in love. I would like to take my brush and write a letter on a flat shell and send it (*tairagi*). (The puns are between okuri*tai* "I want to send", *taira* "flat" and "*tairagi*" "flat-shell", the *pinna japonica*.) When her mouth opens

182

and her red (lips) (*aka*) smile ha-ha (*hoya-hoya*), my heart goes to her (*kokoro-yose*). Ah, if I could be (with her)! (*itara*). (You) draw me to you steadily (*sugai*) but my love is one-sided like the abalone (*awabi*). Oh, cruel one! I would like to give you a taste of my fist (*sazai*) in your monkey-face (*sarubō*)! Plum-blossom shells (*mume no hana*), cherry-blossom shells (*sakura*). Unable to sleep, I spend the night (*aka-nishi*) alone. For whom do I wait (*mate*)? I am sorry I saw the person (*mirukui*) and (would like to) forget (*wasure*). (But) the two of us lying in bed (*tokobushi*) could sink (*shizumi*) in one another's arms, and (whisper words of) joy (*iwai*). We would celebrate (*hora*, literally, "trumpet") our happy departure, and (we would there know) bliss (*yorokobi*).

The words in italics are all names of shells. Usually the word *kai*, "shell", is added to the italicised names, and I have tried to keep the feeling of a catalogue by adding the word in my translation.

57. The word *hamaguri* 蛤 "clam" is also written with the character 蜃 in which case it means a kind of dragon. The property of forming castles belongs doubtless to the second class of *hamaguri*.

58. The peaceful appearance and low chirps of shrikes in marshland grasses gave rise to this expression. (*Cf.* Ueda: *op. cit.*, p. 164).

59. Buddha taught that one must exert discipline over one's mind, body and mouth.

60. The story of Hui-k'o (d. 593) may be found in volume 4 of Hozumi's *Naniwa Miyage*. Hui-k'o (also known as Shen-kuang) went to see the famous teacher Bodhidharma to ask for instruction in Zen Buddhism, but the teacher would not see him. Hui-k'o continued to wait in Bodhidharma's garden even though it snowed so heavily that the branches of bamboo broke under the weight of the snow. Bodhidharma took pity on him and asked what he wanted. Hui-k'o begged to be instructed, but the master did not think him worthy of teaching. Hui-k'o thereupon cut off his forearm and placed it before the master as a sign of his deep sincerity. Chikamatsu (or Watōnai) has mixed up the story. It is used here as an example of sudden enlightenment such as Watōnai then experienced.

61. The battle of the shrike and the clam has been discussed in Chapter IV, p. 79.

62. The strategem was advocated by Chang I, a counsellor of the state of Ch'in, and was successful in winning all of China for the ruler of Ch'in.

63. The *Taiheiki*, or "Chronicle of Great Peace" belies its name, and is actually an account of the disorders during a period of terrible civil war in Japan. It has been attributed to Ko ima Hōshi, and is believed to have been written about 1360.

64. The Emperor Go-Daigo (ruled 1318-39) was the chief figure in the *Taiheiki*. An energetic ruler before his successful revolt against the domination of the Hōjō family, he was led by success to the carelessness in administering the state with which Watōnai reproaches him.

65. Hōjō Takatoki (1303-33) (here called Sagami Nyūdō) was the agent of the Shogunate government at Kamakura until his defeat by the forces of Go-daigo.

66. Kusunoki Masashige (1294-1336) and Nitta Yoshisada (1301-38) were two loyal generals of the imperial cause. They defeated Hōjō Takatoki's forces, but were later defeated in turn by those of Ashikaga Takauji (1305-58).

67. Dogs are regarded in Japan as lascivious animals, rather than as the faithful friends of man. Kissing is considered a highly erotic act.

68. Benzaiten (or Benten) is a Buddhist goddess of beauty, known in Sanskrit as Sarasvatī.

N

69. The words as here used have no meaning, and merely represent Chinese sounds as they seem to a Japanese. They are derived, however, from a Buddhist sutra the *Senjū-darani-kyō*, or "Sutra of the Thousand-Armed Dharani". The sounds in the original are *Na mu ka ra tan nō tō ra ya ya a a ri ya*...Chikamatsu has Komutsu follow Sendan's speech with the words "Ariya, nan to iu o-kyō ja" (What sutra is *that?*) where *ariya* is at once a continuation of the words of the sutra and the colloquial contraction of *are wa*. The next speech by Sendan is entirely without meaning. The *tomo* (however) in the middle of it was undoubtedly intended as a comic touch.

70. The Sumiyoshi shrine at Matsura was celebrated because according to mythical tradition, the Empress Jingū was said to have stopped there for several days on her way to conquer Korea. The treasures of the temple include the ebb-pearl and flow-pearl for governing the tides. For the history of the shrine, see *Higashi-Matsura-gun-shi* (supplement), p. 58.

71. A proverb, "En ni tsurureba kara no mono kuu". This means, literally, "To eat Chinese food because of a relationship", and means that one is dependent on some distant person because of a relationship to him. Here, the proverb ends with the word *kui*. This word serves as a pivot for the following: *Kui no yachi tabi kurikaesu*. *Kui* thus at once means "to eat" (Chinese food) and "sorrow" (many times repeated).

72. I have translated the word *ri* as "mile" because it is used here and elsewhere in the play with such vagueness that no careful consideration of the actual length of a *ri* is necessary. The distance between China and Japan, for example, is stated variously as one, two and three thousand *ri*.

73. This is the seventh hexagram in the *I-ching*. Legge says of it (in *Yi King*, p. 72) "The conduct of military expeditions in a feudal kingdom, and we may say, generally, is denoted by the hexagram Sze."

74. The first quotation is from Mencius. I have adopted bodily the translation of Legge (in *Chinese Classics*, Vol. I, p. 208). The second quotation is originally from the *Wang-ming-lun* quoted in *Han Shu* book 100, 1, 4a ff. It is also found in *Tsure-zure-gusa*. (Ueda: *op. cit.*, p. 462.)

75. The account of the Empress Jingū's conquest may be found in the ninth volume of the *Nihonshoki*.

76. From the Nō play *Semimaru*. "A flower seed buried in the earth will grow into a thousand sprays of blossoms." (Ueda: *op. cit.*, p. 408.)

77. An invention of Chikamatsu's, probably influenced by the saying, "Tora wa senri no yabu ni sumu", "A tiger lives in a thicket of a thousand *ri*".

78. This sentiment seems to prevail among some Japanese wives even to-day. Compare with this passage from *An Adopted Husband* by Futabatei Shimei (tr. Mitsui and Sinclair), p. 193. "Isn't this too much? Aren't you too cruel?" Shaking him, "Do you hate me so much? If you hate me so, I'd rather—" in a crying voice, "be killed at a blow ... Come," pulling herself nearer and crying, "please kill me at a blow".

79. In Japanese novels jealous women frequently turn into serpents to plague the new favourites of their lovers.

80. The following lines were probably derived from a similar scene in the Nō play *Shunkan*. (Ueda: *op. cit.*, p. 406.)

81. Literally, the "Watching for Husband Mountain" in the province of Anhwei in central China. In ancient times there was a man who went far away from home. Years passed and still he did not return. His wife climbed this mountain to look for him, and remained there so long that she turned to stone.

82. At the time of the Emperor Kimmei (reigned 540-72) there lived a man named Ōtomo Sadehiko. When he was sent by the court to Korea, his wife, in deep sorrow over their parting, climbed a mountain and, taking off her scarf, waved it to him. Since then the mountain has been known as "Scarf-Waving Mountain". It is located in Matsura County in Hizen. An account of this incident is found in the fifth volume of *Manyōshū*, poem 871.

83. Sea-fire or "shiranui" is used both as an epithet for Tsukushi (Kyūshū) and as a pivot-word "funaji no sue mo shiranu-hi", where it means "not known".

84. The word ōgo has in it the sound of the word *au* "to meet", and thus there is the play on words, "a *protection met* with".

85. There is a proverb "Nishiki wo kite kokyō ni kaeru" which means that when one returns to one's home town after years of absence one should make people believe that one has prospered.

86. From the Nō play *Yuya*, "The grasses and trees obtain their nourishment from the generosity of the rain and the dew, which are the parents of the flowers". (Quoted in Ueda: *op. cit.*, p. 426.)

87. Kanki, or Kan Hui, was one of Coxinga's ablest lieutenants. See Chapter III p. 49.

88. Hsin-yang now called Kiukiang. The reference to orang-outangs is from the Nō play *Shōjō*. (Ueda: *op. cit.* p. 608.)

89. *The Red Cliff* was a prose poem in two parts by Su Tung-p'o (1036-1101). Although Tung-p'o was exiled to a number of places, the Red Cliff (in modern Hupei Province) was not one of them. Partial translations of the two parts may be found in Clark: *Su Tung-p'o*, pp. 47-56.

90. An invention of Chikamatsu's.

91. *Shirakumo* is used as a pivot-word for *hōkaku totemo shirakumo*, where the *shira* has the force of *shiranu*, "unknown".

92. The peculiar expression *hōto kuwa wo nukasu* is explained by Ueda (pp. 320 and 110) as meaning *hoto-hoto* (very) and *kuwa wo nukasu* "to be so distracted as to let one's rake fall".

93. Rice boiled with red beans was a dish associated with foxes. In children's stories there are accounts of people who are bewitched by foxes and fed by them with rice boiled with red beans.

94. From the *I-ching* (Legge, *Yi Ching*, p. 411). "Clouds follow the dragon and winds follow the tiger:—so the sage makes his appearance and all men look to him."

95. When Yang Hsiang was fourteen his father was seized in its jaws by a tiger. Yang Hsiang rushed forward, intending to sacrifice himself to the tiger and thus save his father. The tiger was startled and left both of them alone. For his virtue he was declared one of the twenty-four examples of filial piety.

96. In *Classic of Filial Piety* (tr. Legge: *Sacred Books of the East*, Volume III, p. 461). "Our bodies, to every hair and every bit of skin, are received by us from our parents, and we must not presume to injure or wound them: this is the beginning of filial piety."

97. The Isuzu River flows by the Great Shrine of Ise. The first sound of *I*suzu is used for *i* meaning "to be": the gods *are* in your body.

98. In the first book of the *Kojiki* may be found the account of how the god Susanoo, to spite his sister Amaterasu, flayed a piebald colt backwards and threw it into her halls. Here used as symbol of strength.

99. A proverb (*gaki mo ninzu*) meaning there is a time when even a hateful creature like a devil may be of use.

100. Watōnai is making fun of Ri Tōten's name. Tokoroten is a kind of jellied noodle served cold in summertime.

101. Literally, his "five bodily parts". These were the head, the hands, and the feet, or, by a different reckoning, the muscles, the veins, the flesh, the bones and the hair.

102. The expression "Niō tachi ni naru" is translated in Kenkyūsha's Dictionary as "to draw oneself up to one's full height".

103. The debt of one's rulers. There is a debt of one generation to one's parents and two generations for husband and wife.

104. When a boy reached the age of fifteen, his head was shaved and his personal name changed. This ceremony was known as *gembuku*.

105. The expression "*Sashizoe no shōto hazusashi*" contains the names of three types of short swords (italicised), but may also be translated "to take off the short sword by the side" by using other meanings for the words.

106. *Itobin* and *atsubin* were two styles of hairdress popular in the Tokugawa Period.

107. A puzzling phrase—"futakushihan no haragegami". One commentator suggested that it meant "to give the dishevelled locks two and a half strokes with a comb". Another thought that the locks were dishevelled because they only had two and a half combs. I prefer the explanation that they were left with two and a half combs' worth of hair, as contrasted with the four combs of a Japanese woman.

108. Japanese given names of the period commonly ended in -zaemon or -bei. Another system of given names involved a series beginning with *tarō* (or *ichirō*) for the eldest, *jirō* for the second, *saburō* for the third etc. down to *jūrō* for the tenth.

109. The names are sometimes difficult to decipher. Honan for Horunan and Chaul for Charunan are doubtful. Unsun was not the name of a place but a kind of game of cards played by the Dutch. (See Ueda, pp. 50-1 for details of the game.) I do not know what Sunkichi stood for. Kitani (in *Watakushi no Chikamatsu Kenkyū*, p. 188) found an interesting parallel between the easy surrender of these assorted nationals and that of the Americans and English to the Japanese in 1941 and 1942!

110. The justification of this sentence lies in the use of *toru* in three senses "to hold the reins", "to gain (a name)" and "to conquer".

111. From a poem by Ts'ao Chih (192-232 A.D.) in the nineteenth book of the *Wen Hsüan* (quoted Ueda: *op. cit.*, p. 544) "The kind father cannot love a worthless son; the benevolent ruler cannot collect worthless ministers".

112. Dolphins (usually gilt) decorate the roofs of many castles in Japan.

113. Japanese novels and plays often contain wicked stepmothers.

114. The mistiness is, of course, in Ikkan's eyes.

115. These are nonsense words designed to sound menacing.

116. Literally, "the way a dog or a cat is kept".

117. A proverb. The ends of Japanese tiles were round and had markings on them like those on a coin, and thus a worthless broken tile has a certain resemblance to precious coins; this may have been the origin of the proverb.

118. Prisoners were led to jail by a rope about their waists. Golownin (in *Memoirs of a Captivity in Japan*, Volume I, p. 76) describes the Japanese method of binding prisoners. "We were all . . . placed on our knees and bound in the cruellest manner, with cords about the thickness of a finger: and yet this was not enough; another binding with smaller cords followed, which was still more painful . . . There were loops round our breasts and necks; our elbows almost touched each other, and our hands were firmly bound together; from these fastenings proceeded a long cord, the end of which was held by a Japanese, and which on the slightest attempt to escape required only to be drawn to make the elbows come in contact, with the greatest pain, and tighten the noose about the neck to such a degree as to produce strangulation."

119. The former gate led to paradise, the latter was the gate to this world of delusion.

120. There is a tiresome series of plays on the words *kayou* "to visit" and *musubu* "to tie".

121. Ten sins: see note 41. The five great crimes were: murdering one's father, murdering one's mother, wounding Buddha's person, killing his immediate disciple, and murdering a Buddhist priest.

122. Chinese sew by pushing the needle through the cloth, while Japanese sew by pulling cloth over the needle. This creates a different pattern of stitching (from Professor S. Elisséeff).

123. "Yamato", the old name for Japan, is written with two characters 大和 that have the literal meaning of "great gentleness".

124. The longan is a southern Chinese fruit and is considered a great delicacy. The dishes enumerated are designed by the author to give an effect of oddness. Translations are approximate.

125. *Musubi* are rice-balls, but the word, written with other characters, may mean a third-rank wrestler.

126. I have translated *sanki shōgun* 散騎将軍 thus, although I cannot find any evidence that it was ever so employed. In any case that is probably what Chikamatsu thought it meant.

127. Literally "whose womb I did not borrow".

128. Literally "a century-plant guest" (except that the *udonge* blooms only once in three thousand years instead of a mere century!)

129. Kusunoki, Asahina Yoshihide, Musashibō Benkei (d. 1189), are famous Japanese heroes. K'ung-ming (Chu-ko Liang), Fan K'uai and Hsiang Yü are Chinese military heroes, the first named being revered as the greatest of strategists. Literally "I shall penetrate the entrails of K'ung-ming and borrow the marrow of Fan K'uai and Hsiang Yü".

130. The sacred ropes (*shimenawa*) are hung before shrines to sanctify them.

131. Meaning, she wept tears of blood. *Namida* "tears" is used as a pivot-word, as is so often the case. "Yaru kata namida", where *nami* has the effect of *nashi*, "there was no way". It says literally "her tears were [like] the crimson leaves [redder] than rouge".

132. From an anonymous poem, number 283, in the *Kokin-waka-shū*. "Tatsutagawa, momiji midarete, nagarumeri, wataraba nishiki, naka ya taenan." "In the Tatsuta River, the red leaves seem to flow by in confused patterns. If I should cross, the brocade would be cut through the centre."

133. Watōnai is henceforth in the play called Coxinga (Kokusenya). A change in function always seemed to require a change in name. For the actual historical background, see Chapter III, p. 46.

134. Mo Yeh was the name of one of a pair of famous swords, the other having been Kan Chiang. Kan Chiang was considered the male, and Mo Yeh the female of the pair. See article by J. J. L. Duyvendak in T'oung Pao, 1948, pp. 305-6.

135. For the story of Kuai-chi Mountain, see note 19.

136. There is a saying, "The quick and the dead travel along different roads". (Cf. Giles: Chinese Immortals, p. 82.) The phrase may have the additional meaning here, "Both the quick and the dead (taught) the same teaching", where dō means "way" as a teaching as well as a road.

137. Two proverbs meaning to supply an already powerful creature (or wise one) with additional power.

138. From Ta Tai Li-chi (tr. Wilhelm as Li Gi, p. 146, "Wo Edelsteine in einem Berge wohnen, da sind die Bäume grün. Wo Perlen in der Tiefe wachsen, da wird das Ufer nicht trocken.")

139. Chikura designated the region in between Korea and Japan, and more specifically, Quelpart Island, but it came to be used as a general term for people or things which belonged neither to Japan nor Korea (nor China), much like our expression "neither flesh nor fowl".

140. Negi was a Shintō official of the second rank charged with the superintending of national shrines. I do not know why Komutsu's appearance especially suggested that of a negi or of an unguent vendor.

141. mizu in mizuasagi (light blue) is a pivot-word, and used to mean "did not seem" with the previous expression.

142. This is a tricky phrase. The "four inches and eight inches" (shisun hassun) are taken by Ueda (p. 168) to mean agile, in that one comes within a few inches of one's enemy's blade as one lunges in.

143. Ushiwaka was the name by which Minamoto no Yoshitsune (1159-89) was known as a youth.

144. See note 70.

145. The name by which Po Chü-i is most commonly known in Japan. The story of his supposed visit to Japan is told in the Nō play Haku Rakuten, translated by Waley in The Nō Plays of Japan. The two poems may also be found in the Nō play (p. 211 of the translation). They are both Japanese poems (although one is written in Chinese) and have nothing to do with Po Chü-i. (See Ueda: op. cit., p. 414.)

146. A poetic name for Japan.

147. For a discussion of these lines, see Chapter I, p. 7.

148. There is a pun imbedded in the text here. "Futaba ni misete" means literally "showing in two leaves", and refers to the proverb "Sendan wa futaba yori kōbashi" (The sendan-tree is fragrant from the time it puts forth two leaves). Here, however, the primary meaning must be that the two women have different thoughts.

149. A rare case of a pun that works in both Japanese and English. mirume is a kind of seaweed; miru means "to see".

150. The wild goose was the traditional bearer of tidings from distant places. This passage is discussed in Chapter II, p. 42.

151. "three, four, five" serve to introduce mutsumajiku (where mutsu means "six") and the Pool of the Seven Rapids.

152. There is a play on words contained in kakurembō, "hide-and-seek", where kakure is used as a full verb "to hide". "The devil" was the "it" of the game.

153. The usual pun on "waiting" and "pine-tree". Here, the name Matsura has the pine-tree element (*matsu*). *Chika no ura* is the name of a bay, but *chika* is used for its meaning of "near".

154. The play on words is here between *taguri* "to haul in" and "*Kuriya*" the name of the river.

155. The word "string" (*ito*) is a pun for the adverb *ito* meaning "very".

156. A reference to a poem by Po Chü-i, "When, on the night of the fifteenth, moonlight bathes anew the sky, I think of old friends two thousand miles away". (Quoted in Ueda: *op. cit.*, p. 550.) Chikamatsu's text says literally, "The memory of old friends, two thousand miles away, though this is not the night of the fifteenth. . ." I have supplied the rest to make the translation more easily intelligible.

157. "white waves" (*shiranami*) serves as a pivot-word, where *yukue mo shiranami* means "not knowing the direction". *shiranami* thus stands for *shiranai*.

158. The twelve islands of Kikai are a small archipelago south of the province of Satsuma in Kyūshū. All the islands mentioned belong to the group except for Two Gods (Futagami-shima).

159. Shikishima is a "pillow-word" for Japan, an epithet modifying Akitsushima ("The Land of the Dragon Fly").

160. These boats were used by the gods; described in *Nihonshoki*, Volume I.

161. Sung-chiang was famous for its carp, as is shown by the Su Tung-p'o poem, *The Red Cliff* (Second Part). "One of my friends replied, 'This very evening I pulled in my net and caught a fish, large-mouthed and small-scaled, in appearance like the carp of the Sung River'. " (Clark: *op. cit.*, p. 55.)

162. *Sumiyoshi*, means literally, a "pleasant place to live". The pivot-word is *sumi* used as the name of the god and for the verb "to live".

163. T'ao Chu-kung was another name for Fan Li (for whom see note 19). The first sentence is taken word for word from the Nō play *Funa-Benkei*. (Ueda: *op. cit.*, p. 419.)

164. From a poem by Wang Chien in the collection *Poems in Three Forms*. Here used to show the contrast between the life of a prince in the world of beautiful things, and the gloomy life of an exile. (Ueda: *op. cit.*, p. 527.)

165. *kumomizu* is a pivot-word meaning "journey", with *kumo* also used for "cloud".

166. Chūgenzen is an intermediate dhyāna stage. I do not know why Chikamatsu used the term here.

167. An allusion to the poem by Po Chü-i, "How happy I am I have my three friends! Who are my three friends? When I've had enough of my lute, I lift my cup of wine. When I've had enough of wine, I chant my poems. My three friends succeed one another in turn." (Quoted Ueda: p. 539.)

168. In the Astronomy Section of the *Chin Shu* there is the statement, "The blue sky is like a round lid, the earth is like a *go*-board". (Quoted Ueda: p. 478.) Another account (*ibid.*) of 1668 states, "The surface of the board is our transitory world . . . The black and white stones are the day and the night. The 360 intersections are the number of days in a year, etc." There are actually 361 intersections.

169. Literally, Shūmisen, the Japanese name for Sumeru, which was the central mountain of the Buddhist universe. It rose to a height of 80,000 yojanas, or about two million miles.

170. In the *Shu-i-chi*, a collection of strange stories by Jen Fang (460-508 A.D.), there is the account of Wang Chih of the state of Chin who went out to cut wood in the mountains. There he saw several boys playing *go*. They gave him something like a jujube stone. When he swallowed it he ceased to feel hunger. By the time the game was over, his axe-handle had completely rotted. When he got back home, his seventh generation descendant was on the throne. (Ueda: p. 559.) "Nights and days" are pivot-words, continuing the previous thought about the black and white stones, and pointing ahead to the man who forgot about time.

171. From the poem, number 56, in the *Kokin-waka-shū*, by Sosei Hōshi 素性法師. "When I look out, the willows and the cherry-blossoms are blended together; the capital is decked in the brocade of spring." (Ueda: p. 443.)

172. 石頭城 (Shih-t'ou-ch'eng), a place near Nanking.

173. Literally, "Left tiger-dragon" and "Right tiger-dragon". Probably these are no more than Chinese-sounding appellations.

174. From the poem in the *Pillow Book* of Lady Sei Shōnagon. "Yo wo komete, tori no sorane wa, hakaru to mo, yo ni Ōsaka no, seki wa yurusaji." A rough translation would be, "The dawn has not come; even though you imitate the crowing of of the cock, you won't be able to get through Osaka Pass where we might meet". This refers to the story of a nobleman who did get through the Pass at night because one of his entourage so well imitated a cock's crowing that the gate-keeper thought it was dawn.
  The effect of divided speech was probably achieved by having assistants to the chanter.

175. The Bunji era was 1185-89. The following passage is based on a scene in the Nō play *Ataka*, translated by Sansom as *Benkei-at-the-Barrier* (in *TASJ* XXXVIII, pt. III, pp. 151-65). Many of the words are identical in the two versions.

176. After the death of Yang Kuei-fei, the Emperor Hsüan Tsung had a magician from Lin-ch'iung search for her ghost. *Cf.* Jenyns: *op. cit.*, pp. 13-4. T'ai-chen was a name given to Yang Kuei-fei.

177. Bit-crickets. *Kutsuwa-mushi* is defined as "a noisy cricket" in dictionaries. I have used "bit" because it is used as a pivot-word—"the pony's *bit*" "*bit*-cricket".

178. A fan used by officers, especially cavalry, to give commands.

179. Kurikara was the scene of a battle in 1183 between Kiso Yoshinaka and Taira Koremori. Minamoto no Yoshitsune's force staged a famous cavalry charge down a precipitous slope at Ichinotani in 1184. Yashima was the scene of a battle of 1184 in which Minamoto no Yoshitsune forced the Taira clan to flee.

180. *hōrokubiya.* Described in Brinkley's Dictionary as, "A projectile weapon consisting essentially of a copper shell filled with explosives and thrown among the enemy".

181. The Hsien-yang Palace was the residence of Ch'in Shih-huang, the first emperor of China. It was burnt by Hsiang Yü, "the man from Ch'u" (233-202 B.C.)

182. From a poem by Fujiwara Sadaie in the sixth *kan* of the *Zoku-Goshūi-shū* "Itsuwari no, naki yo narikeri. Kannazuki, ta ga makoto yori, shigure someken." "It is a world without deceit. In the month of No-gods on account of whose honesty has the autumn rain started?" The poem would seem to be a play on the name of the month. That is, in the month when there are no gods about to supervise one's honesty, who is it who is responsible for starting the disagreeable autumn rain? The month of No-gods was the tenth month.

183. A fictitious place, in the Chikamatsu manner.

184. Either Min or Ken might refer to Fukien; probably Chikamatsu was not too sure of his Chinese geographical terminology.

185. *Mizu-kagami* is a pivot-word, with the *mi* serving as part of *miru*, "to see".

186. See Chapter IV, p. 79.

187. The katsura (or Japanese Judas-tree) is always associated with the moon. The moon was often considered the world of the dead.

188. From the Nō play *Tōru*, virtually word for word. (*Cf.* Ueda: *op. cit.*, p. 413.)

189. From Su Tung-p'o: *The Red Cliff*. "But do you understand the water and the moon? . . . The latter waxes and wanes but does not really increase or diminish." (Tr. Clark: *op. cit.*, p. 48.)

190. "Shines in the heavens" is at the same time the name of the goddess, Amaterasu.

191. The usual pun of the two *matsu*'s.

192. From Ōtomo Yakamochi's poem in the sixth volume of the *Shinkokinshū*, "Kasasagi no, wataseru hashi ni, oku shimo no, shiroki wo mireba, yo zo fukenikeru". "When I see the whiteness of the frost on the bridge the magpies have built, I know the night is far advanced." The magpie bridge is connected with the legend that on the seventh night of the seventh moon magpies flock together to form a bridge in the sky over which the Herd Boy can cross to the Spinning Maiden (two stars). (*Cf.* Ueda: *op. cit.*, p. 453.)

193. A famous bridge, supposedly built by the god of Katsuragi Mountain. Because of his ugliness, the god was ashamed to appear during the day, and worked only at night.

194. *Kake-hashi*, "a bridge over a gorge" has the pivot of *kake*, which is used in *koe wo kake*, "to let out cries".

195. Burckhardt (in *Civilization of the Renaissance*, p. 91) tells of how King Dardanus struck Attila dead at Rimini with a chess-board.

196. Satō Tadanobu was famed as a horseman. He was said to have been able to get the four legs of his mount on a chess-board. Chikamatsu wrote a play *Goban Tadanobu*.

197. The terms used *yotsume-goroshi*, *nakate*, *shichō*, *seki*, *hama* and *kō* are technical ones of the game of *go*.

198. Mencius. (Legge: *The Book of Mencius*, p. 142.) "In such a thing as taking the T'ai mountain under your arm and leaping over the north sea with it, if you say to people, 'I am not able to do it', that is a real case of not being able. In such a matter as breaking a branch from a tree at the order of a superior, if you say to people, 'I am not able to do it', that is a case of not doing it. It is not a case of not being able to do it."

199. Yung Li. For an historical account of this Ming pretender, see Chapter III, p. 53.

200. From the *Minshin Tōki*. See Noma: *op. cit.*, p. 637.

201. For a discussion of Go Sankei's and Kanki's plans, see Chapter IV, p. 79.

202. Komutsu in her guise as a soldier. See note 143.

203. Hatsumotoyui. This was the cord used for tying up the queue at the time of the *gembuku* ceremony.

VIII

BIBLIOGRAPHY

(a) Text

Although there are numerous editions of *Kokusenya Kassen* available, they fortunately are virtually uniform. The one exception is that prepared by Mizutani Yumihiko 水谷弓彦 in *Chikamatsu Kessaku Zenshū* (Tokyo, 1910) which has a number of minor variants, none of which I have seen reason to adopt. The most reliable text of the play is that of Fujii Otoo 藤井乙男 in *Chikamatsu Zenshū* (Osaka, 1925). I have found it more convenient, however, to use the text in the Yūhōdō Bunko entitled *Chikamatsu Jōruri-shū* (ed. Tadami Keizō 忠見慶造) (1926), controlling it with Fujii's text and the one edited by Wada Mankichi 和田萬吉 in the Iwanami Bunko (1928). Other editions include:

Kitani Hōgin 木谷蓬吟: *Dai-Chikamatsu Zenshū*, Volume III, Tokyo, 1922.
Sekine Masanao 關根正直: *Kokusenya Kassen*, Tokyo, 1926.

There have also been a number of translations of the play into modern Japanese. These translations are generally of little help as they skip or fail to explain the difficult passages. The one by Teruoka Yasutaka 暉峻康隆: *Gendai-yaku Nihon Koten: Chikamatsu-shi* is perhaps the most recent (1942), but extraordinarily poor. In English, there is a rough paraphrase-abridgement-translation in Miyamori: *Tales from Old Japanese Dramas*. Like most other Tokugawa texts, *Kokusenya Kassen* has suffered from neglect by Japanese scholars, who have perhaps thought it too easy to require their attention. The student of Chikamatsu may therefore count on very little assistance from his predecessors.

(b) Japanese works

NOTE: Obvious titles are not given in characters

1. Akizato Ritō 秋里籬島: *Shūi Miyako Meisho Zue* 拾遺都名所圖繪 (in *Nihon Zue Zenshū*) Tokyo, 1928.
2. Andō Jishō 安藤自笑: (*Fūzoku*) *Keiseiya Gundan* in *Kokusho Kankōkai* series *Kinsei Bungei Sōsho*, Tokyo, 1911.
3. Arai Hakuseki 新井白石: *Shinsho* 紳書 (in Vol. VI, 3rd series; *Nihon Zuihitsu Taisei*), Tokyo, 1930.
4. Asakawa Kanae 朝川鼎 (Zen'an 善庵): *Zen'an Zuihitsu* (in Vol. I, *Nihon Zuihitsu Zenshū*) Tokyo, 1927.

5. Atsumi Seitarō 渥美清太郎: *Zoku-zoku Gidayū Kyōgen-shū* (Vol. XXXVII of *Nihon Gikyoku Zenshū*), Tokyo, 1932.

6. Ejima Kiseki 江島其磧: *Kokusenya Minchō Taiheiki* (in *Teikoku Bunko: Kiseki Jishō Kessaku-shū*) Tokyo, 1894.

7. Fujimura Tsukuru 藤村作: *Chikamatsu no Geijutsu no Gendaiteki Igi* (in *Bungaku*, Vol. III, No. 3) Tokyo, 1935.

8. Fujimura Tsukuru: *Chikamatsu Oboegaki* (in *Waseda Bungaku* No. 250) Tokyo, Nov., 1926.

9. Futagion Shujin 二木園主人 (pseud.): *Gikyoku Shōsetsu Tsūshi*, Osaka, 1928.

10. Hamamatsu Utakuni 濱松歌國: *Nansui Manyū Shūi* 南水漫遊拾遺 (in *Kokusho Kankōkai Sōsho*), Tokyo, 1911.

11. Hayashi Nobuatsu 林信篤: *Kan'ei Shōsetsu* 寛永小說 (in Kondō: *Zoku-Shiseki Shūran*) Tokyo, 1930.

12. *Higashi-Matsura-gun-shi* 東松浦郡史, Karatsu, 1915.

13. Higuchi Yoshichiyo 樋口慶千代: *Chikamatsu Monzaemon no Gakushiki* (in *Waseda Bungaku* No. 250), Tokyo, Nov., 1926.

14. Hozumi Ikan 穗積以貫: *Naniwa Miyage* 難波みやげ (ed. Ueda Kazutoshi 上田萬年), Tokyo, 1904.

15. Ichiraku 一樂 (pseud.): *Chikuhō Koji* 竹豊故事 (in Vol. VI, *Shin-Gunsho Ruijū*) Tokyo, 1907.

16. Ihara Toshirō 伊原敏郎: *Meiji Engeki-shi*, Tokyo, 1933.

17. Iizuka Tomoichirō 飯塚友一郎: *Kabuki Saiken*, Tokyo, 1926.

18. Inō Yoshinori 伊能嘉矩: *Taiwan Bunka-shi*, Tokyo, 1928.

19. Ishihara Dōsaku 石原道作: *Nihon Kisshi* (乞師) *no Kenkyū*, Tokyo, 1945.

20. Ishihara Michihiro 道博: *Taiwan Teishi Shōyu Ruson Shimatsu* 台灣鄭氏招諭呂宋始末 in *Tōyō-shi Shūsetsu*, Tokyo, 1942.

21. Kanagaki Robun 假名垣魯文: *Kokusenya Ichidai-ki*, Edo, 1855.

22. Karasue Masaji 烏江正路: *Isetsu Machimachi* 異說まちまち (in Vol. IX, *Nihon Zuihitsu Taisei*), Tokyo, 1927.

23. Katō Junzō 加藤順藏: *Chikamatsu Kenkyū*, Tokyo, 1938.

24. Kawatake Shigetoshi 河竹繁俊: *Kawatake Mokuami* 河竹默阿彌, Tokyo, 1925.

25. Kitani Hōgin: *Dai-Chikamatsu to Takemoto Masatayū* (in *Waseda Bungaku* No. 250) Tokyo, Nov., 1926.

26. Kitani Hōgin: Introductions in *Dai-Chikamatsu Zenshū*, Tokyo, 1922.

27. Kitani Hōgin: *Jōruri Kenkyū-sho*, Tokyo, 1941.

28. Kitani Hōgin: *Watakushi no Chikamatsu Kenkyū*, Osaka, 1942.

29. Kōda Rohan 幸田露伴: *Sōrinshi no Nimen* (in *Waseda Bungaku* No. 250), Tokyo, Nov., 1926.

30. Koizumi Tōzō 小泉藤造: Articles in *Nihon Bungaku Daijiten*, Tokyo, 1933.
31. Kondō Tadayoshi 近藤忠義: *Kamigata Edo Jidai* (in *Iwanami Bungaku Kōza*) Tokyo, 1932.
32. Kuroki Kanzō 黒木勘藏: *Chikamatsu Igo*, Tokyo, 1942.
33. Kuroki Kanzō: *Chikamatsu Jidaimono Kenkyū* (in Katō: *Chikamatsu Kenkyū*).
34. Kuroki Kanzō: *Chikamatsu Monzaemon*, Tokyo, 1942.
35. Kuroki Kanzō: *Jōruri-shi*, Tokyo, 1943.
36. Maki Bokusen 牧墨仙: *Isshōwa* 一宵話 (in Vol. XVII, *Nihon Zuihitsu Zenshū*) Tokyo, 1928.
37. Matsuzaki Gyōshin 松崎堯臣: *Mado no Susabi Tsuika* 窓の須佐美追加 (in *Yūhōdō Bunko*), Tokyo, 1927.
38. Miyake Shūtarō 三宅周太郎: *Bunraku no Kenkyū*, Tokyo, 1930.
39. Mizutani Yumihiko: Introductions in *Chikamatsu Kessaku Zenshū*, Tokyo, 1910.
40. Nishikawa Joken 西川如見: *Ka'i Tsūshō-kō* 華夷通商考 (in Takimoto: *Nihon Keizai Daiten*), Tokyo, 1928.
41. Nishikawa Joken: *Nagasaki Yawa-sō* 長崎夜話草 (in *Iwanami Bunko*), Tokyo, 1943.
42. Nishizawa Ippōken 西澤一鳳軒: *Miyako no Hirune Shohen* 皇都午睡初篇 (in *Shin-Gunsho Ruijū*, Vol. I), Tokyo, 1906.
43. Nishizawa Ippū 一風: *Konjaku Ayatsuri Nendai-ki* (in Vol. VI, *Shin-Gunsho Ruijū*), Tokyo, 1907.
44. Noma Kōshin 野間光辰: *Kokusenya Gozen Gundan to Kokusenya Kassen no Genkyō ni tsuite* (in *Kinen Rombunshū*) Kyoto, 1934.
45. Ōe Tadafusa 大江匡房: *Kairaishi-ki* (in *Gunsho Ruijū*), Tokyo, 1904.
46. Ōta Nampo 太田南畝: *Ichiwa Ichigen* 一話一言 (in *Nihon Zuihitsu Taisei*), Tokyo, 1928.
47. Saitō Gesshin 齋藤月岑: *Seikyoku Ruisan*, Edo, 1847.
48. Saitō Setsudō 拙堂: *Kaigai Iden*, 1850.
49. Sasa Seisetsu 佐佐醒雪: *Zokkyoku Hyōshaku*, Tokyo, 1910.
50. Satō Tsurukichi 佐藤鶴吉: *Chikamatsu no Kokugoteki Kenkyū* (in *Iwanami Bungaku Kōza*), Tokyo, 1931.
51. Shidehara Hiroshi 幣原坦: *Kokusenya no Taiwan Kōryaku* (in *Shigaku Zasshi*, Vol. XLII, No. 3) Tokyo, 1931.
52. Shuzui Kenji 守隨憲治: *Chikamatsu Jōruri no Keishiki* (in *Kokugo to Kokubungaku*, Vol. VII, No. 4), Tokyo, Apr., 1930.
53. Shuzui Kenji: Articles in *Nihon Bungaku Daijiten*, Tokyo, 1928.

54. Sonoda Tamio 園田民雄: *Jōruri Sakusha no Kenkyū*, Tokyo, 1944.
55. Takahashi Hiroshi 高橋宏: *Chikamatsu no Gikyoku Taiyō* (in *Bungaku*, Vol. II. No. 4), Tokyo, 1934.
56. Takano Hanzan 高野班山: *Chikamatsu no Ongaku-jō ni okeru Taishūsei* (in *Kokugo to Kokubungaku*, Vol. I, No. 6), Tokyo, 1924.
57. Takano Masami 正巳: *Chikamatsu Jidaimono no Sandamme ni tsuite* (in *Bungaku*, Vol. II, No. 4), Tokyo, 1934.
58. Takano Masami: *Kinsei Engeki no Kenkyū*, Tokyo, 1941.
59. Takano Tatsuyuki 辰之: *Chikamatsu no Kushō* (苦笑) (in *Waseda Bungaku* No. 250), Tokyo, Nov., 1926.
60. Takano Tatsuyuki: *Edo Bungaku-shi*, Tokyo, 1935.
61. Takano Tatsuyuki: *Jōruri-shi*, Tokyo, 1900.
62. Takano Tatsuyuki: *Nihon Engeki no Kenkyū*, Tokyo, 1926.
63. Takasu Yoshijirō 高須芳次郎: *Kinsei Bungaku Jūnikō*, Tokyo, 1925.
64. Takayama Chogyū 高山樗牛: *Chikamatsu Sōrinshi* (in *Chogyū Zenshū*), Tokyo, 1905.
65. Tanabe Mitsuzō 田邊密藏: *Chikamatsu Monzaemon no Shoshutsu ni tsuite* (in *Kokugo to Kokubungaku*, Vol. II. No. 8), Tokyo, 1925.
66. Tanabe Shigeaki 茂啓: *Nagasaki Jitsuroku Taisei* (in Koga: *Nagasaki-shi*) Nagasaki, 1928.
67. Tanaka Shinji 田中辰二: *Chikamatsu to Jidai* (in *Kokugo to Kokubungaku*, Vol. II, No. 1) Tokyo, 1925.
68. Terashima Ryōan 寺島良安: *Wakan Sanzai Zue*, 1715.
69. Tōgi Tetteki 東儀鐵笛: *Ongaku-jō yori mitaru Kokusenya Kassen* (in Tsubouchi *et al.*: *Chikamatsu no Kenkyū*).
70. Tokutomi Iichirō 德富猪一郎: *Sesōhen* 世相篇, Tokyo, 1936.
71. Tsubouchi Shōyō 坪內逍遙 *et al.*: *Chikamatsu no Kenkyū*, Tokyo, 1900.
72. Tsubouchi Shōyō: *Shōyō Senshū*, Tokyo, 1921.
73. Ueda Kazutoshi and Higuchi Yoshichiyo: *Chikamatsu Go-i* (語彙), Tokyo, 1930.
74. Udagawa Bunkai 宇田川文海: *Chikamatsu Okina to Mikkyō no Kōsō* (in *Waseda Bungaku* No. 250), Tokyo, Nov., 1926.
75. Wakatsuki Yasuji 若月保治: *Chikamatsu Ningyō Jōruri no Kenkyū*, Tokyo, 1934.
76. Wakatsuki Yasuji: *(Ningyō) Jōruri-shi Kenkyū*, Tokyo, 1943.
77. Wakatsuki Yasuji: *Kinsei (Shoki) Kokugeki no Kenkyū*, Tokyo, 1944.
78. Wakatsuki Yasuji: *Ko-jōruri no Shin-kenkyū*, Tokyo, 1943.
79. Yamaguchi Gō 山口剛: *Edo Bungaku Kenkyū*, Tokyo, 1933.
80. Yamaguchi Gō: *Edo Bungaku to Toshi Seikatsu*, Tokyo, 1924.

81. Yamaguchi Gō: *Kokusenya Kassen no Beni-nagashi ni tsuite* (in *Edo Bungaku Kenkyū*).

82. Yoshida Sumio 吉田澄夫: Articles in *Nihon Bungaku Daijiten*, Tokyo, 1928.

(c) Chinese Works

83. Cheng Chü-chung 鄭居仲: *Cheng Ch'eng-kung Chuan* 鄭成功傳 in *Li-chou I-chu Hui-chi* 梨州遺著彙集, Shanghai, 1909.

84. Chiang Jih-sheng 江日昇: *T'ai-wan Wai-chi* 臺灣外記, Shanghai, n.d.

85. Chu Hsi-tsu 朱希祖: *Cheng Yen-p'ing-wang Shou Ming Kuan-chüeh K'ao* 鄭延平王受明官爵考 (in *Kuo-hsüeh Chi-k'an* 國學季刊 Vol. III, No. 1), Peiping, 1932.

86. Hsieh Kuo-chen 謝國禎: *Wan-ming Shih-chi K'ao* 晚明史籍考, Peiping, 1932.

87. Huang Tsung-hsi 黃宗羲: *Ssu-hsing Shih-mo* 賜姓始末 in *Li-chou I-chu Hui-chi*.

88. Li Chieh 李介: *T'ien-hsiang-ko Sui-pi* 天香閣隨筆 (*c.* 1660).

89. Liu Hsien-t'ing 劉獻廷: *Kuang-yang Tsa-chi* 廣陽雜記, Shanghai, 1937.

90. Shen Yün 沈雲: *T'ai-wan Cheng-shih Shih-mo* 臺灣鄭氏始末, Shanghai, 1934.

91. Wang Chih-hsin 王治心: *Ts'ung Kuo-nan Shuo-tao Cheng Ch'eng-kung* 從國難說到鄭成功 (in *Fu-chien Wen-hua*, Vol. I, No. 3), 1932.

92. Wei Yüan 魏源: *Sheng-wu-chi* 聖武記, 1844.

93. Yang Shu-fang 楊樹芳: *Cheng Ch'eng-kung Shih-chi K'ao* 鄭成功事蹟考 (in *Fu-chien Wen-hua*, Vol. III, No. 17), 1935.

94. Yang Ying 楊英: *Ts'ung-cheng Shih-lu* 從征實錄 (ed. Chu Hsi-tsu), Shanghai, 1931.

(d) European Works

95. Alcobendas, Severiano: *Las Misiones Franciscanas en China*, Vol. V, Madrid, 1933.

96. Allan, C. Wilfrid: *Makers of Cathay*, Shanghai, 1909.

97. *Archief voor de Geschiedenis der Oude Hollandsche Zending*, Utrecht, 1884.

98. Baldaeus, Philippus: *Naauwkeurige Beschrijvinge van Malabar en Choromandel*, Amsterdam, 1672.

99. Beaumont, C. W.: *Puppets and the puppet Stage*, London, 1938.

100. Biot, Edouard: *Tcheou-Li*, Peking, 1940 (reprint).

101. Blair, E. and Robertson, J.: *The Philippine Islands* (Vol. XXXVI), Cleveland, 1906.
102. Boulger, D. C.: *History of China*, London, 1882.
103. Bowra, C. A. V.: *Some Episodes in ihe History of Amoy* (in *China Review* XXI, No. 2), Hongkong, 1894.
104. Boxer, C. R.: *The Rise and Fall of Nicholas Iquan* (in *T'ien Hsia Monthly*, Vol. XI, No. 5), Shanghai, 1941.
105. Brewster, Dorothy: *Aaron Hill*, New York, 1913.
106. Brinkley, F.: *A History of the Japanese People*, New York, 1915.
107. Brinkley, F.: *An Unabridged Japanese-English Dictionary*, Tokyo, 1896.
108. Burckhardt, Jakob: *Civilization of the Renaissance*, Oxford, 1945.
109. Campbell, William: *Formosa Under the Dutch*, London, 1903.
110. Careri, J. F. G.: *Voyage Round the World* (in Churchill: *Collection of Voyages and Travels*), London, 1704.
111. Chavannes, Ed.: *Mémoires Historiques de Se-ma Ts'ien*, Paris, 1895-1905.
112. Cordier, H.: *Histoire Générale de la Chine* (Vol. IV), Paris, 1921.
113. Cramer, M.: *Borts Voyagie*, Amsterdam, 1670.
114. Davidson, J. W.: *The Island of Formosa*, Yokohama, 1903.
115. Diaz, Casimirio: *Conquistas de las Islas Filipinas*, Valladolid, 1890.
116. Dryden, John: *Works*, ed. Scott, rev. Saintsbury, Edinburgh, 1883.
117. Elisséev, S. and Iacovleff, A.: *Le Théâtre Japonais*, Paris, 1933.
118. Ferrando, Juan: *Historia de los PP Dominicos*, Vol. III, Madrid, 1871.
119. Futabatei, Shimei: *An Adopted Husband*, tr. Mitsui and Sinclair, New York, 1919.
120. Galang, Zoilo M.: *Encyclopedia of the Philippines*, Manila, 1935.
121. Giles, H. A.: *A Personal Memory of Formosa* (in *China*, Vol. II, No. 1), Amsterdam, 1927.
122. Giles, H. A.: *China and the Manchus*, Cambridge, 1912.
123. Giles, Lionel: *A Gallery of Chinese Immortals*, London, 1948.
124. Golownin, W.: *Memoirs of a Captivity in Japan*, London, 1824.
125. Greslon, Adrien: *Histoire de la Chine sous la Domination des Tartares*, Paris, 1671.
126. Grube, Wilhelm: *Chinesische Schattenspiele*, Munich, 1915.
127. Haguenauer, M. C.: *Mélanges Critiques* (in *Bulletin de la Maison Franco-Japonaise*, Vol. II), Tokyo, 1930.
128. Helmers, J. F.: *Nagelaten Gedichten*, Gravenhage, 1823.
129. Heras, Enrique: *La Dinastia Manchú en China*, Barcelona, 1918.
130. Herport, Albrecht: *Reise nach Java, Formosa, Vorder-Indien und Ceylon, 1659-1668*, Haag, 1930.
131. Hill, Aaron: *Dramatic Works*, London, 1760.

132. Hill, S. C.: *Notes on Piracy in Eastern Seas* (in *The Indian Antiquary*) London, 1923-8.
133. Hobson, H. E.: *Fort Zelandia* (in *JNCBRAS*, New Series, Vol. XI), 1876.
134. Hsieh Kuo Ching: *Removal of Coastal Population* (in *Chinese Social and Political Science Review*, Vol. XV, No. 4), 1932.
135. Hummel, A. W., ed.: *Eminent Chinese of the Ch'ing Period*, Washington, 1943.
136. Ides, E. Y.: *Three Years' Travels from Moscow Overland to China*, London, 1706.
137. Imbault-Huart, C.: *L'Ile Formose*, Paris, 1893.
138. Jenyns, Soame: *A Further Selection from the Three Hundred Poems of the T'ang Dynasty*, London, 1944.
139. Kaempfer, E.: *The History of Japan* (tr. Scheuchzer), Glasgow, 1906.
140. Kure, B.: *The Historical Development of Marionette Theatre in Japan*, New York, 1920.
141. Lamartine, A. de: *Graziella*, Paris, 1888.
142. Lee, Vernon: *Studies of the Eighteenth Century in Italy*, London, 1880.
143. Legge, James: *The Chinese Classics* (2nd ed.), Oxford, 1893-95.
144. Legge, James: *Sacred Books of the East*, Vol. III, Oxford, 1879.
145. *Lettres Edifiantes et Curieuses* (Nouvelle Edition), Toulouse, 1810.
146. Liao, W. K.: *Han Fei Tzŭ* (Vol. I), London 1939.
147. Lombard, F. A.: *Outline History of the Japanese Drama*, London, 1928.
148. Maas, Otto: *Cartas de China*, Sevilla, 1917.
149. Macaulay, W. H.: *Kathay*, New York, 1852.
150. Mailla, Joseph: *Histoire Générale de la Chine* (Vol. II), Paris, 1780.
151. Miyajima, Tsunao: *Contribution à l'Etude du Théâtre des Poupées*, Osaka, 1928.
152. Miyamori, Asataro: *Masterpieces of Chikamatsu*, London, 1926.
153. Miyamori, Asataro: *Tales from Old Japanese Dramas*, London, 1915.
154. Montanus, Arnoldus: *Atlas Chinensis* (tr. Ogilby), London, 1671.
155. Montanus, Arnoldus: *Ambassades Mémorables de la Compagnie des Indes Orientales des Provinces-Unies vers les Empereurs de Japon*, Amsterdam, 1680.
156. Montero y Vidal, José: *Historia General de Filipinas*, Madrid, 1887.
157. Murillo, Pedro: *Geographia Historica de las Islas Philipinas* (Vol. VIII), Madrid, 1752.
158. Murry, J. M.: *Shakespeare*, London, 1948.
159. Navarrete, D. F.: *Tratados Historicos, Politicos, Ethicos y Religiosos de la Monarchia de China*, Madrid, 1676.

160. Navas del Valle, F.: *Catalogo de los Documentos Relativos a las Islas Filipinas*, Vol. IX, Barcelona, 1936.
161. Nieuhof, Johan: *Het Gezantschap der Neerlandtsche Oost-Indische Compagnie aan den Grooten Tartarischen Cham*, Amsterdam, 1693.
162. Nomsz, J.: *Anthonius Hambroek of de Belegering van Formoza*, Amsterdam, 1775.
163. Orléans, P. J. d': *Histoire des deux Conquérans Tartares*, Paris, 1688.
164. Palafox y Mendoza, Juan de: *History of the Conquest of China by the Tartars*, London, 1671.
165. Parker, E. H.: *Letters from a Chinese Empress* (in *Contemporary Review* CI) London, 1912.
166. Parker, E. H.: *Maritime Wars of the Manchus* (in *China Review* XVI), Hongkong, 1887-8.
167. Paske-Smith, M.: *Western Barbarians in Japan and Formosa*, Kobe, 1930.
168. Pastells, Pablo: *Historia General de Filipinas* (in Navas del Valle, *op. cit.*), Barcelona, 1936.
169. *Peking Gazette for 1875*, Shanghai, 1876.
170. Pelliot, Paul: *Michel Boym* (in *T'oung Pao*, Second Series, Vol. XXXI), Leiden, 1934.
171. Pelliot, Paul: *Reviews* (in *T'oung Pao*, Second Series, Vol. XXVIII, XXIX, XXXI), Leiden, 1931-4.
172. Phillips, George (G.P.): *Life of Koxinga* (in *China Review*, Vol. XIII, No. 2), Hongkong, 1884.
173. Ponsonby-Fane, R. A. B.: *Koxinga, Chronicles of the Tei Family*, (*TPJSL*, Vol. XXXIV) London, 1937.
174. Ross, John: *The Manchus or the Reigning Dynasty of China*, Paisley, 1880.
175. Rougemont, François de: *Historia Tartaro-Sinica nova*, Lovanii, 1673.
176. Sansom, G. B.: *Benkei-at-the-Barrier* (in *TASJ*, Vol. XXVIII, pt. III), Tokyo, 1919 (reprint).
177. Sansom, G. B.: *Japan* (Revised Edition), New York, 1943.
178. Streit, Robert: *Bibliotheca Missionüm* (Vol. V), Aachen, 1929.
179. Takeda, Izumo: *Chushingura*, (tr. Jukichi Inouye), Tokyo, 1910.
180. Tavernier, J. B.: *Recueil de plusieurs Relations et Traitez*, Paris, 1679.
181. Thevenot, M.: *Relations de Divers Voyages Curieux* (Vol. II), Paris, 1696.
182. *Tweede en Derde Gesandschap na het Keyserryck van Taysing of China* (Second Embassy written by Jan van Kampen and Konstantijn Nobel, Third Embassy by Olfert Dapper), Amsterdam, 1670.

O

183. Van der Aa, A. J.: *China en Zijne Bewoners*, Amsterdam, 1845.
184. Van der Chijs, J. A. and others (ed.): *Dagh-Register gehouden int Casteel Batavia*, Batavia, 1887-1907.
185. Van den Wyngaert, A.: *Sinica Franciscana*, (Vol. II, III), Firenze, 1933-6.
186. Van Doren, Mark: *The Poetry of John Dryden*, New York, 1920.
187. Vixseboxe, J.: *Een Hollandsch Gezantschap naar China in de Zeventiende Eeuw*, Leiden, 1946.
188. Vizetelly, F. H. (ed.): *New Standard Encyclopedia*, New York, 1934.
189. Vojeu de Brunem, M.: *Histoire de la Conquête de la Chine par les Tartares Mancheoux*, Paris, 1754.
190. Waley, Arthur: *The Nō Plays of Japan*, New York, 1922.
191. Wilhelm, Richard: *Li Gi*, Jena, 1930.

ADDENDUM TO THE BIBLIOGRAPHY

During the twenty years since this book was first published many important studies of the puppet theatre and of the art of Chikamatsu have appeared in Japan. It has not been possible to revise the book on the basis of the information that has newly been made available, nor is it possible even to list all the Japanese publications here. (The most important are given in the bibliography of my book, *Bunraku, the Japanese Puppet Theatre*.)

The following are the titles of books written in English since 1951 that deal directly with the subject matter of *The Battles of Coxinga*.

Araki, James T.: *The Ballad-Drama of Medieval Japan*, Berkeley and Los Angeles, 1964.
Dunn, C. J.: *The Early Japanese Puppet Drama*, London, 1966.
Keene, Donald: *Bunraku, the Japanese Puppet Theatre*, Tokyo, 1965.
Keene, Donald: *Major Plays of Chikamatsu*, New York, 1961.
Shively, Donald H.: *The Love Suicide at Amijima*, Cambridge (Mass.), 1953.

IX

GLOSSARY OF JAPANESE WORDS
USED IN THE TEXT

bukyoku 舞曲 The name given to the texts used in the *kōwaka* dance drama.

bunya-bushi 文彌節 A kind of *jōruri* noted for its highly sentimental quality. The name is derived from that of its chief exponent, Okamoto Bunya.

bushidō 武士道 The modern name for the code of etiquette of the Japanese warrior class.

ebisu-kaki, ebisu-mai 夷舁，夷舞 Names given to early forms of puppet entertainment.

jidaimono 時代物 A general name given to historical plays as opposed to contemporary and generally domestic plays.

jō 掾 An official title of the second rank bestowed on some of the outstanding *jōruri* chanters.

jo, ha, kyū 序，破，急 The three phases of action distinguished by Japanese critics in the progress of a Nō play.

jōruri 淨瑠璃 The art of the puppet drama. The name is derived from that of the Princess Jōruri, the heroine of a story which was first used for puppet presentations.

kabuki 歌舞伎 The popular theatre which had its origins late in the sixteenth century.

keisei 傾城 A word meaning "courtesan" which often appears in the titles of plays, generally serving to show the play is set in the demi-monde.

kōwaka 幸若 A kind of dance drama.

kyōgen 狂言 A short comic play often presented between Nō plays in a programme. Also, the comic interludes sometimes interpolated in the body of a Nō play itself.

michiyuki 道行 A section of a Nō or *kabuki* or *jōruri* play which consists of a fanciful travel description.

Nō 能 A short play, chiefly in poetry, and usually on a religious or historical subject of an elevated nature. Also, the theatre itself, patronised by the aristocracy.

samisen (or *shamisen*) 三味線 A musical instrument with three strings, rather resembling the mandoline. Used to accompany *jōruri* recitations.

samurai 士 A member of the warrior class.

sekkyō 説經 A kind of morality play originating in Buddhist sermons.

sewamono 世話物 A domestic play as opposed to the historical play (or *jidaimono*).

shinjū 心中 The name given to the double suicides so prevalent at the beginning of the eighteenth century in Japan.

shōjō 少掾 A title of the third rank similar to *jō* in its use.

-tayū 太夫 An affix frequently added to the names of actors. Originally *-tayū* denoted an important official, but it came to be used quite indiscriminately.

INDEX

DATE DUE

DEMCO, INC. 38-2931